"A spectacular biography! This book is special. A must read for women entranced by strength and independence, and for men who want to understand such exotica!"
Kitty Kelley, author

"Evelyn Kaye has recorded the incredible life of adventure of Victorian Isabella Bird with sensitivity, skill and suspense. This book is a must for young women—and young men—who dream of traveling."
Ruth Gruber, author

"Skillfully describes Bird's adventures and important explorations without sacrificing the freshness of Bird's prose or overwhelming one with quotes. Evelyn Kaye is at her best in her focus on the complexity of Bird's character. Will delight Bird's fans and new readers alike."
Journal of the West

"Tells the amazing adventures of a courageous woman, who defied the Victorian controls placed on women and blazed her own trail. Recommended reading, especially for all who are interested in learning about women who achieved in spite of the culture of their times."
Litchfield County Times, CT

"Adventurous life and daring exploits of the demure Isabella Bird (1831-1904), presented in engaging detail in this American biography of the writer and world traveler."
AB Bookman's Weekly

"A wonderful new biography of a small Englishwoman with a bad back who lived one heck of a life in an age which offered so few opportunities to women with talent, intelligence, and courage. Author Evelyn Kaye tells Bird's story with enthusiasm, wonder, and delight."
Old West Traveler

"Makes for a good read. The reader gains a grand overview of late nineteenth century travel destinations, both popular and remote. Not only does it depict life all over the world during the latter half of the nineteenth century, but it is a worth-while addition to women's history and to travel history."
Colorado Libraries

"Kaye, the author of this straightforward, competently written biography, argues that Bird's ailments were a response to her narrow domestic prospects. This book will be of interest to the general reader as well as specialists in women's studies."
Library Journal

"First American biography of her journeys, providing a fine and detailed account of her endeavors and her Victorian times. An excellent, involving account."
Midwest Book Review

"Enlightening biography about Bird, a fascinating Victorian adventurer, chronicles her worldly travels and is a good read."
Travelin' Woman

"I can't wait to take this one home and spend the weekend with Isabella Bird."
Feminist Bookstore News

"An easy book to read, easy to pick up and put down at will."
The Pilot, NC

Also featured on radio stations around the country, and in the Boulder *Daily Camera*, *Denver Post*, Estes Park Library Newsletter, *Littleton Independent*, *Rocky Mountain News*, *Maiden Voyages* , and other publications.

Isabella Bird on her wedding day, 1881

AMAZING TRAVELER ISABELLA BIRD

The biography of a Victorian adventurer

by Evelyn Kaye

"I am doing what a woman can hardly ever do—leading a life fit for a man." Isabella Bird in Hawaii, 1873

 Blue Panda Publications

Published by
Blue Panda Publications

Tel: 303 449-8474

Photographs of Isabella Bird reproduced by permission of the Denver Public Library, Wesern
History Department, Colorado, and John Murray Publishers, London, England.

The book was designed by Christopher Sarson
Cover design: George Roche Design

© Copyright 1999 by Evelyn Kaye
Second Edition
Printed in the United State of America

Publisher's Cataloging-in Publication
(Provided by Quality Books, Inc.)

Kaye, Evelyn, 1937-
  Amazing traveler Isabella Bird : the biography of a Victorian adventurer /
      by Evelyn Kaye. -- 2nd ed.
    p. cm.
  Includes bibliographical references and index.
  LCCN: 98-94942
  ISBN: 0-9626231-4-8

  1. Bird, Isabella L. (Isabella Lucy),
  1831-1904. 2. Women travelers--Great Britain--
  Biography. I. Title.

  G246.B5K39 1999   910.92 [B]
                  QBI99-288

Books by Evelyn Kaye

Free Vacations & Bargain Adventures in the USA, 2nd edition
(Blue Panda Publications, 1998: 1st edition, 1995)
Active Woman Vacation Guide (Blue Panda Publications, 1997)
American Society of Journalists and Authors 50th Anniversary Journal,
Editor (ASJA, 1997)
Travel and Learn: The New Guide to Educational Travel 1994-5,
3rd edition (Blue Penguin Publications, 1994)
Family Travel: Terrific New Ideas for Today's Families
(Blue Penguin Publications, 1993)
Eco-Vacations: Enjoy Yourself and Save the Earth
(Blue Penguin Publications, 1991)
College Bound with J. Gardner (College Board, 1988)
The Parents Going-Away Planner with J. Gardner (Dell, 1987)
The Hole In The Sheet (Lyle Stuart, 1987)
Write and Sell Your TV Drama! with A. Loring (ALEK, revised 1993)
Relationships in Marriage and the Family, with Stinnett and Walters
(Macmillan, 1984)
Crosscurrents: Children, Families & Religion (Clarkson Potter, 1980)
The Family Guide to Cape Cod with B. Chesler (Barre/Crown, 1979)
How To Treat TV with TLC (Beacon Press, 1979)
The Family Guide to Childrens Television (Pantheon, 1975)
Action for Childrens Television, Editor (Avon, 1972)

The Author

Evelyn Kaye's travels began when she sailed to Canada from England as a child with her grandmother and ended up living in Toronto for four years. She's traveled ever since.

After school in England, she lived for a year in France, and in Israel. She explored Europe, Scandinavia, Mexico, Ecuador, Australia, New Zealand, and India. She's sailed round the Galapagos Islands, camped in an Amazon rainforest, rafted through the Grand Canyon, and horsepacked in Colorado's Sangre de Cristo Mountains. She can find her way around New York City, Chicago, Los Angeles, San Francisco, Denver, Washington DC, and Boston. She visited Antarctica to observe icebergs, penguins and seals from a Russian research ship. She recently traveled through Japan, following Isabella Bird's 1878 route.

As a writer and journalist in England, she was the first woman reporter in the *Manchester Guardian*'s newsroom, and worked for Reuters News Agency in France. In the United States, her articles have been published in the *New York Times* as well as in *McCalls, Travel & Leisure, Glamour, Ladies Home Journal*, and other major publications. Founder of Colorado Independent Publishers Association, she is also past president of the American Society of Journalists and Authors, and is listed in *Who's Who in America*.

CONTENTS

LIST OF ILLUSTRATIONS

THANKS AND
ACKNOWLEDGMENTS

During the years I spent researching this book, I traveled to England, Scotland, Colorado, New York, Chicago, and Hawaii to follow the paper trail Isabella left in her travels, books, magazine articles, speeches, and hundreds of letters.

In England, I appreciated the co-operation and assistance of Virginia Murray at John Murray Publishing, the house that published Isabella's travel books in the 19th century. Today John Murray VII heads the company. Murray's father, John Murray VI, remembered Isabella Bird and told me she visited his grandfather for advice on what kind of tricycle to buy, and practiced riding one up and down Albemarle Street. The company offices are still at 50 Albemarle Street, London. I sat in the same gracious room where Isabella used to visit, read her scrawled letters from Persia and other distant destinations, and looked through bound hand-written ledgers listing her royalties and finances.

In Colorado, many thanks to Denver Public Library Western History Department staff who provided excellent materials, and reproduced the photographs for this book. In Boulder's Carnegie Library, Connie Walker found and played an audio-tape of Charlotte Seymour, granddaughter of Sylvester Downer, one of the two young men who climbed Longs Peak with Isabella and Rocky Mountain Jim in 1873. Many years later, Downer was playing golf in St. Andrews, Scotland, when he heard that Isabella lived nearby. He wrote her a letter describing himself as "one of the rude young men"; she invited him to visit and they reminisced about the climb of Longs Peak.

I shall always remember my first meeting with Angela Overy of Colorado who invited me to enjoy an Isabella Bird tea, complete with English cucumber sandwiches and two of Isabella's devoted readers, Madeline O'Brien and Ann Lowdermilk. Thanks also to the Colorado Historical Society, Longmont Public Library, the University of Colorado Western History Department, Estes Park Public Library, and the Estes Park Museum, where there's a marble bust of Isabella Bird and a display about her.

Special appreciation to Emily Earley of Wisconsin who sent me a copy of the hand-written journal Isabella kept on her first visit to America in 1854.

For assistance in tracking down Isabella's published works, my sincere appreciation to the overworked staff at the New York Public Library on Fifth Avenue, and the Newspaper Annex around the corner. Also thanks to the Newberry Library in Chicago with their superb collection of 19th-century publications.

My thanks to the National Geographic Society library, American Geographical Society at the University of Wisconsin in Milwaukee, New Jersey's Bergen County library network, New York Academy of Medicine Library, and Union Theological Seminary Library in New York.

Thanks also to the British Library, Manuscript Collection, and the India Office Records. The Royal Geographical Society in London searched for, but could not find, the original plates of Isabella's photographs which she left to the Society in her will.

In Scotland, on the island of Mull, I visited Isabella's lovely cottage in Tobermory, and met Jean Whittaker, author of a guide to Tobermory, and Philip Bird of the Western Isles Hotel, who may be a distant relative. Thanks also to the Mull Museum; Ian and Jennifer McLean of Aros, Tobermory; the Western Isles Islands Council, Stornaway; the Harris Tweed Association; and Derek Martin, Ardvourlie Castle, Harris. In Edinburgh, my thanks to the National Library of Scotland, the Scottish Record Office for Isabella's will, the Royal Scottish Geographical Society, and to Edinburgh residents for not knocking down the Georgian houses where Isabella lived.

In Hawaii, Patrick McNally at the Hawaiian Collection at the University provided transcripts of Isabella's Hawaiian letters, donated by Alphons Korn. Also thanks to Mary Jane Knight, librarian at the Hawaiian Children's Mission; Ruth Horie, Bishops Museum; and the Hawaii State Library.

Several people replied to my request for information in the *New York Times Book Review*. My appreciation to Gladys Para of Gig Harbor, Washington, a descendant of the doctor's family with whom Isabella lived in Colorado; Hilda Boehm and James Davis at the University of California at Los Angeles Research Library, where there is an unpublished book of Isabella's stunning photos of Persia; Sandra Dallas Atchison; Helen F. Brooks; Jerome Clauser; Gloria Goldblatt; Katherine Hartnett; Julian Kaplow; Ella Pfeiffer; Lois Ann Rovira:;Priscilla Silber; Paul Snowden; Helga Wall; and Rita D. White.

Some questions were also answered by the Public Archivist office on Prince Edward Island; the Metropolitan Toronto Reference Library, Canada; American Museum of Natural History; Boston Public Library; Cleveland Public Library; Holt-Atherton Center for Western Studies; Jackson Library, University of North Carolina; the Library of Congress; the New York Historical Society; Northern Illinois University Library; Pierpont Morgan Library; Rare Book and Manuscript Library, Columbia University; Van Pelt Library of the University of Pennsylvania; and Dena Bartoleme, Mountain Travel.

Writer friends were most supportive. My thanks to Boulder Media Women at Friday morning coffee, who listened to my enthusiasm for Isabella and encouraged me to publish the book; to friends in the American Society of Journalists and Authors, in particular Ruth Bayard Smith, Dodi Schultz, and Eloise Engle; and to Janet Gardner, who read an early draft of the manuscript and suggested it could be a great movie.

Special appreciation to my family in Colorado, David and Lisa, Claire and Spencer, Katrina and Nick, and in particular my husband Christopher, who designed the book, and provides support, ideas, hugs, encouragement, food, and drink at exactly the right moments laced with quantities of love and laughter.

This book has had an adventurous history, rather like Isabella's own life. The original book proposal submitted by my agent was accepted for publication by E. P. Dutton where I worked with two excellent editors, Leslie Wells and Britt Hollander. On the day I handed in the final corrections, E. P. Dutton was swallowed up in a dramatic take-over by a larger company. The manuscript languished in literary limbo. Today, I have my own publishing company specializing in quality travel books, and I am gratified to be able to bring readers Isabella Bird's inspiring story.

INTRODUCTION TO THE SECOND EDITION

A Celebration of Isabella Bird

Since the first edition of *Amazing Traveler Isabella Bird* was published in 1994, many women have told me how much the biography has inspired them. It's wonderful to discover that Isabella Bird's story still excites people, and that her adventures are as astonishing today as they were in the past.

Why is Isabella Bird such an inspiration? She's quite different from other heroines. She was not renowned for being breathtakingly beautiful, brilliantly clever, irresistibly sexy, fabulously talented, extremely rich, or adorably young. Her childhood was depressing, and her love life almost non-existent. She was a short, plump, solid, rather plain woman. She worried about her health, her looks, and her abilities. However, her one passion was adventurous travel, and her skill was to write about her travels passionately. For women everywhere, her books are a breath of intoxicating and entertaining fresh air.

At Carnegie Library in Boulder, where I had done research for the book, the first "Celebration of Isabella Bird" was held to mark the publication of *Amazing Traveler Isabella Bird* on October 7, 1994, the 90th anniversary of Bird's death. At the Celebration I spoke about my travels researching the book. Linda Batlin, a storyteller dressed in 19th century costume, re-enacted Isabella Bird's climb of Longs Peak. So many people wanted to attend that we had to turn them away, and give a second presentation the following week. It was a wonderful evening.

We listened to the voice of Charlotte Seymour of Boulder, who died in 1988. A long-time Boulder resident, she had been interviewed for the Carnegie Library Oral History Collection. She was the grand-daughter of Silvester Spelman Downer who climbed Long's Peak in Colorado with Isabella Bird in September, 1873. Downer had just graduated from Columbia Law School, and came to Colorado on vacation with his friend, Platt Rogers. Later, Downer became a lawyer and judge in Boulder, while Rogers was elected mayor of Denver, Colorado. Charlotte Seymour said: "My grandfather came out to Colorado immediately after graduation from Columbia Law School. He must have been 20 or 25 years old at that time. He climbed Longs Peak with his partner, Platt Rogers. Isabella Bird thrust herself upon them, unwilling though they were to have her. Isabella has a very different view of the trip in her book, where she praises the guide and says what rude young men they were, and all that sort of thing. The truth of it was that Rocky Mountain Jim, their guide, invited her without asking them. They had not very much money and they had laid it all out to have the trip, and they were not a bit happy about having her. She praises Rocky Mountain Jim, because he's her hero, and says he's had his eye clawed out by a bear, which is not true—it was shot out by an irate husband. She did get up the Peak with Jim helping her up and down the entire way."

Mabel Downer Durning of Longmont, Colorado is the last living link with Isabella Bird. She is a great-niece of S. S. Downer. At the Celebration event she expressed her views:

"I am a great admirer of Isabella Bird. She wrote beautifully. Her descriptions of Colorado are outstanding. No one can fault her for anything she wrote about describing her trips and the mountains and the beauty and the sunrise and the sunsets. But she, like many people, embroidered a little bit when she got down to writing the story. Nothing should take away from her writing skills, but let's face a few facts.

"Isabella Bird was very short, I use the word dumpy, travel worn, courageous, pushy, prone to gross exaggeration, middle-aged, and had a spectacular imagination as well as being an incurable romantic. Isabella was not burdened by humility or an inferiority complex or a lack of assertiveness. She was way ahead of her time. She was constantly sending her stories to all the newspapers all over the west, and she was writing part truth, part fiction, anything to make it interesting. Before she got through with her trip, everybody in Colorado knew her by name. Her reputation preceded her, and she was thoroughly enjoying every bit of the publicity she got on her trip.

"You have to remember that Isabella went to Cheyenne where she was horrified by the wild west, and a lovely English lady came and rescued her. Then she got to Greeley and she was horrified by these horrible new settlements. Then she went to Chambers and she stayed almost a week, and she had a terrible time there. They called her stupid, they didn't kowtow to her, she just had a terrible time. And finally she got on her horse and came to Longmont, where she found a hotel room and prevailed on the hotel manager to talk these two young men into getting her a ride to Estes Park. She went with them. They did not go with her."

When the biography of Isabella Bird's adventurous life was published, I thought the book was completed. But it's taken on a life of its own as more and more people read it and respond to it. I was invited to visit Sylvan Dale Ranch, in Loveland, Colorado, where the owners showed me the remains of the old kitchen in the original Chambers house where Isabella stayed before she reached Estes Park. In Boulder's Museum of History I found an authentic 19th century ladies riding costume, with bloomers, long skirt and jacket, just like the one Isabella wears in the sketch in her book. A woman at Colorado University told me her family in Scotland had known Isabella Bird so she had always been fascinated by her life.

I recently traveled through Japan following the route Isabella Brid took in 1878. I discovered to my surprise that her book is available in Japanese, that her name is well know in the communities she visited, particularly among the Aino on Hokkaido, and that her photo hangs on the wall of the elegant Kanaya hotel in Nikko.

INTRODUCTION

I discovered Isabella Lucy Bird in a church parking lot at a summer book sale in 1982. I collect old travel books, so I was browsing through the boxes on the tables and that's how I found *A Lady's Life in the Rocky Mountains.*

I read the first few pages and felt a sense of high excitement at discovering a great writer. Here was an Englishwoman who responded to America as I had when I arrived from Britain. She traveled through California and Colorado and she too was overwhelmed by the magnificence of the natural scenery—the stunning grandeur of mountains and forests, the breath-taking beauty of rivers and lakes, the spaciousness and drama of the land—just as I had been. She too ignored the cities and reveled in the vast wilderness, so different from the manicured coziness of English gardens. She too loved the challenge of the wild weather, open skies and untouched landscapes. And she described what she saw with a detail and clarity that made me feel as if I were standing next to her.

When I began to research her life, I found her trip to America in 1873 was only the beginning of her travels. This demure soft-voiced minister's daughter traveled alone through Australia, New Zealand, Hawaii, Japan, Malaya, Sinai, Tibet, Persia, Korea and China at a time when ladies were supposed to be helpless and submissive. Discovering her other travel books was a revelation because she described her amazing adventures with an enthusiasm, vitality, and freshness of outlook that was unique. I was determined to tell her story.

Her style and her approach convinced me to write an "oral biography" of her life, using her words as much as possible to illustrate who she was and what she did. I wanted to capture her informal, personal and emotional approach, and not impose my own modern interpretation of her life. Though her roots were in the Victorian era, she was a strong and courageous woman whose voice spoke to all ages. Her life of adventure and literature is an inspiration to women everywhere, particularly older women, since she had some of her most dramatic journeys when she was over 60.

Every incident, comment and adventure has its source in her books, letters and other original materials. There are no fictional inventions. Isabella's reactions and observations were always personal and so intimately reported that her readers felt as if they were going through the experiences with her.

The books she wrote about her travels were so extraordinarily successful that she became one of the best known travel writers of her day. Her adventures in Asia brought her international acclaim. She addressed British Members of Parliament at the House of Commons on her experiences of the cruelty of the Turkish Kurds. Her accounts of the Korean Queen's assassination and Japan's invasion of Korea were major news stories. Her book on Korea became the standard reference work for years after its publication in 1898. She was the first woman to travel up the Yangtze River and overland through the mountains to China's border with Tibet. In 1892, she was the first woman to be appointed a Fellow of the prestigious Royal Geographical Society in London, and in 1897, the first woman ever to address a meeting of the Society.

There were dozens of British and American Victorian ladies gallivanting about the world in the late 19th century: Mary Kingsley, Ida Pfeiffer, Fanny Bullock Workman, Alexandra David-Neel, Annie Taylor, Annie Smith Peck. For many of them, like Isabella, travel was the only escape from a life which offered so few opportunities to women with talent, intelligence and courage. The reason they attracted so much attention and criticism was because they were so very different from the thousands of women trapped within the narrow confines of a rigid society.

The fascination of Isabella for me was the dichotomy between the free-wheeling independent traveler and the ailing, helpless and despondent woman at home. Brought up to believe women ought to be submissive and obedient, she felt guilty about her intense longings for travel and adventure. Depression made her ill. So her doctors prescribed "a change of air" and a sea voyage, fashionable remedies for ailing ladies. They assumed she would go to Brighton, or perhaps the south of France. Instead she took off for Australia, Persia and Tibet. And once free to leave, her aches and pains disappeared, and her unquenchable energy and enthusiasm returned.

Isabella traveled in the last half of the 19th century when Victoria was on the throne and the sun never set on Britain's vast Empire. Before television and movies arrived, books and magazine articles described the wonders of India, Malaya, Africa, the Caribbean islands and other distant outposts of the colonies. The British loved to read about the mysterious Orient and the exotic lushness of tropical jungles, so different from the placid English countryside.

Isabella learned to describe everything she saw with compelling accuracy, based on her extensive research. She gave the botanic names of every flower, plant and tree along the way and provided a detailed summary of the geography and history of the places she visited and the people she met.

Her approach was quite different from other travelers. She never believed the world would be a better place if everyone were British. She expressed frank criticisms of colonial officials who failed to meet her high standards of dedication, and despised the Great Game where Britain and other major powers plotted to take over weaker countries. She felt sympathy with those she met on her travels and respected their unique traditions, and she was particularly interested in the everyday lives of the women and children. Isabella learned to avoid colonial centers where the British read *The Times*, played croquet, and sipped afternoon tea. She chose to travel off the beaten track into what she believed was the real world.

Isabella's books were based on her letters home. She wrote first to her sister, and after Henrietta's death, to women friends, and to her publisher John Murray. She made sketches as she traveled, which artist Charles Whymper turned into the illustrations in her earlier books. On her trip to Persia with Major Sawyer, she used a camera for the first time.

In London, she took photography classes. Then, on her next travels to China and Korea, she carried a heavy tripod camera with her, and developed her photographs along the way. She learned to take scientific instruments to make accurate measurements of temperature, altitude and other data, and to keep a log of her travels with mileage and place names.

She published ten books of travel, scores of articles, and two books of photographs. I read her published works, as well as the reviews and articles related to them. I read her original letters in London, Edinburgh, Hawaii and Colorado. I tracked down her articles in 19th-century magazines, sometimes without her byline, sometimes with I. L. Bird, and sometimes as Mrs. I. L. Bishop after her brief marriage. In London I sat in her publisher's office in the same room she used to visit, looking out through the French windows on to Albemarle Street below, and read the long hand-written letters she sent him from Persia and India and Turkey.

Isabella never had a boring trip. If she boarded a boat, it was sure to be tossed about in a wild gale. If she galloped off in winter, she was certain to find herself struggling through chest-high snowdrifts. If she set out in summer, she would wilt in the unbelievable heat. Her books are a litany of catastrophes, disasters and excitement.

She had a natural tendency to dramatize and exaggerate everything that happened to her, and emphasize every detail. Nothing was ever plain and straightforward. You or I might take a boat trip, and find the crossing a little rough. Isabella, on the same trip, would notice the waves slapping at the sides, the spray breaking over the bow, the wind whistling in the sails, the china rattling on the tables, the clouds lowering on the horizon. She wrote with a dramatic intensity because she saw everything with a sense of heightened excitement.

Certainly she attracted crises and catastrophes. She did, after all, travel to some of the most dangerous and outlandish places in the world. Yet reticence and understatement were not her style. If it rained, Isabella would see a torrential downpour, rivulets of water pouring off the roof, vast puddles flooding the streets. Once out traveling, everything appeared to her as if under a spotlight, with unrivaled clarity and color—the houses, the insects, the scenery, the food, the people, the weather, the adventures. She exaggerated because that was how she experienced them herself. She never had a dull trip or an uneventful voyage and chose to emphasize every detail of the excitement.

It's interesting to speculate whether she really stayed a virgin all those years. Was there was more between her and Rocky Mountain Jim than she confessed to her sister Henrietta? Was that tense conflict between her and Major Sawyer caused by sexual clashes? Did she ever experience a secret passion on her travels?

It is unlikely. Isabella avoided sex. It was so alien to the image she struggled to preserve as a lady, and to her values. Though not a prude, she was devoutly religious and throughout her life held fast to her Christian faith. She learned to suppress her sexual feelings and accepted the boundaries of conventional behavior. She grew up in an age when it was indecent for a man to see a woman's ankle, let alone touch a woman affectionately. Isabella experienced her deepest and most intense relationship with her sister, whose faith and morals adhered to even higher standards than Isabella's. When Henrietta died, Isabella's only intimate bond was broken and she could never replace it.

Her marriage to John Bishop was a respectable Victorian partnership where each lived independently. She had—reluctantly—agreed to marry him on condition that he did not interfere in any way with her travels and writing, and he had wholeheartedly agreed. From all that is known about John Bishop, it is unlikely that the gentle doctor ever forced himself on the strong-willed explorer. Their marriage was one of agreeable compatibility.

Today, Isabella has not been forgotten. Her books have been reissued in paperback, and she is frequently included in anthologies of outstanding women of the past. Her writings speak directly to us today because they were based directly on her original letters, and capture the freshness of her first impressions, recreating her moments of immediate discovery. You can still see the image of her washing her hair in the Rockies on a day so cold that her braids froze to her head. You can visualize her admiring the single perfect flower in a vase in her room at a Japanese inn. You can hear the sounds of gunshots from attacking tribesmen as she rides through the desolate plains of Persia. You can feel her excitement as she climbs the Himalayas.

Isabella is still remembered in Tobermory on the windswept isle of Mull in Scotland. The cottage where she spent her summers and wrote her books still stands. As the ferry steams over from Oban you can glimpse the white cottage behind the trees at the top of the steep hill. And on the curving harbor road, there is a simple clock tower, erected in memory of Isabella's sister Henrietta. Every hour the clock chimes, the gentle sounds echoing across the waves to those far distant shores where Isabella loved to travel.

Clock Tower at Tobermory

Section I
STRUGGLES 1831-1874

Chapter 1
Childhood and America

Isabella's upbringing. Her ailments and bad back. Writes articles. A trip to America. John Murray publishes first book. Second trip to America. Death of her father.

Isabella was born on October 15, 1831, to Edward Bird, an evangelical minister in the Church of England, and his wife, Dora, in Boroughbridge, Yorkshire.

Her earliest memories were of the years with her parents and younger sister Henrietta in the peaceful village of Tattenhall in northern England. Her father used to sit her in front of him on his horse, and take her riding along the country lanes, the sunlight dancing through the leaves and on to her dark hair. The curving branches of oak and chestnut and willow trees shaded the lanes. On either side, the bright pinks and yellows and purple of wild flowers glowed among the shrubs, the fresh scent of mown hay drifted over from the fields, and in the soft, gray skies, the cries of birds floated down.

Looking down at his eager little daughter, Edward Bird pointed out the plants and trees along the way, showed her the difference between horse barns and dairy barns, explained the workings of a water wheel, and how wheat was grown. Then he asked her what he had told her. If she did not know, he would repeat it, and then ask her again. Soon, Isabella could tell him the names of every flower peeking through the grass, every tree along the lane, and every crop growing in the fields they passed. In later years she always attributed her observational skills to those childhood rides and her father's questions.

She was a lively, intelligent and articulate child. When she was about six, a local politician came round to persuade Reverend Bird to vote for him, and complimented the younger daughter, Henrietta, saying she was a lovely child. Isabella sized up the situation, and then marched forward, asking in a clear voice: "Did you tell my father my sister was so pretty because you wanted his vote?"

Her education came from her mother who gave both daughters lessons in reading, writing, painting, sewing, and religion. After Isabella learned to read, she loved to spend hours lost in a book. She had the freedom of her father's library and devoured his books on law—for he had trained as a lawyer and served as a judge in India—and history and religion. One evening, when she was about seven, she did not appear for dinner; her father found her curled up in the barn reading a history of the French Revolution.

She was always eager to try new things, while her sister Henrietta preferred to observe. Every summer, they traveled to their grandparents' house in Taplow Hill for a big family reunion. Isabella romped with her young cousins, rode ponies in the fields and was recognized as a leader in their games, while her sister sat quietly at the side.

The Birds were a remarkable family. One great-grandfather, Sir George Merttins, had been Lord Mayor of London; a cousin, William Wilberforce, had led the fight to abolish slavery in England; two relatives became Bishops in the Church of England.

Isabella's grandfather Robert Bird had made his fortune in India and America, and settled down as a gentleman farmer in Berkshire. Isabella's father, Edward Bird, was one of ten children. His unmarried sisters lived at Taplow Hill, strong-minded women who refused sugar in their tea to protest the use of slaves in the sugar industry. One sister became a missionary and another married a minister. There was a strong religious emphasis at Taplow and every day began with morning prayers.

Isabella loved the time after breakfast with the family sitting around the big table when Grandfather Bird brought in the mail. Letters from abroad were written to be read aloud to eager listeners. Isabella's dark eyes glowed with excitement as she listened to the accounts of life in India where two of her uncles lived, or the unbearable heat of a Cincinnati summer where friends had emigrated, or the news of a new mission in Africa. She saw how letters brought alive distant places and created vivid images of scenes quite different from Taplow.

When the summer ended, it was time to go back to Tattenhall and parish life. The parish faced a growing crisis because of Edward Bird's unwavering determination that there could be no exception to the commandment to keep the Sabbath as a day of rest. In Tattenhall, the dairy farmers knew they had to milk their cows every day. They told Reverend Bird so. He told them that God's law was more important and urged them to give up all work on the Sabbath.

His congregation dwindled week by week. Finally, he was asked to leave. For eleven-year-old Isabella, it was a terrible shock. She admired her father, and believed in him implicitly, but she hated to leave the only home she had known. Fortunately, a Bird relative, the Bishop of Chester, found her father a new parish in Birmingham with over 16,000 people. Edward Bird's annual stipend fell to sixty pounds from three hundred, but like many young men of the gentry, he lived on investments from his wife's inheritance and saw his ministry as his mission, not a means of earning money.

By the middle of the 19th century, England was divided into the aristocracy, the wealthy landowners, the gentry, the new tradespeople, and the poor. It was a pyramid of class and wealth. At the top of the pyramid, a few thousand members of the royal family and aristocracy owned most of the land and the wealth, and controlled Parliament. Below them were the gentry, wealthy members of the upper classes who, like Robert Bird, lived in comfortable luxury on vast acres of farmland, with income derived from investments and family inheritances. The eldest son usually inherited the land, and the wealth was divided among the rest; younger sons of the gentry often went abroad to the colonies, went into the church, or became lawyers or politicians. Beneath the gentry were a small but growing middle class of trades-people, shopkeepers and bankers. At the bottom of the pyramid was the vast majority of the population, the lower classes, working as underpaid laborers on farmlands or in factories in the city.

By the time Edward Bird's family moved to Birmingham, growing unrest and demands for better conditions were beginning to disturb the equanimity of the long-established social system.

In 1843, as the Birds' carriage rattled into Birmingham, Isabella looked out to see row upon row of houses crowded close together, narrow cobbled streets, and dark smoky air produced by the new factories. It was a dramatic change from the rolling green fields of the countryside. The minister's house however was set in a large garden with apple trees, and the house was a spacious mansion. The Birds hired a gardener, several maids and a cook to help run it. Like most well-brought up girls of that time, Isabella accepted that servants performed all the household tasks—buying and preparing food, serv-ing meals, cleaning, lighting the fires, and bringing pitchers of water for washing. There was no system of piped water so there was no running hot water, and no indoor plumbing. Isabella used chamberpots emp-tied by servants, and took hip-baths in her rooms.

Birmingham was in the midst of the Industrial Revolution, with factories producing woollen goods and woven cloth. At the same time, the workers in overcrowded housing and underpaid jobs began to protest their exploitation. One group, the Chartists, demanded im-proved working conditions and more pay. Marchers tore up the iron fence railings around the church to arm themselves with spikes on their way to attack a mill. Isabella was fascinated by the protests by the mill workers and the conditions in the factories, and studied the issues. Should there be protection for the workers with a guaranteed wage and limited hours of work? Or should the "laissez faire" attitude prevail, the philosophy of a free market and profits above all?

Though intelligent, Isabella could not go to school or college because there was nowhere for girls to go. English universities did not accept female students and there were no girls' schools. Isabella's education came from her parents and her own reading. At fifteen, she wrote her first serious essay discussing the issues of worker protection versus a free market. She presented both sides of the case as if in a court, with "Chief Justice Common Sense, Baron Public Opinion, Mr.

Humbug and Mr. Mock Philanthropist." Her father later had it published privately as a pamphlet, and proudly sent copies to family and friends.

At first, the Birmingham ministry was very successful. Edward Bird's dedication and devotion to his congregation was appreciated. Many children attended Sunday School and Isabella was appointed a teacher though her students were almost as old as she was.

Though most of the shopkeepers supported the minister's dedication to keeping Sunday as a Sabbath and signed the church pledge to close, two merchants persistently refused to shut their stores. Edward Bird, with his usual passion and commitment, could not accept their decision. In a misguided moment of zeal, he took out a police summons against them and delivered it himself.

This high-handed approach infuriated the community. As he walked home one day, a crowd of angry parishioners waylaid him, shouting abuse, and pelted him with stones and mud. He came home devastated by the response.

Emotionally shattered, Edward Bird collapsed. The doctor urged him to go away to regain his strength. The family moved, and Isabella found herself adjusting to a quiet seaside village. This time she could not help wondering why they had once again lost their home. At fifteen, she was old enough to understand that her father had failed.

One afternoon, her uncle Robert, her father's older brother, came to visit. He suggested that Edward might prefer a country parish, like the one in Wyton near Cambridge offered by their friend Lady Olivia Sparrow. It was peaceful rural parish with only 300 villagers.

Isabella was sixteen when they arrived at Wyton Rectory, set on a slope overlooking a lake in the fen country. A friend who lived nearby wrote:

"Her favorite outdoor occupations were riding and rowing, and we used often to meet along the roads and on the river. Isabella was a fearless horsewoman, and would mount any horse, however spirited. When visiting our house, she more than once rode a horse which no lady had mounted before, and she seemed to enjoy it all the more."

Throughout her childhood, she was often ill. Now, though happy to be back in the country, she frequently complained of tiredness and pain. At Wyton, her backache, headaches and other ailments grew worse. Her new doctor diagnosed a fibroid tumor near her spine, and recommended an operation to remove it.

It was a dangerous proposition. Victorian surgeons used knives and saws without anesthesia, and the basic facts of antiseptics were unknown. An operation was always a last resort, because the death rate from infection was high. Isabella talked it over with her father, to whom she was closest, and decided to have the operation to ease her pain. That spring, at the age of eighteen, a fibroid tumor close to her spine was removed. She recovered from the operation, but throughout her life she suffered from backaches and other ailments.

The all-purpose medical remedy for sickness was "a change of air." When Isabella's doctor recommended mountain air as a change from the damp low-lying fens, Edward Bird took his family to the Scottish Highlands for six weeks. As soon as Isabella arrived amid the heather-covered hills, she completely forgot her pain and spent hours scrambling up the steep, narrow trails and trekking over miles of rocky, mist-covered mountains. She took a ferry to the islands of Skye, Harris and Mull. She walked along the shore, the wind blowing in her face. Her speedy recovery in a new place with mountains and outdoor activity was a pattern that repeated itself throughout her life.

That fall, back in Wyton, Isabella began to think of sending an account of her travels in the Scottish Highlands to one of the family magazines. She loved to write, and she saw that travel was a popular topic in 19th-century publications, as well as articles on schools for middle-class girls which opened in 1850, the efforts of women to study at university and qualify as professionals, and concerns for married women's property rights. Isabella's religion taught her that women should be subservient to men, but she could not have avoided reading about the new ideas for change.

Her first article was accepted, and delighted, she went on to write for *The Family Treasury, Good Words,* and *The Sunday Magazine,* published anonymously. She traveled to friends and relatives around the country to research her articles. In Portsmouth in 1854 she watched Queen Victoria bid farewell to soldiers going off to the Crimean War and described it for readers of *Leisure Hour* in two long articles.

But her back pains, headaches, and sleeplessness reappeared. Her symptoms were real to her, but they also reflected her emotional despair. Like many capable, intelligent women, she was eager to do more but had no opportunity. She could not go to university as her father had done, nor become a lawyer or judge, as Edward Bird had for several years before turning to religion. Her life was bounded by the narrow routine of home and the acceptable limits of behavior for ladies in society. Florence Nightingale, who lived in the same era, wrote: "I craved for some regular occupation, for something worth doing instead of frittering time away on useless trifles," adding: "Women don't consider themselves as human beings at all."

A 19th-century American writer, Charlotte Gilman, in one of her stories, *The Yellow Wallpaper*, described a wife bored with her empty life at home who declared: "I believe that work, with excitement and change, would do me good."

Isabella would have agreed. Her reaction was to focus on her numerous aches and pains, which depressed her, and made her feel even worse. The cycle is typical of hypochondria or, as it was often called, hysteria, of which 19th-century women frequently complained. Yet Isabella's ailments offered her an escape.

The medical wisdom of the day held that illness was caused by unhealthy air or bad smells. The only remedy: "a change of air." Her doctor recommended a long sea voyage. That spring, Isabella was entertaining some cousins from Canada and they urged her to sail back with them across the Atlantic and discover the beauties of the New World. It sounded an excellent idea.

She discussed it with her father. Concerned about her health, he gave her a hundred pounds and said she could stay away as long as it lasted. On a warm June day in 1854, Isabella, now 22, boarded a boat in Liverpool for Halifax, Nova Scotia. With her were some carefully packed boxes of clothes and a red leather-bound notebook, for she dreamed of—perhaps—writing a book about the journey.

Her first weeks were spent on her cousins' farm on Prince Edward Island in Canada. Isabella rowed over to investigate the Indian village across the lake, staring at the wigwams thatched with birchbark, women carrying papooses and men smoking pipes. She hiked round the undeveloped northwest of the island, eating lobsters cooked in a huge cauldron over the fire with a farmer and his family. She explored untouched woods and paddled in a still, dark, crystal-clear lake that looked as if it had been undiscovered since the beginning of time. Yet as the weeks slipped by, she longed to visit America.

Her cousins warned her of the dangers of traveling alone and of the threat of cholera. But with quiet determination she packed her things and went down to the quay to board a boat going south to Portland, Maine. That evening, a tremendous gale blew in, which she described vividly.

"Crash went the lamp, which was suspended from the ceiling, as a huge wave struck the ship. Rush came another heavy wave, sweeping up the saloon, carrying chairs and stools before it, and as rapidly retiring. The hall was full of men, clinging to the supports. Wave after wave now struck the ship. The wind sounded like heavy artillery, and the waves, as they struck the ship, felt like cannonballs. I heard the men outside say, 'She's going down, she's water-logged, she can't hold together.' A wave striking the ship, threw me against a projecting beam, cutting my head and stunning me, and I was insensible for three hours."

The boat tossed and rolled for ten hours, with the crew pumping desperately to keep the water down. Finally, they reached port in the early morning. Isabella thankfully collected her belongings, feeling as if she had narrowly escaped death. But she did not think for a moment of giving up the trip. Indeed, it was clear that she enjoyed the excitement.

In Maine, she caught the train to Ohio, and described riding through a forest fire, with flames licking up the scorched trunks of the trees, smoke thick in the air, and huge branches crashing to the ground. Aboard the train, the men she admired were the "prairie men", or cowboys, who were:

"Tall, handsome, broad-chested, and athletic, with aquiline noses, piercing grey eyes, and brown curling hair and beards. They wore leathern jackets, slashed and embroidered, large boots with embroidered tops, silver spurs, and caps of scarlet cloth, worked with somewhat tarnished gold thread. They could tell stories, whistle melodies, and sing comic songs without weariness, chivalrous in their manners, and as free as the winds."

From Ohio she went to Chicago and Detroit, took a boat across Lake Erie and went to visit Niagara Falls. Her first view was disappointing: "There is a great fungus growth of museums, curiosity shops, taverns, and pagodas with shining tin cupolas. Not far from where I stood, the members of a picnic party were flirting and laughing hilariously, throwing chicken-bones and peach-stones over the cliff, drinking champagne and soda-water."

But the sight of Horseshoe Falls was exhilarating with their immense, frothing, hissing billows and the sheets of water throwing up huge columns of spray before falling into a cauldron of foam and mist far below.

Ever adventurous, she decided to go behind Niagara. Draped in borrowed oilskins and rubber boots several sizes too large for her, she followed her guide down a spiral staircase, to a narrow path of rock and shale. Clouds of spray whipped at her face. A fierce wind tugged at her coat. The rushing water poured down in torrents, drenching her, filling her boots and soaking her face and hair. Almost deafened by the roar and hardly able to breathe, she struggled on to Termination Rock, gasping for air and terrified she might slip and fall.

Isabella's printed certificate declared she had "walked for 230 feet behind the great fall," but she decided: "The front view is the only one for Niagara—going behind the sheet is like going behind a picture frame."

Isabella traveled on to Montreal and Quebec, and then to New York City. Through friends, she met Mrs. DuBois, a sculptor and leader in New York's artistic community whose Friday night receptions at the elegant DuBois home on Gramercy Park were so popular people fought for invitations. Isabella met Washington Irving, magazine editors, historians, explorers setting out for the Arctic, and travelers who had just come back from Russia.

It was time to leave. She took the train to Boston, with an introduction to the poet Longfellow. At his house in Cambridge, they sat talking, the middle-aged poet and the admiring young English traveler. When Isabella asked if he would visit England again, he sighed and said "there were six encumbrances in the way" and gestured to his six children.

It was December when she reached the port of Halifax. She had covered more than 6,000 miles, an amazing journey for a young woman. Isabella had discovered her natural talent for traveling.

Fierce Atlantic storms buffeted the boat, forcing most of the passengers to moan in their bunks or lie helpless on the sofas in the saloon. Isabella found she was an excellent sailor. So was a dashing young Canadian soldier, Captain Robinson, who enjoyed the weather as much as she did. He was on his way to join his regiment assigned to the Crimean War in Turkey. The two of them spent their days together and their evenings walking the decks.

"It was the most beautiful night I have *ever* seen at sea, though nothing to some later in the voyage," Isabella wrote in her journal after a moonlight stroll. "The moon glittered on the water. It was a glorious night, a compound of all that was bright and beautiful. Never before had I felt the romance of the sea."

But at Liverpool, Captain Robinson left to join his regiment and Isabella took the train back to Wyton. She never heard from him again, and he, like thousands of others, may have died on the bleak battle-fields of the Crimean War. She once told a friend that it was the only time she had been in love.

Her parents and sister welcomed Isabella home and listened eagerly to her stories and adventures. Friends came to visit, and she regaled them with her experiences. Her father encouraged her to write a book.

In the 1800s, hundreds of British men and women went to America, as immigrants seeking their fortunes or as visitors eager to see the New World. Frances Trollope, the novelist Anthony's mother, went to open a fashionable department store in Cincinnati, hoping to make enough money to save her husband and family from bankruptcy in England. But the venture was a complete failure. She returned home penniless. Desperate to gain something from her years there, she wrote *Domestic Manners of the Americans* in 1832, frankly expressing her opinions about the vulgar, unappreciative, uncultured, and unedu-cated Americans. The book caused a great furor and was extremely successful.

In 1842, Charles Dickens arrived in America. A famous author, he was greeted by an avalanche of publicity as he and his wife toured New England, New York, Virginia, St. Louis and the prairies. But he hated the crowds and didn't like roughing it in the wild. In the American scenes for his book on *Martin Chuzzlewit*, his hero met conniving tricksters and offensive boors, and declared Americans have lost "the natural politeness of a savage, and that instinctive good breeding which admonishes one man not to offend and disgust another."

Isabella however had been impressed with much of what she saw, and loved the freedom of traveling through a strange country. Her journal described in exuberant detail her delight in the magnificent scenery and the people she met, noting their patterns of speech and comments with the fresh liveliness of a young woman on her own for the first time.

Settling down at a table, with pen and ink, she started writing her first book, which she called *The Car and the Steamboat*. She worked steadily on, day after day. On a weekend visit to her relative, the Bishop of Chester, she met John Milford at the house, an author of books on travel in Norway and Spain. He thought his publisher, John Murray, might be interested in her book.

In October, Isabella sent the manuscript to John Murray, with a note from Milford. Murray agreed to publish it but called it *An Englishwoman in America*. In January 1856, a few hundred copies were published.

The book was reviewed in *The Times* and in several Canadian newspapers. An American admirer sent her a beautiful bracelet to thank her for what she had written about his country. And as the checks began to arrive, for in those days authors received two-thirds of the profits, Isabella earned a great deal of money.

Isabella was pleased but confused by her success. She had been brought up to believe that a woman's role was to be selfless, do good works, and help others. It was an era when people in the upper classes rarely worked to earn money, but lived on their investments, lands, and family fortunes. Isabella's parents lived on inherited wealth from their families, and her father devoted himself to the church while his wife was his dutiful supporter. For Isabella, it was difficult to accept that the thing she loved to do, travel and write, now gave her success and wealth. She was convinced she could not spend the money on herself but must give it to those who really needed it.

Her attitude was in keeping with the high-minded principles of her upbringing. It also reflected the attitude of a society which considered it quite improper for a well-bred woman to earn money instead of being supported by her husband or her father. Only lower-class women were forced to work for wages.

Isabella spent her royalties to buy new boats for the impoverished fishermen in Scotland, a decision her parents approved of wholeheartedly. When the Bird family arrived in the Highlands for the summer, their steamer was surrounded by brawny fishermen reaching out to shake Isabella's hand, calling their thanks in their loud strong Gaelic voices. It was a moment she always treasured.

At 26, Isabella had discovered a way of using her talents by traveling and writing. She could then donate her earnings to help others and do good. It seemed as if everything had fallen into place. The following year, when her backaches and sleeplessness reappeared, her doctor immediately recommended a voyage to America. She set off in

1857, eager to explore more of the New World and looking forward to writing another book. She also planned to visit churches for her father who was writing a book about evangelism.

Isabella traveled thousands of miles and sat through hundreds of sermons. From New York she went to Philadelphia, to Washington to attend a session in Congress, and to the Hudson's Bay Territory in the northwest among wild Indians. She crossed the Great Lakes, sailed on the Mississippi, and traveled through Virginia, South Carolina and Georgia where she saw first-hand the realities of slavery. Despite Isabella's staunch anti-slavery feelings, when she attended a conference in Boston organized by William Lloyd Garrison and the Abolitionists, she was shocked by the outspoken criticisms of religion, the unladylike behavior of women, and the fact that they dared to wear Bloomer suits with pants, instead of skirts.

When Isabella sailed home a year later in April 1858, she anticipated a happy family reunion. She was looking forward to busy months of writing her book and the pleasure of giving her father the information she had found for his book. She was warmly welcomed home, but that first evening, her father fell ill with chills and a high fever. The next day, despite his illness, he went out to preach on his favorite topic, Sabbath observance. Isabella and her mother tried to persuade him to rest. But driven by what he saw as his mission he refused to stay at home.

At the end of April, he collapsed. An operation to remove an abscess came too late to save him. He called his wife and daughters to his bedside, and in a weak voice, he commended them to God and prayed they would meet again after life. Only a month after Isabella's return, he died on May 14, 1858.

For Isabella, it was a terrible loss. The driving force of the family had always been Edward Bird. She could not imagine her life without him. She also felt a sense of guilt that it was her fault, and that by going away, she had hastened his death. If she had stayed at home perhaps it would have been different. She did give him a few details about American evangelism and his book, *Some Account of the Great Religious Awakening Now Going On in the United States* was published after his death.

Isabella decided that she had failed her father. By doing what she enjoyed, she had not obeyed her Christian principles of self-denial and sacrifice. She vowed that from now on she would no longer travel and write, but would instead devote herself to good works and helping others, as her father would have wanted.

The family had to leave Wyton Rectory: a new minister would take over the parish and the house. Isabella, her mother and her sister Henrietta moved in with relatives, where Isabella wrote a brief account of her father's life.

Next, she put together her book on her American journey. This time her focus was religion in America. The book lists statistics on Sunday Schools, compares Sabbath observances, and quotes sermons. Now and then there's an incident or two that reveals the adventurous Isabella, but it is a brief interruption to the earnest, preaching tone of dreary account. It reads like a sermon by a minister, not the travels of a lively young woman. It was the book Isabella thought her father wanted her to write.

She sent it to John Murray, but he politely rejected it. *The Patriot* magazine printed it as a nine-part series of articles. In 1859 Sampson Low and Company published the essays as a book called *Aspects of Religion in America*. But there was no review in *The Times*, and no eager readers sending her appreciative notes.

Isabella now took on the role as head of the family. She urged her mother to find a home. Her mother agreed they should move to Scotland.

That winter Mrs. Bird and her two daughters moved into their own home at 3 Castle Terrace, Edinburgh. The house stood in a row of graceful houses close to the center of town. The curving windows overlooked the street and the church opposite. At 29, Isabella was ready to begin her new life.

Dora and Edward Bird, Isabella's mother and father

Chapter 2
Edinburgh and Australia

Isabella settles in Edinburgh. Article writing.
Good works. Death of her mother. Falls sick.
Sea voyage to Australia and New Zealand.
Unbearable heat. Paddle steamer to America.
Arrives in the Sandwich Islands.

Isabella arrived in Edinburgh at a time when it was one of the great intellectual and artistic centers of Europe, a rival to London and Paris. The university was renowned for science and medical teaching, and was one of the first places to advocate the use of anesthesia in childbirth. Sir Walter Scott and Robert Louis Stevenson were well-known literary residents.

There was a lively community of young intellectuals including John Blackie, a professor of Greek, and his wife, Ella, whom Isabella had met on her summer vacations. They introduced her to their university friends, and through her writing she met authors, artists, poets, and editors. Anna Stoddart, an Edinburgh writer who became a good friend and later wrote an admiring biography of Isabella, vividly describes meeting her for the first time:

"Her white face shining between the black meshes of a knitted Shetland veil; her great, observant eyes, flashing and smiling, but melancholy when she was silent; her gentleness and the exquisite modesty of her manner; and, above all, her soft and perfectly modulated voice, never betrayed into harshness or loudness, or even excitement, but so magnetic that all in the room were soon absorbed in listening to her."

Isabella spent her mornings working on magazine articles. Propped up on pillows in bed, she had a flat board on her knees and the floor scattered with notes, letters and sheets of paper. She had no grand travels to describe, so she wrote about religious topics. She spent months researching and writing a series of articles on the history of hymns and the lives of their composers for *The Sunday Magazine.*

Her afternoons were spent "making calls" to friends. In these days before telephones, visitors were welcomed for conversation and either invited in, or they left a card to show they had called. Isabella was also frequently invited to dinners and parties, attended plays and lectures, and church services.

She was delighted to have found a community where conversation and lively discussions were more important than frivolous music or dancing. But she was daunted by the sophistication of those she met. She felt her upbringing in the narrow world of a country parish had taught her few social graces, and she felt inadequate in the company of professors. Though she was well read, she had little experience of parties, social gatherings, and the conversation of educated society. When she confessed to Ella Blackie: "I so constantly feel my deficiencies in cultivation as much as in education," Ella suggested that they meet every Thursday morning to talk over the issues of the day, read books together, and discuss whatever else was on their minds. Grateful, Isabella agreed, and throughout her life, she turned to Ella Blackie, calling her "my dearest friend" in her letters and confiding in her much that she told no-one else.

Isabella's activities, like those of many other unmarried women in their thirties, reflected the constraints of the society in which she lived. Single women could be governesses to a family, or teachers in private schools, but Isabella disliked children. Her writing was the only avenue she could see that provided her with meaningful work and a chance to earn some money.

Marriage seemed unlikely for her or her sister. At that time, young English women outnumbered men, a result of the departure of thousands of well-educated young men to India and other distant shores of Queen Victoria's expanding empire to capture new frontiers, fight natives in bloody battles, or to fall ill from strange tropical diseases.

Isabella read about the Female Middle Class Emigration Society which sent marriageable women across the seas to Australia, New Zealand and South Africa, to work as governesses or nannies, and possibly marry the vast surplus of men living there. But she had vowed at her father's death that she would repress her selfish inclination to travel and instead dedicate herself to helping others. Her writing occupied her mind; she looked for good works to ease her conscience.

Her first effort was to help the Highland farmers. The wealthy Scottish landowners found it more profitable to raise sheep than crops, so they threw the farmers off the land, and left them without a home or any means of feeding their families. Isabella joined a committee of well-meaning Edinburgh ladies to offer the farmers a surprising alternative: send them to farms in Canada to start a new life. Isabella wrote letters to people she knew in Canada, arranged passages aboard transatlantic steamers, raised money, and even sewed kilts for the emigrants to take. Her enthusiasm convinced many dubious farmers that they would find a better life thousands of miles across the ocean. Whether the project was a success is not known, but after a few years the emigration committee closed down.

Isabella found a new cause. Edinburgh was flourishing in a wave of gentrification. The city echoed to the sound of builders pulling down the ramshackle old houses in the poorest neighborhoods to erect elegant homes for the upper and middle classes. The displaced families were driven into the slums of Edinburgh's Old Town, where it was rumored they lived in appalling conditions. Isabella went to investigate and wrote a series of articles about what she found.

"Ascending to the top of a narrow, tortuous, broken, and dirty staircase, entered a foul, low-roofed room, containing not a scrap of furniture. In each corner was a little heap of dirty straw on which nestled, tangled in strange confusion, some children. It was impossible to tell how many, but was easy to tell that all were dirty, sore, covered and infested with vermin. By the low fire crouched two crones, both drunk."

Her *Notes on Old Edinburgh* described the appalling living conditions of the poor families, and her descriptions were included in a book on social issues published in Edinburgh. She hoped that her impassioned writing would result in immediate change. But nothing happened. Isabella even went to the Town Council to lobby for the installation of washrooms and running water as a minimal first step toward improvement, but there was little interest in spending money on the poor. It was a frustrating lesson, and reminded her of her father's failed struggle for Sabbath observance.

She constantly scolded herself for not caring enough about those in need. She longed for "a cheerful intellect and self-denying spirit," and told Ella Blackie: "I feel as if my life were spent in the very ignoble occupation of taking care of myself, and that unless some disturbing influences arise, I am in great danger of becoming perfectly encrusted with selfishness, living to make life agreeable and its path smooth to myself alone."

In 1866, Isabella's mother died. For Isabella at 35, and her sister Hennie, 32, it was a shock. As two unmarried women, their choices were limited. They could live with relatives, as many spinsters did, relying on the kindness and charity of family members. Single women who could not support themselves often moved from house to house without any permanent place of their own, caring for a sick relative, assisting during a family crisis, helping with childcare.

Isabella did not want to do that. She estimated that their inheritance provided enough for both of them to live comfortably but carefully. She knew she could earn money from writing. She decided that she and her sister could manage very well sharing a house together, and keep their independence. Hennie, delighted with the idea, agreed to supervise the household responsibilities so that Isabella would be free to write.

It was a uniquely comfortable marriage of two compatible personalities. Isabella was creative and assertive, an independent, capable, and intelligent young woman, who was making a name for herself as a writer. She was the social, outgoing innovator, persuading her sister to follow her. Hennie was a quiet retiring person, with little interest in company or social life. She was intelligent and artistic, painted watercolors and studied Latin, Hebrew and Greek. Her greatest satisfaction was in selflessly doing good by taking food to the poor and tending the sick, the kind of personal devotion to those less fortunate expected of well-bred ladies.

Hennie and Isabella had grown up together as the minister's daughters, moving from place to place as their father changed his parish, and were often isolated from other children in the communities their father served. They learned to depend on each other as playmates and friends. Now the close relationship deepened. Hennie, who always admired clever Isa, was ready to do anything to help her. Isabella appreciated her sister's unswerving devotion to her well-being, and admired her ability to help others selflessly. Their involvement was so exclusive that it successfully deterred any man who might have wanted a friendship with only one of them.

For a few years, all went well. But in 1869, Isabella knew that a crisis was approaching. She desperately needed something challenging to do. She wrote to her publisher, John Murray: "I long for some more serious and engrossing literary occupation than writing papers for the *North British Review, Good Words*, etc., and if you can suggest anything to me I shall be very glad."

She sent him her five *Pen and Pencil Sketches Among the Outer Hebrides*. John Murray urged her to do what he knew she did best: travel abroad and find new and interesting material. It was twelve years since her father had died but Isabella held to her vow. She considered going on a religious pilgrimage to Sinai and the Holy Land, but felt that even that would be too selfish.

Her body knew what to do. Isabella began to suffer from her backaches and head pains. She went to several doctors. Though she described her numerous symptoms carefully, no one could explain why her back pain, weakness and maladies disappeared completely when she was organizing Scottish emigration, or traveling in America, or climbing narrow stairs in a slum. The only visible symptom was her bad back, and even that was an erratic condition.

Her tremendous anxiety about her health increased. She spent hours worrying over every minor twinge so that she was soon in a state of depression and deep unhappiness. She had acquired enough medical information from the many doctors she had seen so she could converse knowledgeably about her ailments, convincing herself as well as everyone who met her that there was something seriously wrong.

One doctor prescribed a steel net to support her head when she sat up, so that her spine would not have the weight to bear. He urged her to avoid going up and down stairs, and advised her to stay on a boat because the motion would ease her pain.

Isabella dutifully followed his advice. She wore the steel net. She slept on the sofa downstairs. She traveled to the Highlands to find a boat. But there was little improvement. Languishing in bed, she quoted in her diary: "All his days he eateth in darkness, and he hath much sorrow and wrath with his sickness."

In an era before psychology and psychiatry were taken seriously, no one suggested that Isabella's ailments were caused by her environment. It would have been considered laughable to suggest that her physical pain was her reaction to mental conflict between her creative abilities and the lack of any opportunity to develop them within the society she lived. Isabella was trying to conform to the image of a genteel lady, and to fit into the society of Edinburgh's secure middle-class life. But she could not quench her adventurous spirit. Getting sick was her way of coping with intense frustration. Her ill health reflected her emotional anguish.

Hennie, desperately worried by her sister's unhappiness and ill health, urged her to do what had cured her before: go on a sea voyage. Isabella refused, determined not to break her vow. Finally, after months of despair, she gave in to Hennie's pleadings. She would take one ocean trip, and perhaps the change of air might cure her, as it had before. Once again, ill health had given her the excuse to return to the life she loved.

This time she chose the Pacific. She bought a ticket to Australia and New Zealand. From Auckland she planned to go to California and come home across America. She would travel for about a year as she had done before.

She and Hennie agreed to give up their home in Edinburgh. Hennie preferred to spend the summer living in the Scottish Highlands and would stay with friends over the winter. When Isabella came back, they could find somewhere new to live together.

In the spring of 1872 they rented a simple white-painted cottage in Tobermory on the island of Mull. There Isabella packed carefully for her travels. She took boots, underwear, warm stockings and dresses, and a black silk for special occasions. She took her medicines—for she had acquired quite a collection. She also took her sketchbooks, pen and ink, notebook, and sheets of paper and envelopes so she could write long letters to her beloved sister.

She boarded the steamer at Liverpool in July 1872, a slight dark-haired young woman of 39. As the ship slowly pulled away from the land, she watched Hennie grow smaller and smaller on the quay. Isabella was traveling again.

———

Twelve weeks on board a ship with a crowd of drinking and card-playing passengers did not prove an ideal voyage for Isabella. As the boat steamed into Melbourne Harbor on October 5th, she looked out eagerly for her first view of Australia.

"The smell of the land was sweet; the patches of purple and blue color in the shallow water were an artist's dream; and to eyes wearied of sea-green hills heaped together by Antarctic waves, the far-off violet ranges suggested paradise."

Once she disembarked, she found an odd familiarity. There was none of the strangeness which had so fascinated her in America. Here, the voices were English, the clothes were English, the homes were exactly like English houses and, as she found, quite unsuitable for the sultry heat of Australia. She walked along paved streets, like those in England, and saw libraries of stone built to look exactly like the libraries in England, thousands of miles away. She saw town halls, banks, theaters, opera houses, music and dance halls as well as cricket grounds, bar-rooms and restaurants—replicas of all she had left behind. Even the names of places were the same; she saw suburban communities called Kew, Richmond, Brighton, St. Kilda.

Only the weather reminded her she was not at home. That year, a fierce heatwave had invaded the usually pleasant spring months. Blazing, unyielding sun burned down, with a power Isabella had never experienced before. She had wanted Australia to be warmer than Edinburgh. But this was too much. For the first time, she suffered from heat exhaustion.

"The night passed slowly: it was hot, still and airless. The next morning the sun rose fierce and red, and a fiery fog took the place of the sky. All day long the north wind blew with a blasting breath, and the mercury hovered about 90 degrees. Swarms of black flies, juicy and lazy, settled on everything indoors. Another night of heavy heat passed wearily, and the third day of the hot wind was ushered in by an airless dawn."

She tried to be interested in what she found, but the enthusiasm and curiosity which had driven her before was barely visible. She knew that kangaroos, koala bears and crocodiles lived in Australia, but she never tried to see live animals in the bush. Instead she described the stuffed models on display in the museum. Melbourne had a unique Oriental community with temples and shops, but she did not go and investigate; instead she reported what other people told her. It was as if she had forgotten the skills of first-hand observation and immediacy and had completely lost her passion for travel.

She wrote miserably to Hennie: "I don't know anything that could reconcile me to living in this country. The climate and the growths are so unlovely, and from all that I hear, the tone of everything is so low."

Though her back was not aching, she still had headaches and found it difficult to sleep at night. Her letters whined and moaned with unhappiness, complaining to her long-suffering sister about her useless, aimless life.

It was not until an old friend invited her to come "up the country" to visit his farm that her enthusiasm revived. Leaving the steamy streets of Melbourne, she boarded an overcrowded boat to Warrnambool. From the river, she drove through forests of gumtrees, draped with hanging bark that peeled off. Cockatoos with yellow crests, parrots, parakeets, and other brightly colored birds, screeching wildly, flitted among the branches, flashing their scarlet and green and purple feathers. A few stunted trees grew, and the ground was covered with short, velvety grass, the brightest deep green she had ever seen.

The family raised cattle and sheep on sixty acres of rolling land, thirty-five miles from the nearest town. Looking out her window she could see miles of green plains dotted with the wooden cabins of early settlers, and wandering herds of red and black cattle. She found the view enchanting. It was lovely to be away from the hot streets and stone buildings of the city.

Eager to see more, she went to visit a friend who was sheep-herding in the bush at shearing time. Intrigued, she watched as men dunked the sheep in tanks of hot water, rinsed them off with cold water, and rubbed them until the wool was white and clean. Travelling shearers came by, experts with their sharp knives who slit the fleeces off in one piece, and then shook, sorted and folded them into heavy bales.

She heard stories of the wild dingo dogs who snatched sheep from under the very nose of the shepherd, and of terrors in the long nights when men sat watching their flocks. For the first time, she felt at home under the open sky gazing up as the stars of the southern hemisphere sparkled above.

At night, there was a celebration, which she enthusiastically described in a *Leisure Hour* article: "I have seldom enjoyed an evening more than one which I spent with a large shearing party at one of the loveliest and wildest of hill stations, round a great bivouac fire, where huge beefsteaks were broiled over the embers, and pannikins of strong tea circulated freely, and stories were told, and songs sung, and the good fellowship was protracted into the small hours, and a few aborigines, not much darker by nature than the white men were with dirt and sunburn, hung about in the shadow and now and then heaped green logs on the fire."

Back in Melbourne, she could not bear to think of staying another day in the overpowering heat. She heard that New Zealand was usually cooler. She immediately booked a berth on a steamer to Auckland, regretfully admitting that after two months in Australia, she felt no better than when she arrived.

She boarded a small crowded steamer, its decks loaded with a cargo of sheep and horses. When she arrived, she found once again the same overpowering heat.

"A white, unwinking, scintillating sun blazed down upon Auckland, New Zealand. Along the white glaring road from Onehunga, dusty trees and calla lilies drooped with the heat. Dusty thickets sheltered the cicada, whose triumphant din grated and rasped through the palpitating atmosphere. Flags drooped in the stifling air. Men on the verge of sunstroke plied their tasks mechanically. Dogs, with flabby and protruding tongues, hid themselves away under archway shadows. The stones of the sidewalks and the bricks of the houses radiated a furnace heat. All nature was limp, dusty, groaning, gasping."

Lying in her hotel room, she could hardly muster up enough energy to go out. She was taking medicine three times a day. She felt so tired that she could not bear to meet people or do anything. She wrote miserably to Hennie of her numerous problems, complaining of "neuralgia, pain in my bones, pricking like pins and needles in my limbs, excruciating nervousness, exhaustion, inflamed eyes, sore throat, swelling of the glands behind each ear."

In desperation, she decided to go straight to America. She booked a passage on the next boat for San Francisco. She hoped to reach the Rocky Mountains and Estes Park where her friend Rose Kingsley had told her there was a paradise of fresh, cool air and spectacular scenery. She was so anxious to escape that she spent the night before departure on board.

Her boat, the steamer *Nevada*, looked as if it had seen better days. Isabella thought it delightful, "huge, airy, perfectly comfortable, a paddle steamer of the old-fashioned American type, deck above deck, balconies, a pilot house above the foremast."

There were only seven passengers besides Isabella. There was an elderly Scottish doctor, four other men, and a Mrs. Dexter and her son. Isabella listened as her fellow passengers gossiped among themselves: the *Nevada* was sailing without a certificate; her starboard shaft was partly broken; the repairs needed were so serious that the ship had not dared to put in at port for months; the floats of the starboard wheel had been shortened; and she leaked. On the previous voyage, she had nearly sunk, and the passengers had signed a protest against the appalling conditions. Now, hastily repaired, the boat struggled to look seaworthy. Most of the gossip turned out to be true.

The reality of danger and the promise of crisis were the stuff to revive a dispirited Isabella. Faced with the possibility of sinking in the Pacific, she rose to the occasion like a cork in a bottle. Her letters became lively, enthusiastic and full of optimism, and her complaints disappeared.

Two days out from Auckland, a severe hurricane struck. The passengers gathered in the deck house which had windows all round, to watch the sea's fury battering the boat.

"Very little fear was felt," Isabella explained. "We understood by intuition that if our crazy engines failed at any moment to keep the ship's head to the sea, her destruction would not occupy half an hour." The hurricane winds shrieked so fiercely that it was impossible to hear anyone's voice.

The captain, the oldest seaman in the Pacific, said it was the worst he had seen for seventeen years. Part of the front of the boat was carried away, and the iron stanchions were gnarled and twisted. By the time the storm ended, the boat had sunk two feet deeper into the water.

The stewards were so busy on deck that no meals were served until the third day. But the food was hardly edible. There were ants and weevils in the bread. Everything was thrown on the table with a slapdash insolence, as if daring anyone to complain.

Next the engines broke down. The boat rocked silently in the waves for hours while the men worked on them. The passengers were grateful that it hadn't happened during the storm and cheered when the engines roared into life again.

Five days out the *Nevada* entered the tropics. Though the air was about 85 degrees and the water 80 degrees, the temperature on board often reached 110 degrees. Isabella could not avoid the winds blowing smoky air in her face from the two smoke stacks. During the day the sun made the deck surfaces so hot she had to put on boots to protect her feet from getting burned.

In rain storms, water leaked through the roof in the saloon so she wore her waterproof cape and rubber boots. In her cabin, her lumpy mattress often split open, and she used her slippers to thwack the cockroaches crawling around and thumped on the floor to scare off the rats.

Despite the discomforts, Isabella's mood was now light-hearted. The catastrophes brought the passengers together. She sat with them as they read aloud the *Idylls of the King* to each other, talking of the snow and ice of long northern winters. She played games of quoits on deck for exercise. She took cold plunge baths. She played chess. And she never ever mentioned her aches or pains.

Her joyous mood and disdain for everyday life at home was reflected in a letter to Ella Blackie: "The old Sea God has so stolen my heart and penetrated my soul that I seriously fear that hereafter though I must be elsewhere in body, I shall be with him in spirit. I am not joking. My two friends on board the ship have several times told me that I had so imbibed the spirit of the sea that they thought after a time on land I should crave for it again.

"It is the perfect infatuation. It is to me like living in a new world, so pure, so fresh, so vital, so careless, so unfettered, so full of interest that one grudges being asleep, and instead of carrying cares and worries and thoughts of the morrow to bed with one to keep one awake, one falls asleep at once to awaken to another day in which one knows there can be nothing to annoy one. No door bells, no 'please ma'ams', no dirt, no servants, no bills, no demands of any kind, no vain attempt to overtake all one knows one should do. Above all, no nervousness and no conventionalities. It seems to me a sort of brief resurrection of the girl of 21. I cannot tell you how much I like my life!"

Suddenly, the situation changed. Mrs. Dexter's son ruptured a blood vessel in his lungs and began spitting blood. The young man was seriously ill. He was laid out in the deck house, and the passengers rallied round, taking turns to stay at his bedside, fanning him to keep him cool, and giving him water and food.

Isabella realized that the old Scottish doctor was completely incompetent, quite befuddled after years of heavy drinking, and no help at all in giving medical attention. Desperate, Mrs. Dexter urged the Captain to go to the nearest land. The only hope for her son was to find a doctor. They were close to the Sandwich Islands, now known as Hawaii. The Captain turned the boat toward Honolulu.

Frightened at the thought of arriving in a strange country on her own, Mrs. Dexter begged Isabella to come with her. Isabella had no reason to hurry on to San Francisco. She liked the idea of a few days in a place far from most beaten tracks. She had become her competent, energetic self again. She cheerfully agreed to accompany Mrs. Dexter.

The battered *Nevada* chugged across the Equator. It was listing so badly that one of the wheels was almost out of the water. As they lurched through the clear turquoise blue water, cool breezes wafted over the old boat. Isabella, leaning over the rail, glimpsed Oahu in the distance. As they came closer, she saw the peaks of the dark mountains rising tall against the blue sky, the mountain sides slashed by canyons of green, and sparkling waterfalls pouring down like streams of light.

She heard the unceasing pounding of waves on the reef, the crashing of white surf against the ring of coral. It was the eternal refrain of her first tropical island.

Chapter 3
Hawaii

Paradise of beauty. Rides astride. Climbs
volcanoes. Travels through the island staying
with native families. Rejects proposal of
marriage. Leaves for America.

As the boat scudded through the surf into the clear turquoise waters of Honolulu Bay, Isabella discovered all she had dreamed of finding in Australia and New Zealand. In the rippling water, long low canoes sped through the rolling breakers. Brown-skinned bodies swam in the waves, splashing and diving. Far below she glimpsed the vast coral forests of the ocean floor. Ahead, she saw crowds of people on the quay, waving and singing, welcoming the boat as it steamed in.

The bright colors of their clothes were like a gathering of rainbows—the plump women in loose dresses of white, crimson, yellow, scarlet, blue or green, and the lithe men flaunting brightly colored shirts and white pants. Around their necks hung wreaths of beautiful flowers, purple and white hibiscus and oleander, yellow allamandas, pink orchids. Some women slipped scarlet blossoms or garlands of flowers in their long, dark hair. As the boat shuddered into its mooring place on the dock, the crowd jostled forward and climbed aboard, laughing and calling, chattering together. Men and women embraced everyone with a lilting greeting of "Aloha!"

"Fair Paradise of the Pacific!" exulted Isabella. "Bright blossom of a summer sea!" She admired the "rich brown men and women, with wavy, shining black hair, large, lustrous brown eyes, and rows of perfect teeth like ivory," noting: "Everyone was smiling." Even the foreigners looked relaxed and happy, standing on the quay in light, cool clothes, with straw hats and parasols. Within minutes of the boat's arrival, Mrs. Dexter and her son were on their way to a hotel, and requesting a doctor be sent there immediately. Isabella joined two of her friends from the boat for a tour in a horse-drawn carriage.

Along the wide roads, huge trees arched overhead, and patches of sunlight filtered through the leaves in dazzling rays. After the barren heat of Australia, she was ecstatic at the abundant richness of the greenery—the giant leaves of umbrella trees, the feathery fronds of bamboo, the hanging fruit of mango, banana, orange, breadfruit, candlenut and papaya, and the tall date and coco palms, their spreading leaves high above the long straight tree trunks. The air was heavy with the aroma of gardenias, oleanders, roses, lilies and dozens of other flowers. The wide porches of the low houses trailed with yellow and white and pink flowers of vines growing in rich profusion, adding their scents to the heady perfume. Along the streets she saw men and women galloping on small, wiry horses. To her surprise, no one rode side-saddle.

"The women seemed perfectly at home in their gay, brass-bossed, high peaked saddles, flying along astride, bare-footed, with their orange and scarlet riding dresses streaming on each side beyond their horses' tails, a bright kaleidoscopic flash of bright eyes, white teeth, shining hair, garlands of flowers and many colored dresses."

Her first glimpse of the newly opened Hawaiian Hotel revealed a charming low stone building with wide verandas drooping with clematis and passion flowers. The guests included English and American naval officers, planters' families, whaling captains, and tourists from around the world. The staff were friendly and eager to help. In the dining room, the tables were piled high with bananas, guavas, limes and oranges. Isabella sat in a wicker chair, looking out on a distant view of hills and valleys in the setting sun and felt as if she had discovered Paradise.

That evening, a soft breeze rustled the palm trees, wafting in the refreshing scent of flowers and sea. Through the half-open jalousies she heard music from the royal band at the king's palace. Outside, a crescent moon glowed in the velvet sky, and the stars hung in the dark as bright as street lamps. It was idyllic, she thought. But suddenly she heard a familiar buzzing sound. Hastily pulling the netting around her bed, she tied it securely. Even in paradise, there were mosquitoes.

The next morning, she heard that Mrs. Dexter's son was on his way to recovery. After her friends left on the boat for San Francisco, Isabella decided to spend a week exploring Honolulu. Someone at the hotel told her that an American lady, Miss Parker, whom Isabella disguised as Miss Karpe in her book, was looking for a companion on a trip to the volcanoes, and was leaving that day. Mrs. Dexter urged Isabella to go, so she packed hastily and hurried down to meet Miss Parker waiting to catch the inter-island ferry to the Big Island of Hawaii.

The *Kilauea* was a big old 400-ton propeller boat that traveled between the islands on an unpredictable schedule, frequently delayed by engine trouble and heavy seas. After her weeks on the *Nevada*, Isabella felt at home as soon as she boarded. Two essential pieces of tackle gave way as the main sail was hoisted. In her cabin, she saw a giant cockroach looking as large as a mouse crouched on her pillow while another scuttled over the quilt. When she asked the steward for help, he only smiled and shrugged.

Miss Parker succumbed to the rolling waves and lay seasick in her bunk. The boat was crowded with men, women, and children, as well as dogs, cats, wooden pots of Hawaiian "poi," coconuts, bananas, dried fish and an avalanche of flower wreaths. Most people slept on deck. Isabella was amazed to recognize Bishop Willis, whom she had met in Honolulu, stretched out on a mattress among the Hawaiians.

Isabella spent her time reading and asking other passengers about the Sandwich Islands. She learned they had been discovered in 1778 by Captain Cook, that the new King Liloliho had just been crowned, and that the Americans, the British and the Germans were maneuvering for political control. She also listened to strong arguments about the missionaries who had arrived from New England in 1820 eager to crush "unrighteousness, fornication, wickedness, debate." Several passengers believed passionately that they had ruined the innocence of Hawaiian life, while others felt Christianity would bring needed civilization.

As the boat entered Hilo Bay, Isabella was spellbound by the view. Stretching in a perfect crescent for almost two miles lay a band of golden sand edged by the turquoise sea. Along the shore, half hidden by greenery, nestled the grass and straw houses of the Hawaiians. Tall palm trees waved their long plumes in the breeze against the cloudless blue sky.

There was a rapturous greeting for the ferry. Colorfully dressed crowds waved from the quay, and a whaleboat skimmed alongside rowed by eight young men in white linen suits and white straw hats with wreaths of scarlet flowers around their necks who sang songs of welcome.

Hilo had no hotel, so Isabella and Miss Parker went to stay with the Sheriff of Hawaii, Mr. Severance. Walking in his garden, Isabella was amazed by the size of the orchids, ginger plants and palms which she had only seen as spindly specimens in the Edinburgh Botanic Gardens. She could hardly find words to describe the abundance of greenery and lavish luxuriance, the dense woods, the glossy leaves of the breadfruit tree, the palmtrees, the lilies, roses, fuchsias, clematis, begonias, the colors, the textures, the quantity of glorious flowers.

Miss Parker, quite recovered from her seasickness, suggested a ride that afternoon. Isabella sat side-saddle as she usually did, and followed her, but she found riding over the uneven terrain was very painful and she came back stiff and sore. Mr. Severance suggested she ride astride as the Hawaiian women did because it was much more comfortable. Isabella never liked to challenge accepted rules about proper conduct or dress which women were supposed to obey, but she realized she had the freedom to do as she pleased because she was traveling. It was a moment of revelation. She provided a careful explanation for her sister Hennie for her unladylike behavior:

"It was only my strong desire to see the volcano which made me consent to a mode of riding against which I have so strong a prejudice. A great many of the foreign ladies on Hawaii have adopted the Mexican saddle also, for greater security to themselves and ease to their horses, and often wear full Turkish trousers and jauntily-made dresses reaching to the ankles."

Isabella borrowed a riding costume and was dressed and ready at eight the next morning. She sat astride her horse with her wide-brimmed Australian hat, and a blanket strapped behind her borrowed Mexican saddle. Miss Parker rode side-saddle, wore a short grey waterproof, and had a broad-brimmed straw hat tied on with a green veil. The Hawaiian guide was decorated with garlands of flowers and carried the saddlebags with the food and drink. He was convinced Isabella was related to Queen Victoria and treated her with great respect.

As they set off on the slow, steady incline toward the volcano, Isabella found it very difficult to clutch her saddle, guide the horse and keep her feet in the stirrups without going over the horse's head when he stopped suddenly. Miss Parker talked incessantly and Isabella began to detest the sound of her rasping voice: "The typical American traveling lady, who is encountered everywhere from the Andes to the Pyramids, tireless, with indomitable energy, Spartan endurance and a genius for attaining everything."

Twelve hours later, after thirty miles of riding, they reached the inn by the volcano. From the window, she could see the sky lit up by clouds of erupting fires. Isabella, though stiff and tired, stayed up half the night watching the sight. The next morning, the guide led them on foot toward the brilliant glow ahead, the air filled with smoke and the smell of sulphur. Visitors were allowed to walk across the volcano floor even though it was extremely dangerous. Isabella climbed down the side of the crater and carefully crossed the steam cracks, jets of sulphur, blowing cones, and occasional grand eruptions. When she slipped and fell in a hole of sulphurous steam, her strong gloves were burned through as pulled herself up.

"Suddenly, just above, and in front of us, gory drops were tossed in the air, and we stood on the brink of Hale-mau-mau, which was about 35 feet below us. It was all confusion, commotion, force, terror, glory, majesty, mystery, and even beauty. And the color! Molten metal has not that crimson gleam, nor blood that living light!"

She had reached the edge of the active part of the volcanic lake which was in full eruption with terrifying explosions, hissing and crashing and with fountains, waves and jets of molten fire rising and falling continually. She stood transfixed by the unbelievable drama as huge flames were thrown high in the air, overhanging crags fell into the burning liquid, and the fiery spray reached up to forty feet above the lake. Finding a safe place, she stopped and watched the eruption for three hours, mesmerized by its power and drama, unable to tear herself away from the spectacular sight. That evening, she wrote an ecstatic letter to Hennie describing "the most unutterable of wonderful things."

The journey back down the volcano in mist and pouring rain was another achievement for her travel abilities, and she was delighted to have had such a wonderful experience. Charmed by Hilo, Isabella watched a surfing exhibition at the beach as hundreds of young men soared along the edges of the waves, balanced on the top of the curls, rode majestically to the shore.

"The more furious and agitated the water is, the greater the excitement, and the love of these watery exploits is not confined to the young. I saw great fat men with their hair streaked with grey, balancing themselves on their narrow surf-boards, and riding the surges shorewards with as much enjoyment as if they were in their first youth. The sea was so blue, the sunlight so soft, the air so sweet. People were all holiday-making, and enjoying themselves, the surf-bathers in the sea, and hundreds of gaily-dressed men and women galloping on the beach."

For her next adventure, she had a flannel riding costume of Scottish plaid made, hired a horse and set off into the countryside. She told Hennie: "I wish you could see me in my Rob Roy riding dress, with leather belt and pouch, a 'lei' of orange seeds round my throat, jingling Mexican spurs, blue saddle blanket and blanket strapped on behind the saddle."

The Severances gave her an introduction to their friends, the Austins, who lived on a sugar plantation. Isabella loved her visit to the easy-going couple and their four young sons, where meals were prepared by a Chinese cook and Isabella had the freedom to do exactly as she liked.

"In a land where there are no carpets, no fires, no dust, no hot water needed, no windows to open and shut, people live more happily than any that I have seen elsewhere. It is pleasant to be among people whose faces are not soured by the east wind, or wrinkled by the worrying effort to 'keep up appearances;' who have no formal visiting, but real sociability; who regard the light manual labor of domestic life as a pleasure, not a thing to be ashamed of."

She was delighted by everything. "The air is always like balm; the rain is tepid and does not give cold; in summer it may be three or four degrees warmer. Windows and doors stand open the whole year. It is a truly delightful climate and mode of living with such an abundance of air and sunshine. My health improves daily, and I do not consider myself an invalid."

One morning Isabella set out with Deborah, a young Hawaiian woman and her cousin, Kaluna, to visit their Hawaiian relatives in the Waipio valley. Kaluna was an irrepressible young man.

"His movements are impulsive and uncontrolled. He talks loud, laughs incessantly, croons a monotonous chant, which sounds almost as heathenish as tom-toms, throws himself out of his saddle, hanging on by one foot, lingers behind to gather fruits, and then comes tearing up, beating his horse over the ears and nose, with a fearful yell, striking my mule and threatening to overturn me as he passes me on the narrow track. He is the most thoroughly careless and irresponsible being I ever saw."

Hawaiian women and children

Soon after they set out, a sudden rainstorm drenched them, and when Deborah stopped at a Hawaiian grass hut, they were soaking wet. Inside, Isabella found several other wet people crowded into the single room. There was nowhere to dry her clothes. She sat on the matting on the floor and shared a meal of chicken, sweet potatoes and native "poi," a paste made from taro root. The others ate with their fingers, but Isabella used her knife. The only place to sleep was the floor so Isabella rolled herself up in a blanket under the broken window. During the night, cats kept jumping in and walking over her, water dripped on her head, and Kaluna and Deborah stayed up all night, joking, talking, and eating "poi" with the others.

Isabella commented primly: "It was so new and so odd to be the only white person among eleven natives in a lonely house, and yet to be as secure from danger and annoyance as in our own home. I was amused all the time, though I should have preferred sleep."

The next morning, her wet clothes dried in the sun. Riding up steep trails, and jumping across streams pouring down the narrow gulches, she reveled in the magnificent views and spectacular scenery stretching on all sides. The trip was delightful, she thought, and she rode happily, slept in grass huts and ate Hawaiian food.

The morning they planned to ride back, Isabella woke to find fierce winds, torrential rain and the surf thundering on the rocks with huge curling waves pounding on the beaches. Cascades of water leapt from the cliffs with a tremendous noise and crashed down to the sea. Isabella knew that the gulches would be full from the heavy rains, the paths slippery and dangerous from the water pouring down, and suggested they wait a day. Kaluna whined that he was tired and cold. It was Deborah, anxious to go home and see her husband again, who ignored their comments and determined to set off.

The narrow rivulets which they had jumped so easily on the ride in had become fast-moving torrents. Isabella told Deborah it was too dangerous and urged her to go back and wait for the rain to stop. But Deborah assured her that it was easy to cross the swollen streams.

"Spur, spur and keep up the river," she told Isabella. "If horses give out, we let go; I swim and save you."

Isabella followed her down the slippery paths to the rushing whirlpool where the sea met the swirling river. Before, it had been so shallow she had paddled through it. Now, it was a torrent of wild waves and currents. Deborah rode in, the water up to her saddles, shouting to be heard above the roar: "Water higher all minutes, spur horse, think we come through!"

They galloped into the frothing waves, and Isabella saw: "One spinning, rushing, foaming river, twice as wide as the Clyde at Glasgow, and most fearful, the ocean, in three huge breakers, had come in. The roar was deafening. My soul and sense literally reeled among the dizzy horrors of the wide, wild tide, but with an effort I regained sense and self-possession, for we were in, and there was no turning. I saw

Deborah's great horse carried off his legs, my mare, too, was swimming, and between swimming, struggling and floundering, we reached what had been the junction of the two rivers."

Her teeth chattering with cold, Isabella struggled to hold on. She spurred her horse frantically. The water poured over her. She tried not to look at the giant waves rising and breaking thunderously only a few feet away. At last, she managed to guide her soaking horse out of the water, and climbed up on to the sand. "It was a horrible suspense," Isabella confessed.

Her ride back over dangerous gulches, leaping streams and deep chasms was a true test of her abilities. When she arrived at the Austins, everyone was amazed. The dangers of crossing the gulches in a storm were well known. Isabella felt she had proved her mettle and shown she could ride as well as a Hawaiian woman.

Now she was ready to explore the island on her own. She went to Waimea on the northern coast and rode through the highlands. She had no plans and no map. She stayed in Hawaiian villages, ate fruit and "poi", swam in the rivers, dried her clothes in the sun and declared it was "the easiest, freest life I have ever seen," and added: "No man now ever says of any difficult thing that I could not do it!" The Hawaiians admired her bravery, endurance, and skill on horseback.

She confided to her sister: "I saw myself looking so young in a glass that I did not know it was me, just as I have been startled in Edinburgh sometimes by seeing an anxious, haggard face and seeing it was me. I have been thought by everyone lately to be under 30. I have grown thin, and my cheeks have so much color from sunburn and my eyes are so dark and even shining that I look, I fear, younger than you."

The revitalized Isabella arrived at the Spencers' sheep farm to spend a few days. Mr. Wilson, a young Canadian hunter working on the ranch, was delighted to meet her. She enjoyed his stories about his adventurous life and his work. They rode together almost every day enjoying each other's company. In the evenings, they sat by the fire after dinner while she knitted and he talked about Canada.

Isabella planned to catch the next steamer to explore the island of Kauai. Mr. Wilson kept urging her to stay longer but Isabella was eager to travel on. On her last morning he rode with her to the ferry. Suddenly, he stopped and handed her a piece of paper. She read: "Dear Miss Bird, my friend Mr. Wilson is most anxious to propose to you but dare not after so short an acquaintance. I can only say that his character is excellent and that he is about the best hearted fellow on the island. Yours very truly, Frank Spencer."

Isabella was completely taken aback. "I asked him why he liked me, and he said the first time I spoke he felt strange all over, and since I had begun to talk to him he had liked every word I said and every opinion I expressed. He said he had never felt so good and happy as the night before, and that the sight of my knitting needles reminded him of his mother in Canada. He was so perfectly respectful yet so perfectly assured."

Isabella told him firmly "it wouldn't do" and said there were fifty reasons against it, but he was persistent: "He said that if I would stay and tell them to him, he would dispose of them one by one."

Isabella hardly knew what to say. She admitted to Hennie that "for a moment" she was tempted to accept this "manly goodhearted splendid looking fellow," but then she thought of her sister: "What I might have said had it not been for you I don't know." The image of Hennie also reminded Isabella that she was still a proper Edinburgh lady: "I wondered whether I should lecture him on difference in social position or say any stereotyped thing." Fortunately, she did not. Instead she hurriedly boarded the ferry and told him she would write to him and explain. The boat sailed off. Isabella did write. Mr. Wilson wrote back - twice. But that was all.

Isabella had changed. The new Isabella was the one Mr. Wilson had met—a suntanned, energetic woman who rode everywhere, enjoyed the unpredictability of her carefree life, fearlessly explored the unknown, slept in straw huts, and swam in the rivers. When Mr. Wilson expressed his admiration for the new Isabella, she reacted as if she were still living in polite society. Though she was now an independent and unconventional traveler, she held firm to her image of herself as a well-bred Edinburgh lady.

Arriving in Kauai, Isabella was overwhelmed by its beauty: "Walls of peaks, and broken precipices, grey ridges rising out of the blue forest gloom, high mountains with mists wreathing their spiky summits; gleams of a distant silver sea; many-tinted woods festooned and adorned with numberless lianas, and even the trunks of fallen trees took on a new beauty from the exquisite ferns which covered them."

Her descriptions captured the essence of the lush tropical loveliness. Her words recreated the sensual images of the soft, warm climate, the heavy scents of oleander and orange blossom, and the languor of the Hawaiian life. She longed for Hennie to visualize exactly what she had seen, and like the French painter Seurat, she tried to make the picture come alive with the intensity of every dot of detail.

In Kauai, she had a small adobe house to herself, on the grounds of a mission in Koloa, near Poipu Beach. She was the guest of Dr. Smith, an English doctor and his family. She joined them for meals, taught in the mission school, and found that she had become very popular.

"There is something soothing and gratifying in being so much liked. They said I was the best pleased and the most boundlessly good natured person they had ever had among them, that I am so genial, like 'sunshine in their houses.' How very strange it all seems to have drifted like a waif into such a life. It was a plan devised and propelled by no one. If Mrs. D. had not been compelled to land, I should have gone on to San Francisco!"

Henrietta must have found it hard to imagine her sister so cheerful and content after her moaning and ill health at home and the whining letters from Australia and New Zealand. Isabella now headed her letters—some of them ten, twenty or even thirty pages long—with "Nothing annoying in this." She described the details of her "ravages" as she called her wild rides in the islands, and declared: "I delight in Hawaii more than ever, with its unconventional life, great upland sweeps, unexplored forests, riotous breezes, and general atmosphere of freedom, airiness and expansion. As I find that a lady can travel with perfect safety, I have many projects in view."

In her long letters, Isabella called Hennie "My Dearest Pet" and "My Ownest" and commented: "I do so wonder how my pet is getting on. My heart yearns over my good sweet little thing." Isabella called herself "Its Pet" and "Its Ownest," reflecting their close affection. She told Hennie how much she missed her, and longed to see her again. But she could not deny her happiness.

"I am doing what a woman can hardly ever do—leading a life fit to recruit a man. Now with my horse and gear packed upon it, I need make no plans. I can fall into anything which seems feasible. It showed some originality and energy to have devised such a life! I feel energy for anything except conventionality and civilization."

Carelessly, she even suggested that Hennie come out and join her to settle on the islands, adding: "If we lived here, we should be rich residents. We could keep six or eight horses, have abundance of books and periodicals, and you could get about and pay visits quite easily. You would be surprised to find how competent I have grown in cooking, mending, washing, moneying. I can saddle, bridle and pack a horse quite independently. I am quite fitted to live on these islands now."

While the letter sailed slowly across the ocean to Hennie in Scotland, Isabella quite forgot her invitation in the excitement of her next adventure. Mr. William Green, an English scientist who had written a book on volcanoes, invited Isabella to climb the volcano Mauna Loa with him. From Hilo, the red glow of the new eruption was clearly visible. Thrilled, Isabella hastily prepared for the trip. She was warned about altitude sickness and the cold, so she borrowed woollen stockings, blankets, a poncho and saddle bags. She bought cans of salmon, cookies, chocolate and potted tongue. On a June day in 1873 she rode off on her mule up the slow incline of Mauna Loa.

She crossed the rough jagged lava, called a-a, and the swirls of smooth black lava, called pa-hoe-hoe. Smoke, fire and choking gases filled the air as they reached the Hale-mau-mau Crater near Kilauea, which Isabella had visited in January. It had changed dramatically: lava flows had added 500 feet to the crater walls and the lake had sunk about 80 feet. She watched as Mr. Green took several scientific measurements and observations.

The next morning, as they followed the trail under the trees, the ground suddenly shook with an earthquake. Isabella thought it most exciting, like being on a ship in a wild ocean storm. That night they slept in a grass hut. At dawn, they set out toward the summit.

"A fountain of pure, yellow fire, unlike the gory gleam of Kilauea, was regularly playing in several united but independent jets, throwing up its glorious incandescence to a height of from 150 to 300 feet, and at one time 600! You cannot imagine such a beautiful sight. The sunset gold was not purer than the living fire. It was all beauty."

She had reached the edge of the huge crater of Mokuaweoweo. Hundreds of feet below were the burning fires that had been visible from Hilo. A constant roar filled the air. Mr. Green wanted to camp on the edge but Isabella pointed out that pieces of the side fell continuously into the pit so it was dangerous.

She had realized that Mr. Green, expert scientist though he might be, was often quite impractical and even forgot to bring tea. She was surprised to realize: "I have to remind him of everything and I have now written out a list of things which we must take with us or die." The impropriety of spending several days alone with Mr. Green did not disturb her, and, showing a manipulative style that she rarely admitted: "I have led him with a thread of silk and often think how much better it is to travel with a man than with almost any woman."

The tents were set up, dinner served and as darkness fell Isabella lay down. When the moon rose, she slipped out of her tent, shivering in the cold, and sat on the crater's edge. She watched, mesmerized by the glorious fountain of fire, the radiance of the reflections, and the thundering, beating noise like some primeval drum inside the earth.

"Everywhere through its vast expanses appeared glints of fire—fires bright and steady, burning in rows like blast furnaces; fires lone and isolated, unwinking like planets, or twinkling like stars; rows of little fires marking the margin of the lowest level of the crater; fire molten in deep crevasses; fire in wavy lines; fire, calm, stationary and restful." It reminded her of Bible descriptions of hell and damnation as "a lake of fire burning with brimstone."

The next day she rode down the slope back to Hilo. When she arrived, Isabella found herself a heroine for her achievement. She was pleased with her success and felt she had learned a great deal on the expedition. She summed up the journey succinctly: "A splendid week, with every circumstance favorable, nothing sordid or worrying to disturb the impressions received, kindness and goodwill everywhere" and "a travelling companion whose consideration, endurance and calmness were beyond all praise." She was already planning another "thoroughly wild" ride into the countryside when she received a letter from her sister that shook her to the core. Hennie had read everything Isabella wrote about the perfect climate, the beautiful scenery and the joys of Hawaiian life. She liked the idea of settling in the Sandwich Islands, and she was making arrangements to come and join Isabella for a year.

Isabella was stunned. This would never do. She was an impressionist who wrote spontaneously as the mood took her, pouring out descriptions and ideas and suggestions in a deluge of words. Her writing reflected whether she felt happy and enthusiastic, or sad and depressed. She never expected her sister to do anything except stay at home. How could Hennie fit into this paradise of carefree living? Even though Hennie might have enjoyed the experience, Isabella did not even consider the possibility. She could not allow the one stable factor in her life to change.

Henrietta's role, though she did not realize it then, was to stay at home so that Isabella could write to her. She provided the solid anchorage Isabella needed, the link with all that had been left behind, the image of family and fireside which Isabella believed she could not live without. Isabella could travel freely, knowing that someone was waiting for her at home, reading her long letters, caring about her, telling their friends what she was doing and where she was going. Henrietta's role was to be Isabella's audience.

Isabella could not bear to think of her sister arriving in the Sandwich Islands. There was only one solution, and she had no time to lose. She wrote to Hennie firmly: "I shall be in the Rocky Mountains before you receive my hastily-written reply to your proposal to come out here for a year, but I will add a few reasons against it."

She then compiled a litany of complaints about the Sandwich Islands—the conflicts about religion, the pervasive American influence, the local newspapers full of narrow-minded gossipy articles, which Hennie would hate. She even declared the easy-going good-natured Hawaiians were aggravating, careless and never got anything done right.

It was an astonishing letter after the months of enthusiasm and delight. The newly revitalized Isabella had to protect herself and her carefully balanced life from any invasion from the world she had left behind. Hennie's place was to stay at home permanently because otherwise Isabella could not travel and write as freely as she wanted. Isabella believed a solid base at home was essential for her survival. It was a letter of desperation. Yet she was miserable at leaving Hawaii.

"I cannot help howling. Oh the life on breezy hills, on countless horses! This is the life that's meant for me. All my gear and occupations on the saddle, and no thought or care. No more shall I test three horses a day! No more shall I go out with the hunters, or swim rivers, or gallop down mountain sides or fight through forests! No more shall I mingle in the tropical life in latticed houses, or hear the music of the Hawaiian tongue, or sleep soundly on the mats of friendly native houses, or take solitary journeys in perfect security! No more will Kilauea's awful fires thrill my soul or my bed be rocked by earthquakes or my eyes be feasted by the lonely fires of Mokuweweo."

She booked her passage to San Francisco for August 7, 1873. The night before she sailed, she sat tearfully in her hotel room watching the moonlight shining through the feathery leaves of the trees, gazing at the huge lilies growing by her window, listening to the distant sound of the sea and sensing the soft perfumed breeze wafting over her. She tried to rationalize her sudden decision: "I am glad that I am sorry to go. I should have been sorrier to have outlived the fascinations of these islands."

On the quay, she stood waiting to load her boxes and bags on the boat. Around her, crowds of smiling men and women and children in colorful clothes with leis of vivid flowers around their necks waved and called "Aloha," just as they had when she arrived. The dazzling sunshine rippled like flickering diamonds on the curled waves. Long low canoes skimmed through the turquoise water.

It was goodbye. With flags fluttering, the *Costa Rica* steamed slowly across Honolulu Bay toward the coral reef, and out to the ocean beyond. Isabella's tropical dream was over.

View of Mauna Kea from Hilo, 1873

Isabella in her "American Lady's Mountain Dress"

Chapter 4
Rapture in the Rockies

*San Francisco to Colorado by train. Truckee
and Lake Tahoe stop. Arrival in Estes Park.
Meets Rocky Mountain Jim. Climbs Longs Peak
with him. Rides in cattle round-up.*

San Francisco was sweltering in a summer heat wave so Isabella quickly boarded a train going east to Colorado on the recently opened Pacific Line. She stopped in Truckee, California, for the night. The bars were full of boisterous drinking men celebrating the freedom of the still-wild West. The next morning, determined to do what she had so enjoyed in Hawaii, she hired a horse, sat astride and rode off to explore.

She found the cool clear air wonderfully refreshing after the soft balmy breezes of the tropics. Her route followed a wagon trail alongside the fast-flowing Truckee River. She had pulled her horse into the shade of some tall pine trees to rest when suddenly, a huge bear rose up out of the bushes in front of her. Her frightened horse whinnied, threw her off and bolted back along the path. It took her an hour to catch him and remount. But undeterred even by bears, she rode on in the bright sunshine.

The trail led under evergreen trees and over rocks and shrubs. She saw crested blue jays, squirrels, red dragon flies and chipmunks. The rushing stream on one side broadened into a river and slowly widened. Suddenly she saw ahead the sparkling waters of Lake Tahoe surrounded by mountains.

She relaxed on the wide veranda of the inn by the lake: "I have found a dream of beauty at which one might look all one's life and sigh. Not lovable, like the Sandwich Islands, but beautiful in its own way! A strictly North American beauty—snow-splotched mountains, huge pines, red-woods, sugar pines, silver spruce; and a pine-hung lake which mirrors all beauty on its surface. There is no sound but the distant and slightly musical ring of the lumberer's axe." As the sun set she added: "The beauty is entrancing. The peaks above, which still catch the sun, are bright rose-red, and all the mountains on the other side are pink, and pink, too, are the far-off summits on which the snow-drifts rest."

After a peaceful night, she rode back to Truckee. When she caught sight of a bear with two cubs ahead of her on the track, she kept her horse quiet and watched the lumbering animal and her playful young ones splash through the river and disappear into the forest.

Isabella left on the night train. She chose the luxury and comfort of a Silver Palace Sleeping Car with carpeted floors, curtains round the bed, linen sheets and a firm mattress. Hidden behind rich curtains were the other sleeping travelers. A profound silence enveloped the car. Silver lamps hung from the ceiling. The temperature was kept at a perfect 70 degrees despite the sub-zero weather outside.

When she woke, she saw outside vast flat plains dotted with sage brush, and prairie dogs standing on their hind legs by their burrows. The next morning the train arrived in Greeley, Colorado. Isabella planned to ride into the snow-capped peaks of the Rocky Mountains and find Estes Park, which her friend Rose Kingsley had told her was one of the most beautiful places in the world. But it proved extraordinarily difficult to get there.

After a night in a Greeley boarding house with a bed so infested with insects that she slept balanced on two chairs, she took a carriage to Fort Collins. The burning sun and the mountain altitude exhausted her. She took a room in a hotel and slept for the rest of the day. She was not impressed with what she saw in Colorado.

"These new settlements are utterly revolting, entirely utilitarian, given up to talk of dollars as well as to making them, with coarse speech, coarse food, coarse everything," she noted, hating the black flies and locusts everywhere.

Someone mentioned a guest house in the mountains, so she hired a young man with a buggy to drive her and her baggage there. He set off westwards. After driving for hours across the grassy foothills, he reached a canyon with a rushing stream. Across a shaky wooden bridge stood a log cabin much in need of repair.

Isabella inspected the ramshackle place. There were holes in the roof, holes for windows and one wall missing. Inside a couple of shelves covered with straw mattresses served as beds. Mrs. Chalmers, who lived there with her husband and children, said Isabella could stay for five dollars a week if she would "make herself agreeable." Isabella wondered whether it was worth paying for such primitive surroundings, but decided she was closer to Estes Park here than in Fort Collins.

She found the Chalmers rough, rude and unfriendly. Mrs. Chalmers always referred to Isabella as "that woman" contemptuously.

"With a look which conveyed more than words, a curl of her nose, and a sneer in her twang, she said, 'Guess you'll make more work nor you'll do. Those hands of yours ain't no good; never done nothing I guess.'"

Isabella tried to be agreeable, remembering her popularity in Hawaii. She swept the floors, drew water from the river, piled logs on the fire, and sat knitting, mending and writing. She improved her status by making a Hawaiian-style lamp using a piece of rag in a can of fat so they had a light at night. When Mrs. Chalmers grudgingly admired her knitting, Isabella taught her and her daughter how to knit, which moved her up in their estimation.

Isabella slept on blankets on the floor while the family pulled their straw mattresses outside to sleep under the trees. She was nervous at the sounds of roaming wild animals and hated the insects and snakes everywhere. One morning she killed a huge rattlesnake outside the cabin, and was told that seven had been killed since she arrived. But the air was fresh and cool, she ate dried beef and milk, and slept well.

Mr. Chalmers, a lumberman, had come from Illinois nine years ago to cure his consumption in Colorado's healthy climate. He had built a sawmill which he and his sons hoped to develop. But Isabella saw the mill was never in operation because something was always going wrong and Chalmers had little idea how to fix anything: "It is hardly surprising that nine years of persevering shiftlessness should have resulted in nothing but the ability to procure the bare necessities of life."

He hated England intensely, so she avoided mentioning anything to do with England or Queen Victoria, and concentrated on mentioning Estes Park. One day, Chalmers and his wife agreed to take her there, much to her delight, and the trio set off on horseback. At first Isabella reveled in the scenery:

"This is an upland valley of grass and flowers, of glades and sloping lawns, and cherry-fringed beds of dry streams, and clumps of pines artistically placed, and mountain sides densely pine-clad, the pines breaking into fringes as they come down, and the mountains breaking into pinnacles of bold grey rock as they pierce the blue of the sky."

Chalmers proved an incompetent guide. The horses ran off at night because he did not tie them securely, the food ran out, and after two days he admitted he was hopelessly lost. Isabella sized up the situation: "I said I had much experience in travelling and would take control of the party." She found the way and led them back to their cabin, but was still no nearer to Estes Park.

"Oh what a hard narrow life it is with which I am now in contact!" she wrote to Hennie, quoting a favorite poem:

> "Beware of desperate steps; the darkest day
> Live till tomorrow, will have passed away."

An accident brought sudden change. Unexpectedly, Isabella was thrown from her horse. She crushed her left arm, cut her back and was badly bruised and shaken. The Chalmers knew a physician who lived nearby and sent for him. Dr. Hutchinson, whom Isabella called Dr. Hughes in her book, had come to Colorado with his wife and young children. He treated her injuries, and invited her to stay with them.

At their home, Isabella found another world. The Hutchinsons were an educated middle-class English family. Their two-story house had a roof, walls, windows, tables, chairs, beds, and even books, flowers and pictures. A Swiss girl helped with the chores. Yet even with such comforts, Isabella saw that charming educated people were also totally overwhelmed by the demands of pioneer life in Colorado. Every day, the doctor exhausted himself working for hours in the fields. At home, his pregnant wife baked bread, cleaned, cared for the children, and sewed the clothes. Isabella helped as much as she could but decided: "The day is one long grind." Indeed, her enthusiastic descriptions of the Sandwich Islands and the idyllic life of the tropics inspired Dr. Hutchinson. A few months later, when his wife tragically died in childbirth, he took his family to Hawaii and settled there.

The weeks slipped by. It was almost the end of September. People were getting ready for the harsh winter ahead. Isabella saw there was no time to find Estes Park. It would be wiser to go home. Sadly, she packed her bags.

Dr. Hutchinson drove her to Longmont to spend the night, before she caught the train to New York. After dinner in the St. Vrain Hotel, she told the friendly landlord how sad she was that she had never seen Estes Park. He shook his head and said she had missed "the most beautiful scenery in Colorado." Later that evening he knocked at her door.

"You're in luck this time," he said, cheerfully. "Two young men have just come in and are going up tomorrow."

Sylvester Downer and Platt Rogers were young law students on their way to enjoy a long-planned vacation in Estes Park. Riding in from Greeley, they stopped for the night in Longmont. The landlord asked them to take Isabella with them. Early the next morning, the three of them set off on the trail west.

Isabella was delighted, but Platt Rogers was less enthusiastic. "The proprietor of the hotel asked that a lady might accompany us," he wrote later. "We were traveling light and free, and the presence of a woman would naturally operate as a restraint upon our movements. However, we could not refuse, and we consoled ourselves with the hope that she would prove young, beautiful and vivacious. Our hopes were dispelled when, in the morning, Miss Bird appeared, wearing bloomers, riding cowboy fashion, with a face and figure not corresponding to our ideals."

Isabella did not even consider the impression she made on these two young men. She had spent the night worrying that her arm still ached from her fall off the horse, that she didn't know if she would be able to ride twenty-five miles in a day, and that if she reached Estes Park, she might be forced to stay with a family as rude and depressing as the Chalmers.

Once astride a horse, Isabella felt better. Her old free spirit returned. She was exhilarated by the magnificent view of the mountains, and began to enjoy herself again. As the trio rode toward the Rockies, she was awed by the scenery.

"Wild fantastic views opening up continually, a recurrence of surprise; the air keener and purer with every mile. Looking back, it was a single gigantic ridge which we had passed through, built up entirely of great brick-shaped masses of bright red rock, some of them as large as the Royal Institution, Edinburgh, piled one on another by Titans. Beyond, wall beyond wall of similar construction, and range above range, rose into the blue sky. There were chasms of immense depth, dark with the indigo gloom of pines, and mountains with snow gleaming on their splintered crests, and still streams and shady pools."

After a long day's ride, she reached the entrance to the gulch leading into Estes Park, named after Joel Estes, who had been the first to settle there with his family in 1859. At one side stood a rough log cabin, smoke curling out of its roof and window.

Isabella thought the place looked like the den of a wild beast. The mud roof was covered with the furry skins of lynx, beaver and other animals, drying in the sun. A deer carcass hung at one end of the cabin. Deer antlers, old horseshoes and the remains of recently killed animals were scattered on the ground. Rogers and Downer told her that a notorious ruffian and desperado known as Rocky Mountain Jim lived there. A large collie dog lying on guard growled ominously.

As they stood talking, Jim Nugent came out. Isabella saw a broad, well-built man, "about middle height, with an old cap on his head, and wearing a grey hunting suit much the worse for wear, a digger's scarf knotted round his waist, a knife in his belt, and a revolver, sticking out of the breast-pocket of his coat; his feet, which were very small, were bare, except for some dilapidated moccasins made of horse hide."

Downer introduced Isabella, and Jim bowed politely. Isabella asked for a glass of water. Jim brought some in a battered tin, "gracefully apologizing for not having anything more presentable." Isabella was surprised by the gentle tone of his voice and the politeness of his manner. Examining him as she sipped the cold water, she guessed he was about 45. His face was remarkable.

"One eye was entirely gone, and the loss made one side of the face repulsive, while the other might have been modelled in marble. He must have been strikingly handsome. He has large grey-blue eyes, deeply set, with well-marked eyebrows, a handsome aquiline nose, and a very handsome mouth." Above his mouth was a dense mustache, and his long, tawny hair fell in curls on to his collar.

He began talking to her, his soft voice lilting with the trace of an Irish accent. Isabella was entranced: "I forgot both his reputation and appearance, for his manner was that of a chivalrous gentleman, his accent refined, and his language easy and elegant."

He told her that he had lost his eye in a fight with a grizzly bear, which had tried to hug him to death, tore him all over, broke his arm, scratched out his eye, and then left him for dead. Isabella, who had her own encounters with bears, listened spellbound. She hardly noticed Rogers and Downer winking at each other, well aware of how Jim liked to charm women with his stories.

Jim rode with Isabella down the trail, still talking to her. When he turned to leave, he called, "I know from your voice that you are a countrywoman of mine. I hope you will allow me the pleasure of calling on you." It was a proper gentlemanly request, and even though Isabella didn't have a place where he could call, she nodded happily, charmed by this well-spoken man living amid the beauty of the mountains.

On the way into the park, the two young men joked about the stories which surrounded Jim, his flirtation with Griff Evans' daughter, his reputation as a famous scout of the Plains, his years shooting and fighting in the wars with Indians. They told Isabella he had a squatter's claim to land in Estes Park, and made his living trapping beavers and selling their skins, for beaver hats, which were very fashionable then. The local wisdom was: "When he's sober, Jim's a perfect gentleman; but when he's had liquor, he's the most awful ruffian in Colorado."

As the sun began to set in a glory of red and gold, they reached the high ridge at the end of the long gulch. Isabella looked down from a magnificent spur to see 1,500 feet below the place she had dreamed of finding.

"Estes Park!!!" she wrote later ecstatically. "Never, nowhere, have I seen anything to equal the view into Estes Park. Guarded by sentinel mountains of fantastic shape and monstrous size, with Long's Peak rising above them all in unapproachable grandeur, while the Snowy Range, with its outlying spurs heavily timbered, come down up on the

Park slashed by stupendous canyons lying deep in purple gloom. The rushing river was blood-red, Long's Peak was aflame, the glory of the glowing heaven was given back from the earth."

Seized with excitement, she spurred her horse and galloped down the trail over the rolling grass plains to a weathered log cabin beside a lake. Dismounting, she saw a round-faced man running to welcome her. Cheery Griff Evans, an ebullient Welshman, had built a large log cabin and several smaller cabins in Estes Park for hunters, visitors and invalids. Isabella was overjoyed to have a wooden cabin to herself, with a roof, walls, a window and a bed, and learned to ignore the scrabblings of the skunk who lived underneath it.

View of Longs Peak from Estes Park

"From my bed I look on Mirror Lake, and with the very earliest dawn, it lies there absolutely still, a purplish lead-color. Then suddenly into its mirror flash inverted peaks, at first a bright orange, then changing into red, each morning new. The hoar-frost sparkles and the crested blue jays step forth daintily on the jewelled grass. The majesty and beauty grow on me daily."

She spent her first days riding the trails with Griff Evans looking for his cattle, which roamed freely in the unfenced plains. She asked about climbing the craggy mountains circling the park, and was told that only a few weeks earlier Anna Dickinson, the American orator and writer, had claimed the title as the first woman to climb Longs Peak. The mountain was—and still is—one of the most challenging mountains of the Rockies. Over 14,000 feet high, Longs Peak soars starkly up into the sky, with a crest of sharp, pointed splinters.

Isabella eagerly recounted her adventures climbing volcanoes in Hawaii, and decided she would climb Longs Peak too. Downer and Rogers pointed out it was late in the year, a difficult climb, and that a guide was essential. Isabella was determined, and when they told her Mountain Jim guided groups up the mountain, she sent Downer over to Jim's cabin to make arrangements for an ascent. Then, in a fever of anticipation, she watched as Mrs. Evans baked enough bread for three days, cut steaks from the steer hanging up in the kitchen, and packed tea, sugar, and butter.

For the climb, Isabella had only her light Hawaiian riding dress to wear, and borrowed a pair of boots, a quilt and blankets from the Evans. She was ready very early in the morning, waiting for Jim.

"He had on an old pair of high boots, with a baggy pair of trousers made of deerhide, held on by an old scarf tucked into them; a leather shirt, with three or four ragged unbuttoned waistcoats over it; and with his one eye, his knife in his belt, his saddle covered with an old beaver-skin, his axe, canteen and other gear hanging to the horn, he was as awful looking a ruffian as one could see."

To add to the wild picture, he rode a small Arab mare, quite overwhelmed by the equipment loading her down and dwarfed by the large man on her back, and was accompanied by his dog. Yet, despite appearances, within half an hour he was riding along with Isabella, talking to her with the charm and intelligence which had first impressed her.

Isabella was curious to know everything she could about Jim, and he, in his turn, was delighted to impress such an educated and refined lady. He listened as she described her travels among the Hawaiians, her climb up the volcano—a story she often repeated—and her six months exploring the Sandwich Islands.

By early afternoon, they reached the campsite. The horses were unsaddled and tied up securely. Jim dragged logs in for a big fire. As dusk fell, they drank tea from battered meat-tins and ate smoked strips of beef with their fingers.

The flames of the fire crackled and leapt in the dark night air. One of the young men sang a Latin student's song, and two Southern folk

melodies. They both sang *The Star-spangled Banner* and other patriotic songs, to which Isabella, as an English visitor, listened politely. Jim
recited a poem he had written and told stories of his daring exploits with
the Indians.

After supper, Jim told his dog Ring to "go to that lady, and don't
leave her again tonight." Isabella saw that "Ring came to me, looked
into my face, laid his head on my shoulder, and then lay down beside
me with his head on my lap."

That night, she lay under the stars, with a blanket over the soft
pine shoots on the ground, her saddle for a pillow, and Ring at her back
to keep her warm. Jim stretched out by the fire. She looked over at him
and wondered at "the notorious desperado sleeping as quietly as
innocence sleeps."

The temperature fell below freezing, the wind blew through the
pines ominously, and wild animals howled in the distance. "I could not
sleep, but the night passed rapidly," she admitted. As the first streaks
of light slipped across the sky, Jim called her to come and see the
sunrise. Standing on a high rock, she watched as the first rays of
morning light broke over the gray mountain peaks. Jim exclaimed, "I
believe there is a God!" and Isabella felt moved to pray by the beauty
of the moment.

A difficult day lay ahead. By seven, they were on the trail to the
Lava Beds, a vast field of boulders of all sizes sprinkled with early snow.
There the horses were tethered and left. Isabella put on Evans' boots,
which were too large, but Jim found a pair of small overshoes under a
rock to keep the boots on. She followed Jim over the rough boulders
to the Notch, a narrow rock track, only a few feet wide. Then the real
climbing began.

"Two thousand feet of solid rock towered above us, four thousand feet of broken rock shelved precipitously below. Melted snow,
refrozen several times, presented a more serious obstacle; many of the
rocks were loose, and tumbled down when touched. To me it was a
time of extreme terror. I was roped to Jim, but it was no use. My feet
were paralysed and slipped on the bare rock."

Isabella understood now that Longs Peak was very different from
climbing the gradual volcanic slope of Mauna Loa. Here she faced
sheer cliffs and jagged, perpendicular rocks. Isabella knew that she was
not prepared for such serious mountaineering. Rogers and Downer
thought her "a dangerous encumbrance." She begged to be left

behind, but Jim said firmly he wouldn't go up at all if he hadn't decided to take the lady. He told the two young men they could take the quicker more difficult route and then they could wait at the summit until he and Isabella arrived.

Isabella and Jim scrambled up, roped together. The only toe holds were a few smooth granite rocks sticking out here and there. Many were loose and tumbled down as soon as she touched them. Isabella clung to the rope, trying not to slip, and felt like a package that Jim was hauling up.

Lava beds, Longs Peak

"Slipping, faltering, gasping from the exhausting toil in the rarefied air, with throbbing hearts and panting lungs, we reached the top of the gorge and squeezed ourselves between two gigantic fragments of rock by a passage called the Dog's Lift."

Worse lay ahead. "As we crept round a horn of rock, I beheld what made me perfectly sick and dizzy to look at - the terminal Peak itself - a smooth, cracked face or wall of pink granite, as nearly perpendicular as anything could well be which it was possible to climb."

It was the only way to reach the summit. Isabella climbed on to Jim's shoulders and scrambled up, stretching her arms and legs and clinging to rocks until finally her fingers gripped the top ledge. Platt Rogers found that "by alternately pulling and pushing her and stimulating her with snow soaked with ginger, we got her to the top."

The view was a magnificent vista of the Rocky Mountains, snowy peaks and soaring cliffs, stretching to the horizon. The summit of Pike's Peak, more than a hundred miles away, stood out clearly. There were sudden patches of snow, dazzling sun on white snowfields, and to the east, giant gray mountains stretching toward the plains. Isabella could see hundreds of miles in every direction, rivers like tiny threads, tiny clumps of trees and the blue of lakes. She stood panting in the high thin air under the pale blue sky.

"We all suffered severely from the want of water, and the gasping for breath made our mouths and tongues so dry that speech was unnatural." They wrote their names and the date on a piece of paper and put it in a tin set inside a crack in the rocks.

Now they had to climb down. Rogers and Downer took the quicker route again and were soon far below. Isabella noticed that once the students had left, Jim dropped his rough, mountain manner, and treated her with gentleness and kindness. For Isabella, the descent was as grueling as the climb up. Jim went first, Isabella resting her feet on his shoulders, and they slowly scrambled down the cliffs.

"I had various falls, and once hung by my frock, which caught on a rock, and Jim severed it with his hunting-knife, upon which I fell into a crevice full of soft snow." She struggled on. "Sometimes Jim pulled me up by my arms or a lariat, sometimes I stood on his shoulders, or he made steps for me of his feet and hands."

When they reached the horses, Isabella was so exhausted she had to be lifted onto the saddle. Though it was late in the day, the young men were eager to ride home that evening. But at the campsite, Jim said firmly, "Now, gentlemen, I want a good night's rest, and we shan't stir from here tonight."

Isabella was asleep in seconds, rolled in her blankets. She was so stiff that she could hardly move. During the night, she woke and looked around. The moon was shining through the branches, glittering on the snow. Jim was sitting by a huge fire, with Ring at his side. The cold air was very still. The only sound was the crackling of the logs in the flames. Shivering with cold, she got up and went to sit with him.

He gave her a blanket and wrapped it around her. Slowly, as the fire warmed her, they began to talk. The stars twinkled above, brighter and clearer than Isabella had ever seen them before. The moon glittered on the night frost. They sat close together, their voices low and quiet. Jim spoke of his youth, of things he would not dare to tell, of a great sorrow which had ruined his life, and of how he regretted so much of what he had done in his life.

As Isabella listened sympathetically, she noticed: "His voice trembled, and tears rolled down his cheek." He turned and looked at her. She thought then that something happened between them. It was an almost tangible sense of connection, a sudden sharing of feelings and emotion. Isabella confided to Hennie: "For five minutes his manner was such that for a moment I thought love possible, but I put it away as vanity unpardonable in a woman of forty. Afterwards he explained his emotion satisfactorily and never showed a trace of it again. Was it semi-conscious acting, or was his dark soul really stirred to its depths by the silence, the beauty, and the memories of youth?"

She rode back to Estes Park and told Hennie: "A more successful ascent of the Peak was never made, and I would not now exchange my memories of its perfect beauty and extraordinary sublimity for any other experience of mountaineering in any part of the world."

The days flew by. Every morning, Isabella drew a bucket of water from the lake, washed, tidied her cabin, read, and wrote her journal. Almost every day, Jim came by. Tying his horse at her cabin, he strolled in, invited her to ride with him or come and check his beaver traps.

Isabella's letters to Hennie about "Mr. Nugent," as she called him, were unremittingly enthusiastic. He was such splendid company. "You would like him so," she assured Hennie, "he is quick like a needle, a thoroughly cultured Irishman, and can talk on all subjects and has real genius."

She admired his "breezy mountain recklessness in everything," thought him most perceptive in analyzing events and people, felt he had "pathos, poetry, and humor, an intense love of nature, a considerable acquaintance with literature, a wonderful verbal memory." He treated her as a perfect gentlemen should, even when he teased her about what she said, or made her laugh.

Isabella was falling in love. Never in her life had she written so openly about her feelings toward a man. She saw Jim was part actor, telling tall tales and bragging to keep up his image as a wild desperado. But she saw underneath his roughness a persuasive charm, a lively mind and a generous nature. Yet she could not ignore his unhappy past.

"His magnificent head shows so plainly the better possibilities which might have been his," she mused sadly. "His life, in spite of a certain dazzle which belongs to it, is a ruined and wasted one, and one asks what of good can the future have in store for one who has for so long chosen evil?"

Yet ironically, part of Jim's attraction was her feeling that she could reform him. His appeal to her was irresistible—he was an entertaining conversationalist, loved riding and the mountains, was intelligent and interested in writing, admired her abilities as a horse-woman and traveler, and needed help.

She had planned to stay in Estes Park a short time, and then explore the rest of Colorado on horseback. But the weeks slipped by and she kept asking herself: "Shall I ever get away?"

Griff Evans and the others at the ranch gossiped about the romance. Platt Rogers saw that "Jim took quite a fancy to her and she took quite a fancy to Jim." One of the guests at the ranch commented: "What a thorough gentleman Jim is, and how very much he likes you." Both of which, Isabella realized, were quite true.

Isabella spent hours every day riding along the mountain trails with Jim or with other guests at the ranch. She heard that Griff Evans and Jim disliked each other. Jim objected to the scheme Evans had developed with the Earl of Dunraven to buy up Estes Park as a private hunting preserve for English aristocracy. Evans was angry at Jim because Jim flirted with his daughter, and she knew there had been threats of shooting between them.

Late one afternoon, she met Jim on her way home after a long ride. The two of them began racing together, galloping faster and faster, speeding alongside each other in the sharp, frosty air. The horses' hooves thundered on the grass, manes flying in the wind. Isabella was exhilarated by the wildness of it all.

"It is so sad that you can never see me as I am now", she wrote to her sister, "with an unconstrained manner, and an up-to-anything free-legged air."

Griff Evans asked her to help with the cattle round-up. She joined the other stockmen and galloped downhill towards the herd of more than a thousand head of cattle, riding in the line of horses and dogs to direct the animals toward the fenced corral.

"The great excitement is when one breaks away from the herd, and gallops madly up and down hill, and you gallop after him anywhere, over and among rocks and trees, doubling when he doubles, and heading him till you get back again."

Evans was so impressed by her riding skill that he offered to pay her to stay at the cabin through the winter and watch the cattle. She was flattered but politely declined.

That night there was a tremendous snowstorm. Lying in bed listening to the howling wind, Isabella was terrified that the roof would be blown off. Thunder and lightning shook the sky, snow hissed through the chinks between the logs to cover the floor and her bed, and the sheet froze to her lips. In the morning a foot of snow blocked her door. She was trapped until at last some men came to dig her out.

At the big log cabin, the wind forced the tiny, dry, needle-like snow through the chinks. Isabella joined the other guests by the big fire, huddled in coats, cloaks, wraps and blankets to keep warm. For three days the whirling flakes and fierce winds battered the cabins by the lake.

At last the storm blew out, leaving brilliant blue skies and the sun dazzling on the snow. It was almost the end of October. Isabella realized that she would never be able to ride and see the rest of Colorado once winter set in. Jim had gone into Denver with freshly caught trout for his friends, and beaver pelts to sell. Isabella decided to set off on her travels, chose a bay Indian pony she named Birdie, packed a few belongings in a bag, and rode off to explore Colorado.

Chapter 5
Travels in Colorado

Tours through Colorado on her pony. Rocky Mountain Jim says he loves her. Leaves for England.

"Miss Isabella L. Bird, a Scotch lady and a noted traveller in new and strange countries, is in Denver. She has travelled extensively in Australia, New Zealand, the Sandwich Islands and California. For a month past, she has been in and about Estes Park, having ascended Longs Peak on September 30. She travels almost altogether on horseback, and has laid out a pretty good winter's work in Colorado."

William N. Byers, the editor of the *Rocky Mountain News*, was impressed by Isabella Bird when she came to see him. They talked about her climb up Longs Peak—Byers had led the first party to climb the peak in 1868, five years earlier—and her plans for exploring Colorado. He introduced her to Governor Hunt who suggested a circular route around the territory, not yet a state. He suggested she go south across the Arkansas Divide to Colorado Springs, west toward the

Rockies, north across the Breckenridge Pass to Hall's Gulch, and east back to Denver, a journey of some 500 miles on horseback.

Governor Hunt also gave her a letter of introduction and the names of some settlers. There were few hotels, so travelers expected to stay with settlers and pay for their rooms. Sparsely populated Colorado was still virtually unexplored and unmapped. Isabella learned to follow unusual directions: "Keep along a gulch four or five miles till you get Pike's Peak on your left, then follow wheel-marks till you get to some timber, and keep to the north till you come to a creek where you'll find a great many elk tracks; then go to your right and cross the creek three times."

Isabella was surprised by the "great, braggart city" of Denver. Booming from the wealth of the nearby mines, Denver was the final stop of the Kansas Pacific Railroad and had become the region's distribution center. There were stores and wide streets, public schools, a library, a roller-skating rink, a French restaurant, and a selection of saloons and brothels where men like Rocky Mountain Jim, Comanche Bill, and Buffalo Bill came to spend their money in celebration.

Isabella walked along the streets and saw: "Hunters and trappers in buckskin clothing; men of the Plains with belts and revolvers, in great blue cloaks, relics of the war; horsemen in fur coats and caps and buffalo-hide boots with the hair outside; Broadway dandies in light kid gloves; rich English sporting tourists, clean, comely and supercilious-looking; and hundreds of Indians on their small ponies, the men wearing buckskin suits sewn with beads, and red blankets, with faces painted vermillion, and hair hanging lank and straight, and squaws much bundled up riding astride with furs over their saddles."

Denver's altitude and fresh air was reputed to be beneficial to health. Hundreds of asthmatics and consumptives came to spend the summer in the mountains and fill the hotels and boarding houses for the winter. Isabella felt she was now back in society, so rode side-saddle as she thought a lady should, and soon felt overwhelmed by the noise and bustle. She left Denver with relief to go south across the flat grassy plains.

"It was free and breezy, and my horse was companionable. Sometimes herds of cattle were browsing on the sun-cured grass, then herds of horses. Occasionally I met a horseman with a rifle lying across his saddle, or a wagon of the ordinary sort, but oftener I saw a wagon with a white tilt, known as a 'Prairie Schooner,' laboring across the grass, or a train of them, accompanied by herds, mules and horsemen, bearing emigrants and their household goods in dreary exodus from the Western States to the much-vaunted prairies of Colorado."

She stopped to have lunch with a family from Illinois. They had been traveling for three months, their food supply was low, one child had been buried along the way, and several of the oxen had died. She shared her supply of tea with them, and then watched as the wagon moved slowly across the desolate grasslands. As dusk fell, she rode up to a house in Plum Creek to stay for the night. Her bed was a sofa in the living-room. At dinner she met another traveler, the first woman to have settled in the Rocky Mountains who regaled Isabella with stories of her early life in Fort Laramie. But next morning, heavy snow was falling, the temperature dropped, and the day's riding was difficult.

Isabella had an introduction to Mr. Perry, a millionaire cattleman. After hours riding against the icy winds, she was glad to turn off the trail toward his elegant mansion in Pleasant Park near a magnificent gorge. He was away but his daughter welcomed her. Isabella enjoyed a comfortable bedroom, hot water and stewed venison for dinner but woke to find eight inches of new snow, covered with smooth frost. Miss Perry gave her men's socks to pull over her boots so she would not slip. Ahead lay the Arkansas Divide, almost 8,000 feet high.

"Everything was buried under a glittering shroud of snow. The babble of the streams was bound by fetters of ice. No branches creaked in the still air. No birds sang. No one passed or met me. There were no cabins near or far. The only sound was the crunch of the snow under Birdie's feet."

When Birdie refused to cross a bridge Isabella was forced to ride through the half-frozen river. But she heard later the bridge was unsafe. She had nothing but praise for Birdie: "She is the queen of ponies, and is very gentle. She is always cheerful and hungry, never tired, looks intelligently at everything, and her legs are like rocks. She is quite a companion, and bathing her back, sponging her nostrils, and seeing her fed after my day's ride, is always my first care."

She struggled to the summit of the Divide as the sun was sinking. The landscape of glistening snow and a vast frozen lake was bleak. Isabella shivered at the mournful sound of owls hooting among the pines. She rode down in bitter cold to the nearest cabin, one foot frozen to her stirrup. The two German women who lived there helped thaw her out and gave her a room under the roof with a ladder to climb up to it.

Isabella had little idea exactly where she was or how far she had traveled. She had hoped traveling through Colorado would be as interesting as her explorations of the Sandwich Islands. She had to admit that riding in subzero weather over desolate snow-covered mountains was quite different from sunny gallops through tropical Hawaiian valleys. She assured Hennie that she was: "Greatly enjoying the adventurousness and novelty of my tour, but ten hours or more daily spent in the saddle in this intoxicating air disposes one to sleep rather than to write in the evening."

The Great Divide

It took her a week to reach Colorado City, 150 miles south of Denver. She took a room in a boarding house, and the friendly landlady welcomed her. They sat chatting together in the lounge. Opposite, Isabella could see into a bedroom where the door was wide open. A very sick-looking young man was half lying, half sitting on the bed with his feet sticking up at the end. Another equally sick-looking man went in and out of the room, occasionally leaning on the wall looking very depressed. Then the door was suddenly half closed, and someone called out for a candle.

"All this time the seven or eight people in the room in which I was were talking, laughing and playing backgammon, and none laughed louder than the landlady, who was sitting where she saw that mysterious door as plainly as I did. All this time, I saw two large white feet sticking up at the end of the bed. I watched and watched, hoping those feet would move, but they did not. And somehow to my thinking, they grew stiffer and whiter, and then my horrible suspicion deepened—that while we were sitting there a human spirit had passed forth into the night."

Isabella was so shocked to see death treated casually without the rituals and mourning she expected that she could hardly sleep that night, listening to the sobbing of the man whose brother had died. The next morning, she noticed the door of the room was open. Curious, she went in and found the landlady sweeping the floor, children running about, the sun pouring through the window, and, to her horror, haphazardly balanced on some chairs with not even a cloth over his face, the body of the young man.

The landlady told her that people came to Colorado Springs in the last stages of consumption hoping the climate would miraculously cure them, and with no money to pay for food or board.

"It turns the house upside down when they just come here and die," she said frankly. "We shall be half the night laying him out."

Isabella rode off to the west. She traveled over the Mesa, through Glen Eyrie and into the Garden of the Gods where she was not impressed with its grotesquely shaped red rocks. In the summer tourists flocked to the huge hotels by the medicinal springs of the Great Gorge of the Manitou, but Isabella found them deserted and had a luxurious room for six dollars. She traveled on to Bergens Park, Hayden's Park, Twin Rock and Deer Valley to reach Hall's Gulch.

Here she found a ramshackle log cabin, with no fireplace, one very dirty room, and a large shed without a roof. The food was greasy, the owner drunk, and Isabella declared: "This is the worst place I have put up at."

An English hunter arrived, and when he heard Isabella was English too, he tried to impress her and bragged about the elk and buffalo he had shot. Isabella noted crisply: "This gentleman was lording it in true caricature fashion, with a Lord Dundreary drawl and a general execration of everything, while I sat in the chimney corner speculating on the reason why many of the upper class of my countrymen make themselves so ludicrously absurd."

She left early the next morning for a ride of over twenty miles through a narrow gorge. That evening she arrived in Deer Valley and found a warm friendly farmhouse, sparkling clean and bright. Delicious hot meals were served on a table with a tablecloth, and the pots and pans gleamed with polishing. There was even blacking to polish her boots.

Isabella learned it was critical to cross the Continental Divide and reach the Denver road before more snow fell. Next morning she set out in the bright cold air to ride up the steep trail.

"I was at a height of 12,000 feet, where, of course, the air was highly rarefied, and the snow was so pure and dazzling that I was obliged to keep my eyes shut as much as possible to avoid snow blindness. The sky was a different and terribly fierce color; and when I caught a glimpse of the sun, he was white and unwinking like a lime-ball light, yet threw off wicked scintillations. I suffered so from nausea, exhaustion, and pains from head to foot, that I felt as if I must lie down in the snow. We plodded on for four hours, snow all round, and nothing else to be seen but an ocean of glistening peaks against that infuriated blue."

Hardly knowing which track to follow, she and Birdie pushed through the snow, Isabella sometimes walking because it was too deep for the pony. At last she reached the summit of the Great Divide. Riding across it she saw far below the rolling grassland of the prairies and the road to Denver. She cantered down, and a horseman joined her on the way.

"He was a picturesque figure and rode a very good horse," she observed. "He wore a big slouch hat, from under which a number of fair curls hung nearly to his waist. His manner was respectful and frank. He was dressed in a hunter's buckskin suit ornamented with beads, and wore a pair of exceptionally big brass spurs."

Isabella noticed he had several weapons: a rifle across his saddle, a pair of pistols in his holster, two revolvers and a knife in his belt, and a carbine slung behind him. But she found him good company as he entertained her with stories of hunting and Indians.

After he rode off, Isabella stopped at a nearby cabin for a rest. The woman there said: "I am sure you found Comanche Bill a gentleman." Isabella was amazed to learn that her companion was one of the most notorious desperadoes of the west, dedicated to killing Indians to avenge the murder of his family in a massacre. As she rode toward Denver she found herself thinking of Estes Park and wondered what Jim was doing. He would have been such an entertaining companion on this journey, telling her poems and stories. She missed him, but she felt apprehensive about seeing him again, and was worrying about going back home.

She wrote a long letter to Hennie. "I woke at four, feeling very miserable, thinking of so many things past and future. I wish I had anything arranged about writing my travels, so that on returning I might at once begin easy literary work. I dislike going back with nothing fixed for me to do. I am beginning to be so afraid of breaking down as soon as I give up this life."

The day after she took a train to visit the mines west of Denver and rode up to Green Lake, Denver was abuzz with news of financial disaster, the crash of 1873. Isabella could not get her money out of the bank and had no funds to travel home. Griff Evans had moved to Denver for the winter with his family, so she went to see him. He told her he had no money to repay the loan she had given him. He urged her to go to Estes Park and he would bring it up there as soon as he had some money.

It was time to go back. The ride was long and cold. When she reached the gulch, it was dark. Jim's cabin loomed ahead, but there were no lights. Everything was silent. Disappointed, she rode on, listening to the sounds of wolves howling in the distance, and the cracking of snow and ice in the freezing night. She heard a dog barking, and suddenly a large collie leapt through the snow and put his paws up on her saddle, his face nuzzling hers as he barked in recognition. It was Ring. Behind him she saw two men on horseback, and a horse loaded down with valuable furs. She recognized Jim's voice and called to him. He was delighted to see her, and sent his companion on with the furs. Turning his horse, he rode back with her.

Isabella had imagined Estes Park just as she had left it - the jovial welcome, the cheerful guests round the fire, her cabin by the lake, rides in the sunshine with Jim. Everything had changed. Evans and his family were gone, the guests had left, and the lake was frozen. Two men, Kavanagh and Buchanan, were in the log cabin; Evans had hired them to watch the cattle till his return. They were sitting by the fire, smoking, when Isabella walked in. Surprised to see her, they cooked her some supper and she explained she had to stay until Evans brought her money. She put her things in a small room at the side, filled a bag with hay for a mattress and fell asleep.

The next morning, Isabella took stock of the situation. There was little food, and a great deal of work. She and the men agreed to share the chores; she would clean the house and look after the horses; they would cut wood, get water from the lake and hunt for elk. There was only pickled pork to eat, and some milk to drink. Isabella made rolls and a bread-and-butter pudding, and organized the situation expertly.

"The men cook, wash the dishes, clean the kitchen, bring in wood. I do my room and the parlor—each day I have swept it three times taking out shovelfuls of powdered mud—a truly dreadful business."

The propriety of living with two young men under the most intimate circumstances never crossed her mind. Isabella believed she had no other alternative, and declared: "The air is superb and I sleep well, and probably the quiet is good."

Early one morning, as she sat writing alone in the cabin, Jim walked in. Would she like to come with him to check his beaver traps in the Black Canyon? It was the moment Isabella had dreamed about, to go riding with him along the trails again. But he looked so morose that she wondered what was wrong. He had stopped by the cabin once or twice, looking bad-tempered, and one of the men said he was like that before an "ugly fit." Isabella had been too busy to take much notice, but now she was concerned.

"His mood was as dark as the sky overhead, which was black with an impending thunderstorm. He was quite silent, struck his horse often, started off on a furious gallop. No more whistling or singing, or talking to his beautiful mare, or sparkling repartee. We had not ridden more than two miles when a blinding squall came on, and I had to turn back. He turned back a little way with me to show me the trail. Then came a terrible revelation: as soon as I had gone away he had discovered he was attached to me, and it was killing him. It began on Longs Peak, he said."

Standing in the swirling snowflakes, Jim blurted out the terrible story of his life, telling Isabella details of events that horrified her. "It was one of the darkest tales of ruin I have ever heard or read. A less ungovernable nature would never have said a word, but his dark, proud, fierce soul all came out there. It made me shake all over and even cry."

Thick snow flakes whirled about the two of them as Isabella looked at Jim's glowering face: "My heart dissolved with pity for his dark, lost self-ruined life. I told him I could not speak to him, I was so nervous."

Jim was in a blind fury: "He said if I would not speak to him, he would not see me again. He would go and camp out on the Snowy Range till I was gone."

Turning his horse and shouting at Isabella, he rode off. She struggled back alone to the cabin, overwhelmed by the drama of the confrontation.

"I could not bear to think of him last night, out in the snow, neither eating nor sleeping, mad, lost, wretched, hopeless. It is really terrible." He had made her promise never to reveal some of the awful things he told her but "they come between me and the sunshine sometimes, and I wake at night to think of them," she confided to her sister.

Isabella had little experience of confessions of love from admiring men or emotional revelations of past sins. She had responded to Jim's charm, his gentleness beneath the rough facade, and his crying need for help which she longed to give him. Now, she was shattered.

"He is a man whom any woman might love but who no sane woman would marry. I believe for the moment he hated me and scorned himself. Nor did he ask me to marry him. He knew enough for that. He is so loveable and fascinating but so terrible."

Isabella busied herself with washing, sweeping the cabin with a buffalo tail, feeding the cows, watering the horses, making a batch of rolls, cleaning the pans, sewing her clothes. She tried not to dwell on what had happened.

Then Jim came to visit, and offered to show Isabella the trail up one of the most spectacular canyons. She did not refuse. They rode together, and he was polite, but coolly silent. He said nothing about the conversation of the day before. Isabella was confused. Had he been acting then, posing as a man who cared for her to arouse her sympathy? Or was it a real confession?

Isabella did not understand his sudden passionate declaration of love and then this icy coolness. She did not like the strangeness of Jim's moods, and worried that his wildness might lead him to harm her. She decided it was time to end the relationship. After considering what to do, she followed the approved style of well brought-up middle-class ladies, and wrote him a formal note:

"Dear Sir, In consequence of the very blameworthy way in which you spoke to me on Monday, there can be nothing but restraint between us. Therefore, it is my wish that our acquaintance shall at once terminate. Yours truly, ILB."

The reality of her situation—an unmarried woman sharing a cabin with two young men in the most intimate day-to-day contact, and emotionally entangled with a wild hard-drinking hunter in the desolate Rocky Mountains—had no effect on her behavior. She behaved as she would have done at home in Edinburgh society.

That day, Isabella met Jim out riding and gave him the note. He put it in his pocket. Apprehensive about his reaction, she waited. Nothing happened. She wrote to Hennie of a dream she had: "We were sitting by the fire, Mr. Nugent came in with his revolver and shot me," adding hastily: "But there is no such peril." A few days later, a passing trapper stopped at the cabin, and mentioned that Mr. Nugent was very ill. Isabella, concerned, saddled her horse and rode down to visit him. Halfway down the trail she saw him riding toward her.

"He said he did not wish to intrude on me but he was coming down to ask as a favor for an hour's conversation. We rode a little and then got off and sat under a tree. He was perfectly calm and rational and entered into the fullest explanation of his circumstances."

"I told him that if all circumstances on both sides had been favorable and I had loved him with my whole heart, I would not dare to trust my happiness because of whisky. I told him he must not be angry and I told him what I had heard of him from the first, and he admitted everything. He said he would never say another word of love."

Isabella knew that many of his difficulties came from his drinking and urged him to give up whiskey. He replied sadly: "I cannot, it binds me hand and foot. I cannot give up the only pleasure I have." She had seen enough of alcoholism in Scotland to know that his erratic allegations, his sudden remorse, his self-pity and his ability to ignore irrational behavior were all tell-tale signs. She longed to reform him, and had even thought of marriage, but it was too late. She assured Hennie: "You would like him so. He is so charming and can talk on all subjects and has real genius. Poor fellow, he had built such castles in the air of your coming to live here in the mountains." Isabella could not help remembering quiet well-meaning Mr. Wilson in Hawaii, who had wanted to marry her and whom she had dismissed so firmly, and wondered why she found the dark, tempestuous, and terrifying Mr. Nugent so much more fascinating.

Jim told her he planned to leave the park to go buffalo hunting, and would not see her again before she left. He said he felt better now that they understood each other. She agreed.

"I feel quite at ease about him now. He ought not to have told me that he loved me, but it was a mistaken notion of honor, and from my first acquaintance with him until now, he has acted and spoken as a perfect gentleman."

Isabella's frank letters to Hennie about Jim still included affectionate personal notes; "Oh my sweetest, how I long to see Its sweet unworldly face again, It must care for me and be demonstrative. I like names, and to be cared for," and "I generally dream of you and wake so disappointed because you are not there," and "I am always thinking of my one darling. I keep its picture on the table by me and when it says any nice words to me I read them over and over again."

Isabella needed to reassure Hennie that she loved her still, that she was always in her thoughts, and that their deep emotional bond was not threatened. No man could come between them.

Isabella was relieved to have come to such a peaceful agreement with Jim, and rediscovered the joys of Estes Park, riding through the magnificent scenery with the spectacular backdrop of the snow-covered mountains.

"Every day I admire it more, and the melancholy of its winter loneliness suits me. It is such a completely healthful life. Oh, how glorious it was to-night when crimson clouds descended just to the mountain tops and were reflected in the pure face of the snow. I think I never saw the procession of the stars so glorious as here."

She still thought of Jim. "I miss him very much. It is so sad to think of him and no more to see his Arab mare tied in front of the house, as it used to be almost daily. I do like a companion on horseback."

Jim missed her too. He kept postponing his departure for the buffalo hunt. Kavanagh and Buchanan saw him out riding in the mountains, looking miserable. For Isabella, life in the log cabin had settled into a pleasant routine. The young men shot an elk and then a deer, so there were venison steaks for every meal. It was the first time in weeks that Isabella had not felt hungry. One day she made a spiced gingerbread cake, baked three loaves of bread, washed and ironed her clothes and declared: "It is all hollow and sickly that idea of degradation in manual labor. I am quite sure all women would be better for stirring about their own houses."

Isabella invited Jim to the cabin for Thanksgiving dinner. He sighed, and said mournfully he was not fit for society and could not come. Isabella felt: "It really is miserable to see him. I can't do with this at all. I could not prolong my stay here because of him."

Isabella had had quite enough of Jim. It was time to go home. "I am howling frightfully, fearfully about leaving the place and the life, but it will be better when it is over now. I believe I should always be pretty well here, but that whenever I left it would be the same miserable downfall. So what good is there in staying?"

One night, a vicious winter storm blew in. Five calves died in the shed, the milk and treacle turned into ice, and the living room was covered with snow blown in through the chinks. When Isabella washed her hair the braids froze to her head.

It was now December, three weeks since she came back to Estes Park and there was no sign of Evans. Isabella saddled Birdie and rode off in an icy fog to find him and get her money. The pony struggled through the snow, her coat and mane covered with white ice crystals, while Isabella tried to spot the landmarks on the way. A bitter east wind blew fine hard frozen snow directly in her face, freezing her eyelids together with her tears. When she reached the hotel, she was lifted off her horse, her teeth chattering so with cold that she could not speak. But after several cups of hot tea and some food, she stopped shivering, went to bed, and slept through the night.

The next morning she found Evans at the hotel about to leave for Estes Park with his friend, Lord Dunraven. He gave her the money he owed her, much to Isabella's relief. She did some errands in Longmont, flattered to find that everyone had heard of her daring exploits. When the storm cleared, she remounted Birdie for the last ride back to Estes Park, the sun dazzling on the unbroken miles of white snow under a cloudless blue sky.

That night in the log cabin, she and the men cooked dinner and Jim came to join them. Isabella hardly recognized him. He had washed, put on clean clothes, and combed his hair into ringlets. For once, he looked like the gentleman she believed him to be. At the table, he talked and joked with the charm she had always admired, and later joined the others in singing songs around the organ. When he offered to accompany her on her ride out of Estes Park to the coach, she hesitated for a moment, and then accepted.

Next morning, she rode along the familiar trail to his cabin. Jim gave her a present, a soft mouse-colored beaver skin. Isabella rode his mare and they set off, Jim reciting poetry and talking with his old charm so that the time flew by as they rode together through the spectacular scenery.

"I never saw the mountain range look so beautiful—uplifted in every shade of transparent blue, till the sublimity of Long's Peak, and the lofty crest of Storm Peak bore only unsullied snow against the sky. Peaks gleamed in living light; canyons lay in depths of purple shade; a hundred miles away Pike's Peak rose a lump of blue, and over all, through the glorious afternoon, a veil of blue spiritualized without dimming the outlines of that most glorious range, making it look like the dreamed-of mountains of the 'land which is very far off,' till at sunset it stood out sharp in glories of violet and opal, and the whole horizon up to a great height was suffused with the deep rose and pure orange of the afterglow. It seemed all dream-like as we passed through the sunset solitude."

At the inn, Isabella and Jim sat together on the last evening talking quietly in the kitchen about his poetry and her writing. They made an incongruous pair—the neatly dressed English lady and the rough long-haired mountain man. Other guests peered in through the doorway at the dangerous desperado, amazed to see him so gentle and smiling while the innkeeper's children climbed on his knee and played with his ringlets.

The next morning, Jim stood with Isabella outside in the snow. The coach for Greeley arrived. Her baggage was loaded on. Isabella climbed aboard. She settled herself in her seat and the coach took off, rattling across the frozen ground.

Leaning forward, she looked out of the window. There was Jim, his hair gleaming golden in the sunshine, leading the beautiful mare over the snowy plains back to Estes Park, and the life she had loved so much. She never saw him again.

Dr. John Bishop

Section II
ACHIEVEMENTS
1874-1889

Chapter 6
A Journey to Japan

Writes magazine articles about her Rockies adventure. Meets John Bishop. Travels to Japan. Her first servant. Experiences hardships of journey.

Just before Isabella sailed from New York, she commented wryly in a letter to her friend Ella Blackie: "I still vote civilization a nuisance, society a humbug and all conventionality a crime, but possibly I may fall into the old grooves speedily."

Once back in Edinburgh, she did. She no longer gallivanted about in her riding costume, rounding up cattle or battling through snowdrifts.

She became the respectable Miss Bird, living demurely with her sister, visiting friends and doing good works. She spent her days writing. Her old friend John Murray had expressed interest in the Sandwich Islands and was eager to publish a book about her Hawaiian adventures. Sitting by the coal fire in rented rooms in Edinburgh, Isabella edited the letters and notes from the joyous six months in her tropical paradise.

When spring came, she and Hennie left Edinburgh and happily settled in at their white-painted cottage in Tobermory on the island of Mull. By the end of the summer the book was finished. She sent it off to John Murray in London with a certain amount of trepidation.

It was almost twenty years since her two books about America had been published, and both were out of print. She was apprehensive and confided to Ella Blackie: "I think the success of a book by a little known writer on an infinitesimal part of the earth is most problematical."

In February, 1875, 2,000 copies of *Six Months Among the Palm Groves, Coral Reefs and Volcanoes of the Sandwich Islands* were printed and published. From the first, it was received with tremendous enthusiasm.

The Spectator asserted that "everyone who loves scenery and the more detailed beauties of nature, and especially those who do not shrink from the awe-inspiring marvels of natural phenomena on a grand scale, should read this remarkably fascinating and beautifully written book, by a brave and cultivated lady who has seen all that she describes."

Her delight in Hawaii, while exuberant, was balanced, according to *The Athenaeum*. A model tourist, "bent upon seeing, doing, enjoying and describing everything, and devoid of crotchet or bias, she tempers her enthusiasm with judgement and reproduces what she sees with fidelity. We do not know any other book which so completely familiarizes the reader with the aspects of nature and life in the Hawaiian Archipelago."

Isabella's accurate scientific observations were praised by *Nature* magazine. Only *Saturday Review* was unimpressed, sniffing that "under all the vast mass of words there are, no doubt, now and then some interesting passages to be found by those who do not shrink from the trouble of getting at them."

For the rest of the year, reviews of the book appeared in journals everywhere. According to her friend Anna Stoddart: "Her rank amongst the foremost writers of travel and adventure was conclusively established."

Isabella wrote to John Murray: "I assure you I am beginning to think it rather a nice book! Seriously, there has been nothing but what is pleasant connected with it; and as it has been so very pleasant to me, I am glad that you are in a measure satisfied with its sale."

A second edition appeared the following year and seven more editions were published over the next fifteen years. The book is still in print today.

An editor at *Leisure Hour* magazine invited her to write an account of her adventures in the Rockies, so Isabella put together a series of 17 articles. She described the spectacular scenery, her rides in the mountains, the people she encountered in Colorado, and her romance with Rocky Mountain Jim. When the series appeared in print, it was tremendously popular.

But success revived Isabella's guilty conscience. She still believed she should never benefit from doing something she so much enjoyed. She ought to be doing good for others. When friends asked her to help with efforts to build a shelter for cabmen in Edinburgh, she quickly accepted.

The Town Council had voted to erect a shelter on Princes Street, but taken no action. Isabella wrote indignant letters, appeared at a public hearing, and at last the building began. The Cabmens' Shelter was opened on January 31, 1876, and within months was self-supporting. It was the kind of charity Isabella always liked—finding a practical solution to a human problem, and seeing the results working successfully.

Next, she joined a committee to establish a training college for medical missionaries, in memory of explorer Dr. David Livingstone. Dr. John Bishop was member of the committee. While Isabella was gallivanting around Hawaii and Colorado, he had come to Edinburgh to study medicine, qualified as a physician, and set up his practice.

He was, as Isabella later noted, a man of medium height, with a kind face, brown curly beard, gentle eyes behind his glasses, soft-spoken and respectful. A friend introduced them and he was most interested in Isabella's botanic discoveries in the Sandwich Islands. His research specialty was histology, the microscopic study of tissues. Isabella wrote to Ella Blackie that his "noble character compels one's increasing and respectful admiration."

Within weeks, she had acquired a microscope and spent many evenings with John Bishop, peering into the lenses at different specimens. She took a course in histology at the Edinburgh Botanical Gardens, and, to her friends' surprise, even talked of giving up travel for science.

John Bishop was equally enthusiastic. He appreciated her need for independence, and respected her intelligence. Though ten years younger than Isabella, he was convinced that she was the ideal woman to be his wife. Yet when he gently tried to bring up the subject of marriage, she said it was not a topic she ever wished to discuss.

In September he traveled to Tobermory on the island of Mull to visit her. They walked together along the winding country paths under the shady trees, and he once again talked of marriage. Isabella repeated that she did not wish to talk or think about marriage. John Bishop, unlike Rocky Mountain Jim, refrained from dashing off into the mountains on a horse, and calmly said he respected her decision. Isabella, relieved, confided to Ella Blackie: "He behaved so beautifully so that our intercourse will be quite free from embarrassment."

The real barrier to her emotional involvement with any man was her intense relationship with her sister. Their lives were now so intricately interwoven that outsiders were completely excluded. If Isabella was attracted to a man, as she was to John Bishop, she would not dream of disrupting her complicated relationship to Henrietta, the emotional anchor of her life, and thus upsetting the delicate balance of her work, her travel, and the close attachment to her sister.

During the winter, four years after she came home, the damp Scottish weather and her sedentary life reactivated her illnesses and backaches. A missionary friend from Honolulu who came to see her in Edinburgh hardly recognized the once-dynamic Isabella languishing on a sofa, in such pain that she was unable to get up and greet him.

Isabella again consulted several doctors. They never understood the strange paradox: a fragile, sickly, helpless woman who changed into a fearless, untiring, and irrepressible traveler. But they knew what to prescribe: a sea voyage and a change of air.

Given her mandate to escape, Isabella recognized by now that she no longer traveled only to find better health. She knew that it was the best way to find interesting material for her books and articles. She appreciated the fact that her aches and pains gave her a legitimate excuse to travel alone without raising eyebrows because she was a woman unaccompanied by a man. She also understood that away from home she had the freedom to behave in ways that were quite impossible within polite society, and noted: "Travellers are privileged to do the most improper things with perfect propriety."

Isabella searched for a place with enough unusual interest and adventure to provide material for her writing. She wrote to Charles Darwin asking for his advice about travel in South America, hoping to ride through the Andes as she had in Colorado's Rockies. But his reply was not encouraging. She knew Constance Gordon Cummings, another adventurous woman traveler and writer because Isabella had copy-edited her book on India for John Murray. She spoke to her about her travels in the Far East. Isabella was fascinated to hear about the great changes taking place in Japan in 1878. The country was in the midst of a cataclysmic upheaval as the old feudal system was transformed into a modern state. Little was known of the effects of the changes outside the major cities. With a sense of excitement, Isabella decided she would travel through the rural regions of Japan and find out. She also wanted to visit the aboriginal tribe of Ainos, on the northernmost island.

She wrote to John Murray, who was most enthusiastic. The editors of *Leisure Hour* assured her they were eager to publish anything she submitted. So she prepared to leave.

She traveled with very little luggage this time: medicines, riding costume and saddle, a few clothes, new boots, paper, notebooks, sketch pads, pens and ink, and letters of introduction to people in Japan.

She and Hennie gave three farewell parties for their friends in Edinburgh. A special prayer was said in church for Isabella's safe journey. Shortly before the boat sailed, Hennie fell ill. Since their old doctor had retired, Hennie consulted Dr. John Bishop. Isabella told Ella Blackie: "He has treated her admirably, and I am so glad that if the need arise she is now able to have a doctor who has learned something of her very sensitive constitution."

Though Isabella felt guilty at leaving her sick sister, she clung to the official reason for her travels: "I hope I shall get such health as that I may never be long separated from her again." The doctors, it should be noted, never prescribed travel or a change of air to improve Henrietta's health.

Isabella left England in April, 1878, to sail to New York. There, she took a train west to California, stopping in Chicago and Salt Lake City, and reached San Francisco to board a steamer to Yokohama, Japan. She had traveled thousands of miles half-way round the world, and her adventures had only just begun.

———

From the moment she arrived in Yokohama, Isabella realized she was in a new world, and she wasn't sure she liked it. On a walk in the city, she lost her way: she could not see any street signs or find the sequence of house numbers and she could not ask anyone for help because she did not speak Japanese. Unlike her previous travels, she was in a country where no one spoke English, the alphabet was completely different, and she could not read the newspapers, books, or signs.

"Yokohama has a dead-alive look," she concluded. "It has irregularity without picturesqueness, and the grey sky, grey sea, grey houses, and grey roofs look harmoniously dull."

It was not an auspicious start to her travels. The next day her spirits lifted when the British Consul, Sir Harry Parkes, and his wife came to visit her. Parkes had spent thirty years in the Far East, surviving a spell in a Chinese prison and an assassination attempt on his life in Japan. He assured Isabella that her plans to see the countryside were excellent; her only problems would be fleas and poor horses. He gave her a map and when she saw one rural area marked "insufficient information," he said cheerfully: "You will have to get your information as you go along and that will be all the more interesting." It was just the kind of encouragement Isabella needed.

Parkes arranged her travel passport, warned her about the "squeeze," the cut native servants took out of every monetary transaction along the way, and sent her by train to Tokyo to see Ernest Satow, the renowned expert on Japanese history, who would answer her many questions.

Satow explained that for over two hundred and fifty years, Japan was unified by the Tokugawa family. The rulers, Shoguns, had preserved peace inside Japan but cut off all outside contact with the world. In 1854 the United States naval officer Matthew C. Perry forced the opening of trade with the West. The Shogunate collapsed, the Meiji

Restoration returned formal power to the Emperor Meiji in 1868 and a new government was established under samurai leadership. Meanwhile, America was struggling through the years of Civil War and the period of Reconstruction.

Ten years later, when Isabella arrived, Japan was busy modernizing. Satow warned her that the cities were changing rapidly but the new order had hardly touched the villages, where all foreigners were regarded with suspicion.

Isabella was eager to set off. But for the first time, she needed a interpreter and servant to help her. She had to collect her information through the filter of another person and it was important that she trust him. She interviewed several young men for the position, and chose Ito. He was only eighteen, and an inch shorter than her. He said he could cook, write English, walk twenty-five miles a day, and had been on a trip to the interior. His most useful asset was that Isabella could understand his English and he could understand her.

"He has a round and singularly plain face, good teeth, much elongated eyes. He is the most stupid-looking Japanese I have seen, but I think that the stupidity is partly assumed." She hired him on the spot, and they signed a contract.

Lady Parkes helped her pack two light baskets covered with oil-paper, and she took a stretcher bed, a folding-chair, and an india-rubber bath. She also had an air-pillow to sit on, candles, and an Anglo-Japanese dictionary.

On a sunny morning in June 1878, wearing a gray striped tweed skirt and jacket, Isabella was ready. On her head was a Japanese bamboo sun-hat with a light frame inside. Her special passport was tucked in a bag at her waist, and her money was packed away in bundles of notes. Her friends stood outside the British Legation waving as the runners picked up the long wooden handles of her three loaded chariots or "kuramas," and Isabella was on her way to discover the real Japan she longed to find.

Once beyond the city, she bowled along past the flat swamplands. The houses were poor and shabby, with the front open to the street. She saw men and women working in ricefields, up to their knees in slush, as they "puddled" the rice, pulling out the weeds and tangled plants that strung themselves around the rice tufts. On islands above the water, she spotted wheat, onions, millet, beans and peas growing. On the ponds floated huge white lilies and lotus flowers.

After a couple of hours, the runners stopped at a teahouse. Isabella sat in the Japanese garden. Looking around she saw "baked mud, smooth stepping-stones, a little pond with some goldfish, a deformed pine, and a stone lantern." A smiling young woman came to set up a small lacquer table with a tiny teapot and a little cup without handles or saucer. When the hot water was poured on the tea leaves, it turned a soft amber color. Isabella tasted it cautiously, and discovered it had a delicious aroma and flavor. She ate a bowl of cold rice, and watched her runners heat theirs up by pouring hot tea over it. They washed their feet, rinsed their mouths, ate salt fish and pickles and smoked their pipes.

A kurama

After about an hour's rest, her entourage set off. Isabella soon learned to distinguish between the teahouses. There was the "chaya" which offered food; the "yadoya" or hotel; the one-room roadside stands; the elaborate three-story structures with flags and lanterns; and the teahouses where the "vices which degrade and enslave the man-hood of Japan" were practiced, as she noted crisply. By five o'clock after about 23 miles of travel, they arrived at Kasukabe, a derelict, rundown village. On this journey Isabella kept a careful daily log of how many miles she traveled and the names of the places where she stayed.

In Kasukabe, Isabella had her first experience of a Japanese inn. The two-story building was filled with travelers and she noticed an unpleasant smell. She was shown her room, up a steep wooden step-ladder. It was divided from the other rooms by sliding panels covered with opaque paper, and one wall was made of frames of thin paper, with many holes and tears in it. The room was absolutely bare - no shelf, rail, hook, bed or chair. Isabella glanced at the matting on the floor and saw thousands of frolicking fleas. Around her, she could hear the persistent buzzing of mosquitoes.

Ito put up her stretcher bed with its large green canvas mosquito net. He brought her tea, rice and eggs, and took her passport to the inn owner for copying. She tried to write up her notes for the day, but the constant biting of the fleas and mosquitoes was too distracting. Then she saw the sliding screens eased open so that several pairs of dark eyes peered at her through the cracks. Isabella banged the screens shut. She watched as they slowly opened again. She gave up and climbed into her stretcher bed.

On all sides, she could hear strange noises. Nearby, a man chanted Buddhist prayers in a high voice, there was the insistent twang of a guitar, the sound of people talking and splashing, the banging of drums and tomtoms. Several times the fire-watchman passed outside, clapping his hands and beating two pieces of wood together as he walked around the village. Suddenly, she felt her bed giving way: a piece of canvas nailed to the wooden bars creaked and split away from its framework along one side. Not daring to move, she found herself slowly slipping toward the fleas on the matting, and waited apprehensively in case the entire contraption collapsed.

She heard Ito's voice outside the room: "It would be best, Miss Bird, that I should see you." She got up. Outside were two policemen who for unknown reasons wanted to check her passport again. There was also a messenger from the British Legation with a note from Sir Harry. When they left, she lay on her hastily mended bed uneasily waiting for the morning light.

Other travelers might have considered going home. Isabella declared cheerfully: "Already I can laugh at my fears and misfortunes. A traveller must buy his own experience, and success or failure depends mainly on personal idiosyncrasies."

She had been told the trip was rough, and was prepared for discomfort. She found that everywhere in rural Japan the inns were appalling. Fleas and mosquitoes attacked her, noises kept her awake, bad smells permeated the rooms and the food was terrible. It was not until she reached Nikko, famous for its magnificent temples, that she saw a more pleasant side of life.

This time she rented a room with a Japanese family, the Kanayas. The only sounds were the stream rushing by and the twittering of birds. Peonies, irises, and azaleas grew in profusion. The two-story house had gleaming wooden floors and white mats, and was spotlessly clean.

Isabella's large room was enclosed by sliding screens made of sky-blue paper splashed with gold. On one wall was a painting on white silk of a blossoming cherry branch. Hanging on a polished post was a spray of rose azalea in a white vase, and in another vase stood a single purple iris.

The Kanaya's home

The change was dramatic, and Isabella confessed: "I almost wish that the rooms were a little less exquisite, for I am in constant dread of spilling the ink, indenting the mats or tearing the paper windows."

She spent two weeks observing Japanese family life. The women were busy weaving or spinning cotton, caring for the children, talking together. Isabella loved the children.

"I have never yet heard a baby cry, and I have never seen a child troublesome or disobedient. The arts and threats by which English mothers cajole or frighten children into unwilling obedience appear unknown. I admire the way in which children are taught to be independent in their amusements." She watched them flying kites, spinning waterwheels in a stream, and harnessing paper carts to beetles, and visited a school. At a children's party, little girls, dressed in flowered silk kimonos, acted with the gracious politeness of the adults, drinking tea and playing quiet games. The longer she stayed in Japan, the more impressed she was.

"I never saw people take so much delight in their offspring, carrying them about, or holding their hands in walking, watching and entering into their games, supplying them constantly with new toys, taking them to picnics and festivals, never being content to be without them, and treating other people's children with a suitable measure of affection and attention."

The pleasure of Nikko disappeared once she set out again. Now heavy rain poured down day after day. The roads were so bad that travel by "kurama" was impossible. Isabella mounted a Japanese horse, with a shaggy mane and forelock, led by a woman holding a rope tied round its nose. When the ground was rough, the woman tied straw sandals over the horses' feet. Isabella found her saddle made of two packs of straw with a folded cotton futon on top, which forced her to balance about a foot above the horse's back. Her legs hung down over his neck. The trick was to learn how to sit without tipping over. Once, going downhill, she slid over the horse's head into a mudhole. For the first time in her life, she found riding depressing, and was exhausted after hours sitting on the high saddle.

The inns became more primitive. Ito, who had never traveled outside Yokohama to see rural Japan, was so shocked that he told her: "I am ashamed for a foreigner to see such a place."

Isabella's descriptions spared no detail of what she found. She realized that her view of Japanese travel was very different from the romantic accounts by other European travelers and she explained:

"I write the truth as I see it, and if my accounts conflict with those of tourists who write of the Tokaido and Nakasendo, of Lake Biura and Hakone, it does not follow that either is inaccurate. But truly this is a new Japan to me, of which no books have given me any idea, and it is not fairyland."

At one inn, Isabella's sympathies were roused by the terrible cough of the owner's little boy. She dosed him with one of her medicines which cured him. Next morning Isabella found men and women crowded outside her room, holding children with infected eyes, terrible sores, skin diseases, ringworm, and more.

"Sadly I told them that I did not understand their diseases and that I had no stock of medicine," and explained that in her country people kept healthy by washing themselves and their clothes in water.

In the rural communities, a foreigner was a rare creature. As Isabella traveled further north, her arrival attracted crowds of people. They stood staring at her, pushing and peering to see the strange visitor. One evening, when she went out for a walk, hundreds of men and women waited on the street and shuffled behind her in their clogs. Isabella disliked the constant staring and the lack of privacy.

She was also affected by the bad weather and was not feeling well, admitting: "I find it impossible in this damp climate and in my present poor health to travel with any comfort for more than two or three days at a time."

When she reached Shinjo, her left hand and arm were swollen, her back ached, and she had a fever. She told Ito she wanted to see a doctor. Ito brought Dr. Nosoki, who bowed three times to Isabella.

"He asked to see my 'honorable hand' and 'honorable foot.' He felt my pulse and looked at my eyes with a magnifying glass, and with much sucking in of his breath informed me that I had much fever, which I knew before; then that I must rest, which I also knew; then he lighted his pipe and contemplated me."

Suddenly he clapped his hands. A servant brought in a handsome black lacquer chest, fitted with shelves, drawers, and bottles of medicine. The doctor made up a lotion, bandaged Isabella's hand and arm with oiled paper, and told her to pour the lotion over the bandages at intervals until the pain stopped. He gave her a powder to bring down her fever, and told her not to drink any more sake!

Isabella, fascinated, asked about his training. His father had taught him all he knew. His remedies were 'moxa' (herbs that burned the skin), acupuncture, medicinal baths, some animal and vegetable medicines and certain kinds of foods. He showed her his medicines: ginseng, rhinoceros horn, and powdered tigers' livers. Opening a small box with great care he told her it was powdered unicorn's horn which was worth more than its weight in gold. Though skeptical, Isabella found her swollen arm improved and she felt better.

She was now completely dependent on Ito, who had proved to be all that she had hoped. She learned a great deal from him, and he was absolutely reliable. He dealt with rapacious innkeepers, looked out for food along the way, and answered questions from the staring crowds. Isabella gave him her watch, passport and half her money each night. Following her example, he kept a diary which he sometimes read to her, surprising her with his observations. He wrote down new English words as he learned them and questioned her each day about their meanings.

He kept details of all bills and receipts in a special book, and wrote down English transliterations of all the places they visited. When they arrived in a village, he found out the number of houses, the special trades, and other useful information from the police or a local authority. He was most concerned about accuracy, repeating Isabella's maxim: "If it's not true, it's not worth having." Since he did not drink, go out at night, or show any inclination for a rowdy life, he won Isabella's complete approval.

He also dealt pragmatically with Isabella's ailments. When she complained about her backache or other pains, Ito told her frankly: "I'm very sorry for you, but it's no use saying so over and over again. I can do nothing for you." Realizing that Isabella's ills would never stop her traveling, he accepted them as inevitable, and ignored them.

Isabella was far too interested in all she saw to allow mere discomfort to stop her: "I no longer care to meet Europeans; indeed I should go far out of my way to avoid them. I have become quite used to Japanese life, and think that I learn more about it in travelling in this solitary way than I should otherwise."

At Kubota, the rain stopped. Relieved, Isabella rested for a few days. She was honored by an invitation to a Japanese wedding. In the morning, she was shown the rich brocades, wine, and lacquered bowls of the bride's dowry and gifts. In the evening, the 17-year-old bride was carried in a procession to the bridegroom's house. She was dressed entirely in white silk, covered from head to foot with a veil of white silk. Two girls brought her into a large room where the groom, aged 23, sat staring fixedly at the floor. Cups of sake and food were served to the bride, the groom, and the parents, who sat at the side. The girls poured a two-spouted kettle of sake into the mouths of the bride and groom, the symbolic joining of man and wife.

"It was a very dull and tedious affair, conducted in melancholy silence, and the young bride, with her whitened face and painted lips, looked and moved like an automaton," Isabella observed. Only when the wedding guests arrived after the ceremony for the feast was there a sense of celebration.

Traveling on, Isabella reached the harbor where she planned to sail north and find the aboriginal tribes of Ainos. Once again, it was pouring with rain, the rivers were high, and the roads almost impassable. Climbing a steep ridge, she saw huge gray waves breaking on the shore and the island steamer to Hokkaido about to leave.

Isabella boarded quickly. Wrapped in borrowed blankets, she settled herself in a cabin. Fierce winds tossed the boat from side to side, developed into a gale, and battered the steamer on all sides with gust-driven waves. Isabella loved every minute of it. When the boat bounced into the island harbor of Hakodate, the quay was awash with pounding waves and heavy rain poured down.

There was no one to meet her. Consulate officials, alerted by Sir Harry Parkes to the arrival of famous author and traveler Isabella Bird, had assumed the storm was too fierce for anyone to take a steamer crossing. Isabella and Ito walked to a nearby Church Mission House to dry her clothes and find a bed for the night.

Japanese raincoat

Chapter 7
Meeting the Ainos.

Visit to tribe of Ainos. Lives with primitive tribal families. Explores Hokkaido.

When Isabella walked into the British Consulate next morning, the officials fell all over themselves with embarrassment at having failed to meet her. A room was ready for her, and she was invited to a banquet that evening to meet three explorers visiting the island.

At dinner that night Isabella was introduced to Count Diesbach of the French Legation, Mr. Von Siebold of the Austrian Legation, and Lieutenant Kreitner of the Austrian Army. She listened politely as Count Diesbach outlined their plans to map Hokkaido's mountains and visit the tribes of aboriginal Ainos. She too hoped to visit Biratori, one of the largest Aino villages, and study the tribal customs, and to travel inland to confirm the presence of volcanoes.

As the three men bragged about the quantities of food, claret, and heavy boxes they were taking on pack-ponies, she was skeptical about their achievements.

"I predict that they will fail, and that I, who have reduced my luggage to 45 lbs., will succeed! I have planned it for myself with the confidence of an experienced traveller, and look forward to it with great pleasure, as a visit to the aborigines is sure to be full of novel and interesting experiences."

Isabella, usually modest about her successes, had spent four months traveling in Japan to cover over 600 miles of almost unknown territory, and arrived safely. Though she wrote as if she were a woman of limited ability and intellect experiencing travel and adventure almost by accident, she was now a professional and expert at what she did. In Japan, having survived the most challenging journey she had ever undertaken, she felt a new confidence and an appreciation of what she had accomplished.

The next day, Isabella left the consulate with Ito to explore Hokkaido. The island was shrouded in myths and stories of magic. Ito, like most Japanese, called the Ainos "dogs" because they were reputed to be hairy, and repeated to Isabella the rumors of their bizarre religious practices and ritual tattooing.

Female tattooed hand

When they reached a village on Mororan Bay, Isabella saw for the first time the Aino storehouses of woven grass perched on six-foot stilts, and their homes made of reeds tied on a wooden framework, with small windows and high thatched roofs. Three Aino men were hired to pull Isabella's "kurama" to the next village, and she observed:

"They were very kind and so courteous that I quite forgot that I was alone among savages. The two lads were young and beardless, their lips were thick, and their mouths very wide." They reminded her of Eskimos, with long straight black hair falling to their shoulders.

The older man she found "completely beautiful in features and expression, with a lofty, sad, far-off, gentle, intellectual look. His manner was most graceful, and he spoke both Aino and Japanese in the low musical tone which I find is a characteristic of Aino speech. These Ainos never took off their clothes, but merely let them fall from one of or both shoulders when it was very warm."

When they had to cross a deep stream, the older man carried her on his shoulders with great care. At a muddy waterlogged swamp, they held the 'kurama' high in the air so that she kept dry. They helped her into the low flat scow to scull over two rivers they had to cross. Isabella had a wonderful time.

"I enjoyed the afternoon thoroughly. It is so good to have got beyond the confines of stereotyped civilization and the trammels of Japanese traveling to the solitude of nature and an atmosphere of freedom. The breeze came up from the sea, rustled the reeds, and waved the tall plumes of the Eulalia Japonica, and the thunder of the Pacific surges boomed through the air with its grand, deep bass. Poetry and music pervaded the solitude and my spirit was rested."

Ito found clean rooms in a new inn, and cooked broiled salmon for supper. Next morning, Isabella woke to the sound of horses' hooves thudding down the street. Every day, the villagers drove wild horses into a corral for people to select the animals they needed. Isabella settled on a horse, and happy to be riding again, set off toward the next village. Ahead she saw riding towards her Mr. Von Siebold and Count Diesbach, accompanied by an Aino man.

The Count galloped up, jumped off his horse and cried: "The fleas! The fleas!" He had suffered agonies from the fleas, the mosquitoes and the unbearably rough traveling. Lieutenant Kreiter had deserted them. Their plans for exploration had failed completely. They could not wait to get back to the comforts of civilization. Isabella was introduced to Benri, the chief of the Biratori village, who had traveled back with them. He bowed, and assured Isabella she would be welcome to visit his people but he would be away for a few days.

The invitation was more than Isabella had hoped for. With the blessing of the chief, her stay would be far more successful. She immediately set off with Ito, three horses, and a guide following the route through the woods to a river where she climbed into a dug-out canoe. The boat slipped swiftly past several villages along the shores until they reached Biratori, nestled beneath a slope of trees with peaks of mountains beyond. The guide led the way to the chief's house. Benri's nephew, Shinondi, greeted them. The men helped Ito unload the horses and Isabella followed Shinondi into a large one-roomed hut amid several storehouses on stilts.

She was taken to a movable platform in front of the large fireplace, the place of honor. An ornamental mat was unrolled for her to sit on. Shinondi brought her water in a lacquered bowl from the well.

"They said that Benri, the chief, would wish me to make his house my own for as long as I cared to stay, and I must excuse them in all things in which their ways were different from my own," Ito translated for her. Some men spoke Japanese while others only understood the native language.

Aino storehouse

The one person who did not welcome her was the chief's mother, a wizened old woman with a shock of white hair who sat at the side of the hut glaring at Isabella.

"She alone is suspicious of strangers, and she thinks my visit bodes no good to her tribe," Isabella noted. "I see her eyes fixed upon me now, and they make me shudder. She sits there watching, watching always."

That evening, Shinondi returned with a group of men, many of them with full, gray, wavy beards. Each one waved his hands and stroked his beard, the formal welcome, and then sat alongside the fireplace. Behind them seven women sat in a row, splitting bark for weaving.

"I never saw such a strangely picturesque sight as that group of magnificent savages," noted Isabella. "The fitful firelight on their faces, the flare of the torch, the strong lights, the blackness of the recesses of the room, and the row of savage women in the background."

Benri's principal wife, Noma, stood by the fire. She was busy cutting wild roots, green beans and seaweed into a large hanging iron pot, with shredded dried fish and venison as well as millet, water and fish-oil. She stirred it occasionally with a wooden spoon. When it was ready, the women ladled the food from the pot into lacquer bowls, serving the men first. Then men and women sat eating together. After the bowls were emptied, sake was poured in and a finely-carved stick laid across it. Isabella watched as each person waved the bowl and the stick in a ceremonial obeisance to the gods before the wine was drunk.

Isabella handed round some mild tobacco as a gift. She explained that she came from a land "so very far away that a horse would have to gallop day and night for five weeks to reach it," and was interested in learning about their customs for her people. She asked a question in English which Ito translated into Japanese for Shinondi. Shinondi translated it into Aino, and waited for the answer. This often took time as the old men discussed the question among themselves, trying to find an answer on which they all agreed. They begged her not to tell the Japanese government anything, fearful that officials would come and suppress their traditions.

Isabella learned that the center of their religion was the bear, considered a god. They hunted the animal and admired his fierceness and courage. The chief, Benri, was said to be "as strong as a bear" and a brave young man was sometimes called "a young bear."

Isabella had noticed a large bear in a cage near the chief's hut. Outside were tall poles with the skulls of bears on top. The men told her that every year a newborn bear cub was captured and brought back to the village, suckled by one of the women and treated as a household pet. When it grew too big, it was put into the cage to become full-grown for the Festival of the Bear.

On the appointed day, the celebration began. With the men shouting and yelling around the cage, the chief shot an arrow to wound the animal. As soon as the bear was snarling and furious, the cage door was opened. The bear leapt out and the men rushed at him with weapons. Every man tried to cut him in some way because bear blood brought good luck. After a struggle, the huge animal fell to the ground. The men cut off his head, placed it on a pole and divided up the carcass among the tribe. A day of feasting followed. In some villages the woman who had nursed the bear screamed piercingly as he was killed, and hit the men with the branch of a tree.

In the half-light from the flames of the fire, Isabella asked questions, listened intensely to Ito's translation, gazed at the scene before her. As the women cleared away the bowls, Isabella asked about the tattoos she could see on their faces and hands. Every woman had a thick, dark line above and below the mouth, a line across the knuckles, and elaborate bracelet patterns up her arms. The men explained to her that tattooing was part of their religion.

Children were cut above and below the mouth, and soot from the fire was rubbed into the cuts, which were later washed with liquid from tree bark. The arm tattoos began at about age five, and were extended every year up to the time of marriage. The tribe believed that no woman could marry without tattoos.

At last the old men left, waving their arms to her gracefully in farewell. Isabella settled in her trestle bed under the mosquito net, shivering from the cold, listening to the breeze rustling through the trees and the voices of Ito and Shinondi talking quietly together. The other men and women lay down to sleep on the floor of the hut behind screens.

Then Isabella saw the chief's wife, Noma, approach the fireplace, set a lamp with a fish-oil wick on the ground, and sit down to sew strips of blue cloth on to a piece of bark cloth. Isabella looked at her unhappy face and remembered that Benri had taken a second wife because Noma had no children. After she left, Isabella fell asleep.

At dawn she was woken by people coming into the hut. Ito prepared rice for her to eat, while the women served the others from the big pot over the fire. When Isabella offered some rice to the young children in the hut, they asked their parents' permission and waved their little hands in appreciation.

After the meal, the men left to go hunting. The women drew water from the well, chopped wood for the fire, ground millet and dug the soil for crops. Sitting in the hut, Isabella watched several young women sitting on the floor weaving without a loom, using the special tree bark to make coats. The children ran about. At the side, the chief's mother sat scowling.

Ito discovered that two of the young women understood Japanese, though they had not said a word when the men were present. Now, they talked to him, laughing and teasing, eager to answer Isabella's questions. Girls never married before the age of seventeen, and men at twenty-one. The custom was for the man to ask the chief's permission first and if granted, to ask the girl's father. The man gave a present to the father, and the marriage followed, celebrated by songs and sake.

The bride's dowry was a pair of large hoop earrings, and a richly embroidered kimono. The husband provided a house, for couples lived separately from parents. A man could take a second wife if his first was childless, as the chief, Benri, had done. Divorce was permitted, if the chief agreed.

Isabella saw that the women were the same height as she was, about five feet high, and several inches shorter than the men. They had straight dark hair, high foreheads, straight noses, well-formed mouths with small white teeth, beautiful brown eyes with long silky eyelashes that gave them a gentle expression, and though their skin was dark, they looked more European than Asiatic.

As the conversation in the hut became ever livelier, the chief's mother suddenly spoke sharply. She told the women she would tell their husbands they had been talking to strangers if they said another word. At once, there was complete silence. The women went on with their weaving and sewing without saying another word.

Then a young man limped in. He was Pipichari, Benri's adopted son. He had cut his foot on a fishing expedition. The women crowded round, but none of them knew what to do.

Isabella told him it was important to wash and bandage it. He sat impassively as she rinsed the cut with warm water, and wrapped a lint bandage around it. As the pain eased, he bowed low and kissed her hand. When the word of Pipichari's cure spread, several children were brought in for her to examine. Isabella sadly explained she had no knowledge of how to treat a malformed leg or skin disease, but one man begged her to see his wife who was having difficulty breathing. Isabella followed him to a small hut.

"She was lying in a coat of skins, tossing on the hard boards of her bed, with a matting-covered roll under her head. I took her dry, hot hand - such a small hand, tattooed all over the back - and it gave me a strange thrill."

Diagnosing bronchitis, she gave the woman cough medicine. Later that night she was called back again, and dosed her with brandy and beef-tea. She knew if the woman died, they would think she had killed her. Fortunately, by morning the woman felt better.

In gratitude, the husband offered to show Isabella their temple. This caused great consternation among the other men: no outsider had ever seen the temple before. Again they begged her not to tell the Japanese government.

Aino patriarch

Isabella followed the line of men to a steep hill just beyond the village. She scrambled up the remnants of a wooden staircase and helping hands pulled her up to the edge of a cliff. There she saw a wooden shrine made of simple unlacquered black wood. One man drew back the sliding doors. All bowed with much reverence. Inside was a shelf with a figure of a man in a suit of inlaid brass armor. He represented the god Yoshitsune, a renowned soldier. Beside him stood a pair of brass candlesticks, a Chinese painting of a junk, and a bell.

One man rang the bell three times to alert the god to their presence. They all bowed three times, and made six libations of sake. Isabella was invited to bow down but she politely declined saying she could only worship her own god. She realized "No European had ever stood where I stood, and there was a solemnity in the knowledge."

As they huddled on the narrow ledge of the cliff, Benri, the chief, suddenly arrived. The others greeted him with great respect, but he looked angry. He had not wanted anyone to answer Isabella's questions until he returned, and he was very displeased at seeing her by the temple.

He had returned with large quantities of sake which he quickly distributed. Within hours, Isabella saw that most of the villagers were completely drunk, lying unconscious on the ground. It reminded her of the drunks lying on the streets of Edinburgh. She was disappointed in Benri as a leader and disapproved of his own heavy drinking, and his sudden violence.

Benri was renowned as a hunter, and used traps and pits, as well as bows and poisoned arrows, with poison made from monkshood root pounded into a pulp. She asked him to show her how he went hunting, and he grabbed his spear to demonstrate.

"He looked a truly magnificent savage, stepping well back with the spear in rest, and then springing forward for the attack, his arms and legs turning into iron, the big muscles standing out in knots, his frame quivering with excitement, the thick hair falling back in masses from his brow, and the fire of the chase in his eye."

Isabella had stayed for three days in the village, and it was time to leave. The men and women presented a special farewell dance in her honor, slow languid movements to the accompaniment of whining music played on a guitar, the strings made from whale sinews. The villagers pressed gifts on her—cakes of millet, venison fat, a fine bearskin—but she refused them all because she could not carry them with her. As she rode out of Biratori, the entire village stood watching, smiling and waving their hands in traditional style.

Isabella's enthusiasm for the simple life of the noble savage had undergone a radical change. She was forced to admit that it was far from noble. She saw little to impress her in the character of the people she had met, and decided: "They are charming in many ways but make one sad, too, by their stupidity, apathy, and hopelessness. The glamour which at first disguises the inherent barrenness of savage life has had time to pass away, and I see it in all its nakedness as a life not much raised above the necessities of animal existence, timid, monotonous, barren of good, dark, dull."

She rode off to explore Hokkaido. Her goal was to find out if there were ancient volcanoes on the island. When she saw smoke and steam gushing out of cracks in the ground, she noted: "There was light pumice everywhere, but nothing like recent lava. One fissure was completely lined with exquisite, acicular crystals of sulphur. Lower down were two hot springs with a deposit of sulphur round their margins, and bubbles of gas, which from its strong, garlicky smell, I suppose to be sulphurated hydrogen."

When she put her thermometer in a hot spring, the heat registered beyond boiling point and broke the thermometer. She held an egg in a handkerchief on a stick in the water, and timed it: "It was hard boiled in 8½ minutes. The water evaporated without leaving a trace of deposit on the handkerchief, and there was no crust round the margin. It boiled and bubbled with great force."

Reaching a ridge of volcanic tufa cones, she scrambled up to see a deep crater that resembled the old cones on Kauai, proof of volcanic activity on the island.

"I have enjoyed few things more than that exploring expedition. The scenery was magnificent, and after getting so far, I longed to explore the sources of the rivers. I felt an intuitive perception of the passion and fascination of exploring, and understood how people could give up their lives to it. Oh that I had the strength!"

Isabella knew that if she wanted to be taken seriously as an explorer she needed to adopt the methodology and tools of the profession. For the first time, she noted the miles she traveled, the name of every place she stayed, the distances covered and other factual details of exploration as well as the personal adventures, human stories and descriptions of natural beauty.

Visiting different Aino villages, she reached Lebunge. Here the villagers were shorter, with very low foreheads and deep-set eyes, and were sullen and less talkative. Most of them had extremely dark skins, and were almost completely covered with hair. One man looked exactly like the "Missing Link" in the chain of evolution from ape to man, which she had read about in Charles Darwin's *Origin of Species*. Isabella drew a careful sketch, and wrote a detailed description of what she had seen, convinced it was a significant discovery.

Her time on Hokkaido was ending. Ito had to return home to accompany a botanist exploring in China. He asked her: "Are you sorry that it's the last morning? I am." She regretfully agreed with him.

They rode slowly back along the shore and returned to the port of Hakodate. Isabella went straight to the British Consulate to spend a few days writing up her notes and found several letters from her sister waiting for her. Then she took a steamer back to Yokohama.

Chapter 8
Pilgrimage to Sinai

Camel trip in Sinai Desert. Visits site where Ten Commandments were given. Debilitating heat. Returns to England.

Isabella settled easily into the British Consulate in Tokyo without complaining about the comforts of civilization. She wrote long journal-letters to her sister, the basis of her future book, and checked many facts about Japan with local experts. She was invited to dinner parties, visited temples, and even toured the crematorium.

On December 19, 1878, she left Yokohama for England. She planned to sail west through the Suez Canal, which had opened in 1869, to make a complete tour around the world. She watched Mount Fuji's snow-covered peak slowly fade into the mist. The ship steamed on and she watched with excitement as the coast of Asia appeared.

"The mysterious continent which has been my dream from childhood—bare, lofty, rocky, basaltic; islands of naked rock separated by narrow channels, majestic perpendicular cliffs, a desolate uninhabited region, lashed by a heavy sea, with visions of swirling mists, shrieking sea-birds, and Chinese high-sterned fishing-boats, with treble-reefed, three-cornered brown sails."

After a few days in Shanghai, she sailed on to Hong Kong, and Saigon, to be dazzled by the bustle, color and vivacity of Oriental life. She spent several weeks in the Malay States, which were under British protection. As a guest of the British government, Isabella explored villages, rode an elephant through the jungle, and shared her table with tame monkeys.

From Asia, she took a boat to the port of Alexandria in Egypt and traveled south to Cairo. The British were very interested in all things Egyptian. Prime Minister Benjamin Disraeli had persuaded Egyptian Viceroy Ismail in 1875 to sell his Canal shares to the British to ease the country's financial crisis. Grateful, Ismail sent a gift to London of an ancient stone obelisk called Cleopatra's Needle, but continued debts led to the appointment of a British-French controller to take charge of Egypt's finances in 1880. Next the British grabbed political control, and for the next forty years, Britain ruled Egypt under a series of High Commissioners.

British magazines and newspapers published romantic articles about life in the desert and the wandering Bedouins. Novelist Amelia Edwards explored the ruined pyramids and palaces along the Nile for her bestselling book, *A Thousand Miles Up the Nile*. Steamships sailed regularly from London to Alexandria. Thomas Cook organized his first excursions there in 1869. Hundreds of travelers came to see the soaring pyramids, the sunsets on the Nile, and camels striding across the sand.

Isabella's destination was a personal mission. She had grown up with the Bible story of the exodus of the Israelites from Egypt, their wanderings in the desert, and how Moses received the Ten Commandments from the Lord on Mount Sinai. Throughout her childhood, her father had emphasized the importance of those laws. His favorite theme was the sacredness of the fifth commandment, "Remember the Sabbath Day to keep it holy." She planned a pilgrimage across the desert to Mount Sinai as a journey of faith, to see the place where the Ten Commandments were first given to mankind. From the balcony of her hotel room overlooking the spectacularly blue waters of the Red Sea, she gazed across the Gulf of Suez to the opposite shore. There she could see the Sinai desert stretching east, and the Sinai mountains, some 270 miles away.

The hotel manager assured the renowned Miss Bird that the 18-day journey was not too difficult. He arranged an escort of several Bedouin and camels, and Hassan as her personal servant and guide. Isabella packed her own limited supply of food - two tins of condensed milk, two of cocoa-and-milk, some raisins, some flour, a pot of raspberry jam, some rice, and some Liebig's extract of meat - as well as her medicines, some brandy, a white umbrella, a wash-basin, a lamp, a canvas roll with her clothes, her Bible, and Murray's *Handbook of Travel*. Equipped with a large tent for herself and a small one for Hassan, a mattress, blankets, cooking utensils, and a folding chair, she sailed across the Gulf to a ramshackle pier. Though Isabella's books rarely mention her own washing and going to the bathroom under primitive circumstances, the logistics must have challenged her modesty. As soon as she realized that having her own tent provided a shelter for personal privacy, she always took a tent on her travels.

Her guides were waiting—five swarthy Bedouin, wrapped in long white cotton robes with a rope round the waist, and turbans and sandals. Hassan, her servant, spoke a little English. He supervised the loading of her baggage and goatskin waterbags on to the four braying camels, while she set off to walk the few miles to the Wells of Moses, the first oasis. Its black outline of palm trees and tamarisks stood out sharply against the desert sands.

By the time she arrived, her tent was set up. The sun was setting in a blaze of color. Isabella was overwhelmed by the realization that she had walked on the actual sands of the Sinai desert, the name she had repeated so often in reading her Bible. Almost on this very spot Moses had led the Israelites from the green Nile Valley across the Red Sea escaping from Egypt.

"It was most fascinating to sit on the crimsoned sands and be perfectly sure that either somewhat higher up or lower down the pillar of fire guided the host of Israel from the land of bondage to the freedom of the desert," she noted. "How real the Pentateuch has already become!"

Hassan made her dinner. Night fell quickly. Stars sparkled brightly in the velvet dark sky, and white moonlight streamed across the sand. The Bedouin made a fire of dried camel's dung they had picked up along the way. After feeding the camels, they sat around the fire, with the camels looming in the shadows of the flickering flames like misshapen mountains. The men talked and smoked together for a while, and then wrapping themselves in their goat's hair cloaks, lay down to sleep beside the animals.

Isabella lay on her bed in the tent, listening to the dry rustling of the palm trees, and the occasional bray of a camel. She never for one moment worried about the propriety of camping alone in the desert with half a dozen Arab men who did not speak a word of English. She was again on an expedition, had assumed the role of leader, and the rules of propriety could be ignored. That night was surprisingly cold. At dawn, Hassan brought her water for washing, a cup of chocolate and some rice. She felt shivery and nauseous, but refused to admit to the discomfort. She set off to walk a few miles in the cool, morning air while the braying camels were loaded. As the sun came up and the temperature soared, it was time to ride her camel. This proved more difficult than she had expected.

"It does not lie quiet while I mount it, but two or three times, just as I have been getting on, it has jumped up with an angry roar, and has taken the combined efforts of several Bedouin to make it lie down and keep down." The Bedouin clutched the unruly animal, she climbed up the side, and took a flying leap on to the saddle.

"The camel, with a jerk which might dislocate one's neck, jumps on his knees, nearly throwing me backwards, then another violent jerk brings him to his haunches and would throw me over his head but for Hassan's arm, then the forward movement is arrested by another jerk which sets him on his four legs and leaves me breathless on the lofty elevation of his hump."

Isabella rode on a packsaddle resting on top of the hump while a Bedouin led the camel with a rope. Once, she had just grasped the saddle when the camel jerked himself up and threw her over his shoulders, which bruised her badly. Sometimes the camel snarled and lunged at her with his teeth, or jerked up while she was half-way up so she was thrown off, or threw her off sideways. Dismounting, she learned, was just as tricky as getting on. But Isabella had ridden on saddle-horses, pack-horses, mules and elephants, and never questioned her ability to conquer a camel. The camel's slow, swinging gait was much less tiring than the uneven jerks of the Japanese pack-horses. She suffered most from vermin on the animal, which bit her constantly. The Bedouin didn't mind: they never washed because they believed it was a shameful waste of Allah's gift of water.

The sun climbed higher and higher. Isabella watched her elongated shadow shrinking on the ground below. The caravan straggled in single file across the sands. At noon, when they stopped to rest, Hassan showed her how to wriggle under a rock to find some shade. When there were no rocks, he scooped a hole in the sand, into which she scrambled, lying hidden under two blankets to escape the sun. She lay reading her Bible, nibbling raisins, feeling the heat of the sand penetrating her clothes.

They rested for an hour. Then, with the sun still burning down, they set off again. Isabella longed for the fiery red globe to sink so that the shadows would lengthen. Suddenly she saw in the distance a lake with tall, graceful palm trees reflected in it.

"The tantalizing blue water with the mirrored palms beckoned me forward, as the shadows lengthened and the heat and fatigue increased. But the weary tramp brought us no nearer, and before sunset, it faded as a vision, leaving nothing behind but the scorching sand."

After about ten hours of riding, she saw ahead the oasis with true swaying palm trees. She longed for the cool of the night. But the temperature never went down below 90 degrees. There was no breeze.

Isabella's throat was sore, her head ached, she had developed blisters and a rash on her body. She realized she had typhoid fever. At night, she tossed and turned. She suffered from the heat, the rash, her aching head, nausea and exhaustion. But in the morning she was up early, ready to go on, declaring: "I feel this glorious desert, this waste howling wilderness, the new and rich experiences and the prospect of Sinai, are worth them all."

When traveling, nothing could deter her. Hour after hour she looked out at the featureless desert as her camel plodded over the rolling miles of sand. In the noon heat, she rested. At night she camped in an oasis. Ill and dizzy, she forced herself on. Isabella believed that travel for a noble reason, like a pilgrimage to Sinai, justified any discomfort. She was constantly torn between her desire to see places full of interest and excitement, and her need to help others and spread the word of Christianity. She hoped the journey to Sinai would bring both aspects together, and be the highlight of her travel experiences. But in reality, it was extremely monotonous, unlike the variety of Japan, and she felt very ill.

Now a fierce wind began, blowing fine sand in her eyes, nose and mouth, stinging her inflamed skin, filling her mouth with grit. The sun blazed down from a sky that was white in its intensity. During the day, the desert temperature soared to 107 degrees in the shade. Isabella, huddled under two blankets, sympathized with the Israelites.

Ahead, rising starkly from the sands, Isabella saw the Sinai mountains, a range of magnificent peaks more beautiful to her than the ore-stained peaks of the Rockies in Colorado. She marveled at the shapes of their ridges, spires, and towers, and the incredible rifts and chasms, looking as if they had been carved. Elated, she could hardly wait to climb Mount Sinai.

That night, Hassan had terrible news: one of the Bedouin had stolen most of the water in the goatskins. There was only a cupful left. He brought it to Isabella and she looked at the murky, dark fluid with bits of refuse in it. She was so desperately thirsty that she sipped it during the night as she lay tossing in her tent. By now she was almost delirious. Her mind jumped from one thought to another, lines of poems about water kept coming into her mind, phrases of Biblical text repeated in her brain, like the Israelites in the Wilderness of Shur who "went three days and found no water." Once she imagined she heard rain. Struggling up from her bed, Isabella went outside to find it was only the desert wind rustling through the dry, twisted tamarisk trees.

Hassan assured her there would be water at the oasis that evening. He showed her how to put some pebbles in her mouth to give relief from thirst. The sun blazed down unceasingly. The line of camels plodded on. Isabella, her head aching, her body itching from the rash, and hardly able to keep her balance, became dizzy and confused. She tried to ask Hassan to stop but she could not form her words. The minutes crept slowly by in the furnace-like heat.

She was hardly conscious when they reached the oasis, only aware of a man running toward her with a pitcher of water in his hand. She snatched it greedily, gulping it down. The men laid her on a blanket under a palm tree, brought her warm goat's milk, and a water-cooler, urging her only to drink a little at a time. The water was pure, ice-cold, and delicious. She sipped it slowly. Around were green plants, palm trees, fields of barley, the murmur of water from the stream. Exhausted, she soon fell asleep.

With her usual resilience, Isabella was ready to travel on the next morning. Ahead stretched the mountains, craggy rocks formed into fantastic shapes resembling the ruins of abandoned cities, huge yellow boulders against the black and gray rockfaces beyond. On Easter Sunday, 1879, Isabella planned to spend a day in spiritual contemplation. At Wadi Es Sheik, a bleak area of gravel and boulders, about an hour's ride from the highest mountains of Sinai, she rested. Sitting under the shadow of a rock, her Bible on her lap, she read from the book of Exodus to the end of the Old Testament, and noted: "The Bible is to me now, and I hope for my life, a new book vivified, illuminated, intensified, and its credibility is so marvelously enhanced. It is obvious now how the historians and the prophets came to write as they did, and how the story of the wanderings, emphasized by the great feasts and the bloody ritual of the temple, must have tinged the life and thought of even the dullest Israeli—the crossing of the Red Sea, the weary tramp through the burning desert, the thirst, the longing for the green vegetables of Egypt, the murmurings, the discontent with the light, monotonous food, the rapidity and severity of the judgements of God, the halts by trees and water, then the move into the blazing wastes again, and finally Sinai, and the giving of that law which made the whole world guilty before God."

It confirmed all the stories she had heard from her father, reminding her of the eternal truth of the Bible, and her own spiritual and religious upbringing. The day was one of great personal significance for Isabella. She rode on in a state of exultation to the mountains.

At the Pass of the Wind, high walls of almost perpendicular red granite, split and cracked, stood on both sides. Uneven piles of rock lay along the route. The camels plodded among them surefootedly, slowly climbing higher on the steep path. As she emerged from the pass, she saw they had reached the foot of the Sinai mountains. Around her stretched craggy peaks against the evening sky. Ahead lay an avenue of red, black and yellow mountains on both sides of a deep ravine.

Overcome with emotion, Isabella dismounted and thought of taking her shoes off to show her reverence at the holiness of the place. These mountains were what she had dreamed of discovering. This was a moment she would never forget. Gazing round at the high peaks, the stark cliffs, the cloudless sky, and the burning sun, she was filled with a sense of joy and excitement.

At the far end of the long ravine, she could see the thick stone walls, towers and chapels of the Greek Orthodox Monastery of St. Catherine. Dating back hundreds of years to 250 A.D., the craggy fortress was a symbol of Christianity through the centuries. The story went that it was built on the site where Moses saw the Burning Bush and heard the Lord speaking to him.

Riding on excitedly, Isabella came to the open gates of the monastery courtyard. Several untidy-looking monks ran out and began unloading the camels. Hassan said brusquely that she must stay at the monastery. Isabella gestured, explaining she preferred to spend the night in her tent. The monks began shouting angrily at Hassan, and then turned and shouted at her. Hassan said again that she had to stay. Isabella watched the noisy altercation, and noted:

"I tried to be perfectly cool and firm, and told Hassan that I had no money except for "backsheesh", that I could not afford to lodge in the convent, and I knew it was perfectly safe to encamp."

To her relief, after another angry discussion, the camels were reloaded, and marched off to a small plateau of rocks a short distance away. Hassan pitched her tent, and brought her some supper. He told her that through agents at Cairo and Suez, the monks received a cut of payments made by tourists who came to the monastery, and a percentage of the fees paid to the Bedouin or other guides. When camels were hired, they took half of the fee. All travelers were charged for food, lodging and any services. Isabella was shocked to hear she had to pay a fee for drawing water from the well near her tent.

The next morning, after a peaceful night, she watched the sun rise, drenching the mountain peaks in flaming color. Faintly, the sound of silver bells echoed in the still air, calling the monks to prayer. But her visit to the monastery building was far from the spiritual experience she had expected. In the Chapel of the Burning Bush, its jeweled lamps glinting on the diamonds and emeralds in the halo of the effigy of St. Catherine, the monks in attendance kept asking for money. Entering the library, renowned for its ancient manuscripts, she inquired about a book, and a monk burst into an angry tirade against those who stole the manuscripts and published them. At the Bursary, where she had to pay an entrance fee, another monk pestered her so persistently to buy souvenirs, including "manna" made from the desert tamarisk, that she finally bought a small roll of dates and almonds, stitched up in a goat's skin.

Isabella was even more appalled to find that the monks ran a distillery where they made arak, an exceptionally strong spirit made from dates, and in the dining hall she noticed a bottle of wine stood by each plate when she knew wine was expressly forbidden. She was even more shocked to see several drunk and unkempt monks wandering about.

"I almost wish I had abstained from visiting, so painful is the impression I brought away," she confessed sadly. "How much of hollow mockery there is in its gorgeous church, its silver chiming cymbals, its library of precious manuscripts, its ceaseless services!"

Back in her tent, Isabella tried to recapture her mood of spiritual dedication. She gazed out at the mountains as the sun set, and looked forward to her climb up Gebel Musa, the highest point. At dawn, her Arab guide arrived from the convent, "a dried-up, wizened creature not more than five feet three inches in height, lean, shiny, clothed in a cotton garment which had once been white, a dirty turban, and goat-skin sandals, at once pathetic, stupid and melancholy-looking," she observed, and watched him pick fleas and other vermin off his clothes.

She followed him towards Gebel Musa as the first rays of the sun tinged the mountains pink. As she scrambled over huge uneven boulders, moved centuries before into a rough set of steps, she was so short that her guide hauled her up the largest of them by two straps. She drank from the cold, clear waters of the Fountain of Moses, a spring where Moses was said to have watered his flocks of sheep. By the water's edge, she saw tiny blue flowers growing, and in the crevices of the rocks, almost a dozen different flowering plants.

The path turned sharply to the right, under a rocky arch. Scrambling between two walls, she hauled herself up over granite crags and boulders until after an hour, she reached the summit at over 7,000 feet. Looking out at the magnificent view of the craggy peaks, she exulted:

"For how many years, from early childhood upwards, have I thought and dreamed about this mountain top, and have imagined its aspect! It is like and unlike; like in its absolute desolation, but unlike in its grandeur and majesty. It was worth all the desert heat and dreariness, the raging thirst, the relentless hot wind, the burning glare. It is the grandest mountain view I have ever seen. Completely silent, unutterably lonely, awfully solemn."

There were two simple buildings, a chapel and a mosque. Beneath was a cave where Mohammedans believed Moses stayed for forty days and forty nights. Lying on the ground at her feet lay an empty champagne bottle. Disgusted at such profanity intruding on her mood, she threw it over the precipice. She scrambled over the rocks to another plateau, where the chapels of Elijah and Elisha stood. Next she climbed to the summit of Ras Sufsafeh where far below a vast gravel plain stretched for miles. It was there, Isabella imagined, that the millions of Israelites encamped while Moses went up into Mount Sinai. From the ridge she knew that the sound of a great crowd below and the sight of its tents and campfires would have been crystal clear. She sat on a rock, and read and reread the book of Exodus, murmuring the familiar names of the places she had seen. In the stillness, the hours passed.

It was late when Isabella began the climb down. Regretfully, she took a last look of the magnificent mountains, already tinged with the colors of the setting sun. Night had fallen by the time she reached her tent. In the dark, the huge granite cliffs were gray and shadow-filled. The first stars twinkled in the sky. Later, she often spoke of her journey to Mount Sinai as one of the most significant experiences of her life. But it was time to go back to Cairo.

At the port of Alexandria, she boarded a steamer to Liverpool. Almost at once she fell ill with a chest infection and a fever and was very sick throughout the voyage. When she arrived at Liverpool, she was so weak that her friend, Miss Clayton, who came to meet her, took her home to nurse her until she was well enough to travel to Scotland.

Isabella arrived at the island of Mull on May 27, 1879, to find her sister Henrietta waiting anxiously for her on the quay. Isabella had traveled around the world, and been away for a year. She had accomplished all she had hoped to do, and felt refreshed spiritually, if exhausted physically. Once again, the Isabella who dismissed typhoid fever and unbearable heat to travel across the Sinai desert now collapsed helplessly at home. She wrote in a letter from Tobermory:

"My body is very weak, and I can only walk about three hundred yards with a stick, but my head is all right. Nothing but kindness has been my lot all round the world, and, except that my health grew worse rather than better, nothing ever went wrong."

Chapter 9
Unexpected Successes

Summer in Tobermory. Her life with Henrietta.
Rockies book published to acclaim. John Murray
delighted. Completes book about Japan. Winter
in Edinburgh.

Tobermory nestles in a cove on the north shore of the island of Mull, off the west coast of Scotland. In the summer of 1879, it was a thriving community with a population of almost a thousand people. The curving main street faced the harbor and was lined with small stores—the baker, the grocer, the blacksmith, the boot-maker, the tailor, the hatmaker. Steamships from Glasgow arrived loaded with coal and provisions, and took local cattle and wool to sell. Every summer, paddle steamers arrived from Oban filled with tourists, who spent a day or two visiting the island, or came for a month or more to relax in the inns and boarding houses. The imposing Western Isles Hotel overlooking the bay opened in 1883.

For years, the village had teetered on the brink of collapse. In the 1700s, the British Fisheries Institute had tried to develop Tobermory as a major fishing port. Unfortunately the local farm community had no knowledge of fishing and no capital to invest in boats and equipment, so the project failed. After that, the town's only industry was kelp seaweed - selling alkaline ash from burnt kelp to makers of soap and glass - and that collapsed in the 1820s. For years the residents struggled to survive in extreme poverty.

Tobermory's luck changed in 1829. The composer Felix Mendelssohn took a boat trip to Mull, was inspired by the magnificent scenery, and wrote his famous *Hebrides Overture*. His ardent admirer, Queen Victoria, sailed over on her yacht with her beloved husband, Albert, eager to see the inspiration for her favorite composer. It was pouring rain at the time, so she never actually landed, but the news of the Royal Visit blessed Tobermory.

From then on, dozens of companies offered steamer trips along The Royal Route. Boatloads of visitors came to spend a day, a week, or rent a cottage for the summer. They strolled along the sheltered bay with its quaint houses clustered on the slope, gazed at the green hills dotted with grazing sheep, visited farmhouses in sheltered valleys, and walked over the rolling moors rich with purple heather, even in the pouring rain. The golden egg of tourism saved Tobermory.

Isabella preferred to avoid the crowds of visitors. She and Hennie lived at the top of a steep winding road behind the main street. The zigzag road up the cliff led to their two-story white-painted cottage. The windows faced the bay and offered views of rippling waves, rocking boats, and misty skies. There was a garden, with the scent of lavender and snapdragons and periwinkles in bloom. White and yellow wild-flowers and grasses waved in the soft breezes. Pink roses climbed round the doorway.

Isabella loved the peaceful atmosphere of Tobermory. That summer, she was busy writing a book about her Rocky Mountains adventures, based on her articles in *Leisure Hour* magazine. The articles had been published while she was traveling in Japan and proved so popular that John Murray was eager to bring out the book.

She had to add one important explanation. Shortly after she left Colorado, Rocky Mountain Jim had been shot by Griff Evans, and later died from his wounds. Friends had written to her about the event, which had caused a great deal of controversy in Estes Park. Griff Evans was never charged with the murder though Jim wrote an impassioned account of the shooting from his sickbed explaining in detail how he had been shot while passing Evans' house. The story was published in a local newspaper, but the case was dropped after Jim's death. He was buried in an unmarked grave.

Isabella was very upset by the letters from friends giving her the news, and imagined she saw the figure of Mountain Jim bowing to her the night he died. She asserted: "Don't let anybody think that I was in love with Mountain Jim, for I have never, alas, been in love but once, but I felt the pity and yearning to save him."

In her introduction to the book, she added a note: "Some months later Mountain Jim fell by Evan's hand, shot from Evan's doorstep while riding past his cabin. The story of the previous weeks is dark, sad and evil. Of the five differing versions which have been written to me of the act itself and its immediate causes, it is best to give none. The tragedy is too painful to dwell upon. Jim lived long enough to give his own statement, and to appeal to the judgement of God, but died in low delirium before the case reached a human tribunal."

Isabella spent her mornings settled at the big table in the upstairs sitting room as she worked on revisions for the book, scribbling across the pages quickly, her thin slanting handwriting covering closely-written line after line. From the window, she could see in the distance the peak of Speinne Mor, the highest hill in the north of Mull. Below lay Tobermory Bay dotted with the sails of visiting yachts. Outside she could hear the hum of bees, the twittering of birds, and the occasional clattering of horses' hooves trotting down the road. It was perfect weather, warm and mild, and she managed to write for five hours a day.

Henrietta looked after the house, and planned the meals with the cook. Her thoughts were always to meet Isabella's needs. Henrietta knew Isa wanted to write all morning, and that she liked her dinner, the main meal of the day, around 1:30 p.m. However, on the island with its limited facilities, Henrietta admitted: "It is so difficult to get variety, and now and then difficult to get anything. And I like to have everything perfect, and when it falls short of this perfection, I always feel vexed and disheartened."

After dinner, Isabella took a long walk with her sister. They strolled along country lanes, over the heather-covered hills and down the narrow cliff paths, talking together in the sea air scented with the perfume of honeysuckle. Henrietta knew that Isabella's books were based on the letters written to her and she never hesitated to express her opinions and share her thoughts with her sister.

Years later, Isabella wrote of her sister: "One thing among many which made my letters to her what they were was the singular amount of her accuracy, knowledge of countries and their geography and botany. She always read and took notes of the best travellers, comparing them with naturalists and other books on the same subjects. It made her mind so responsive to all one could tell, and from her stories, she could supply so much to fill in or correct the outlines."

Henrietta thought of Isabella as the clever one in the family. From the time they were children together, it had always been Isa who was able to accomplish so much. Henrietta was bright and intelligent, studied Greek with Professor Blackie at Edinburgh University, and read a great deal, but she had always modestly preferred to keep in the background. She was the ideal passive partner for Isabella's more dominating personality.

Henrietta had never looked beyond her affectionate relationship with Isabella. She had always preferred to be alone, and disliked parties and social occasions. Isabella was everything she needed, as she explained in a letter to her parents once when they urged her to be more sociable: "I think for some people it is very good to have a companion, while for others it is very bad. I get on quite well without companions, and therefore I think I can do without them now as much as I did before. I have been blest with a very dear sister, who is young, and to whom I can tell all secrets as well as have profitable conversation, which I could not do with a companion."

She treasured their closeness as much as Isabella did. The sisters called each other "My Ownest" and "My Dearest" and shared private jokes and special words, like "dil" for someone who was dull and inactive, and "annoying" for men who paid them too much attention. The intimacy and understanding which had developed over the years had entwined their lives on so many levels that no one else could have offered the intense affection, companionship, and compatibility they found together.

After their walk, Isabella went upstairs to continue work on her book, while Henrietta read or sewed in her sitting room downstairs. At about seven o'clock, they shared a light supper. Sometimes they went out for a stroll along the harbor in the long summer twilight for a couple of hours. Sometimes they sat talking or reading until it was time for bed. Henrietta's concern was always that Isa have time to write, and told a friend: "Nowhere could she have such quiet and freedom from interruption."

Henrietta never understood why Isabella needed the challenge of the outside world. She often said she would be happiest if she could stay in Tobermory year round, never leaving the quiet village. She had little interest in taking part in the social life of Edinburgh, or in the wider world of travel and writing that Isabella enjoyed. She returned in the winter to Edinburgh to accompany her sister, and rarely took part in the gatherings and activities that Isabella enjoyed, often complaining at how much she disliked them.

Henrietta felt her mission was to help the poor, the suffering, and those in need as she could. In Tobermory, she visited an old man who was paralyzed, and a young boy, dying of consumption. Every day she took them food, listened to their complaints, did their errands. She felt this was the most important thing for her to do, after caring for her sister, and her unassuming simplicity and kindness warmed people's hearts. She had a gentle way of assisting others which made them appreciate her, and a manner that showed she enjoyed what she did.

Once she offered to mend the stockings of a friend who hated to sew. She was horrified to receive dozens of pairs with holes everywhere. She dutifully mended them all, and returned them with a poem:
"Oh ye innumerable holes! Oh toes that mock repair!
Oh gaping heels! Oh tattered soles! Ye drive me to despair!
And now, since patience has no bounds,
So dire the toil and shocking,
Unless you turn your pence to pounds,
I've mended your last stocking."

As the months slipped by amid the peaceful calm of the island, with Isabella busily writing and Henrietta happy in her different projects, the two sisters had found a perfect balance, each fulfilled in her own way, and happy to share their lives.

In June, Isabella sent John Murray the manuscript for the Rockies book. He loved it, added some drawings based on Isabella's sketches, and sent it to the printer.

She immediately began her next project, which was to write a book on her travels in Japan. Murray was anxious to have it quickly because another author was writing on the same subject. Isabella's concern was that the book about Japan would not be interesting enough: "People will find my Japan flat and dull after the Rocky Mountains."

The book was again based on letters to her sister but was much longer than Isabella's other books. Isabella had traveled more than 1,400 miles in Japan, and her experiences had been far more varied. Since much of what Isabella had seen of Japan's primitive conditions was quite shocking and repulsive, John Murray urged her to tone down some of the more lurid details in case she upset her readers. Isabella refused, explaining in her Introduction:

"Some of the Letters give a less pleasing picture of the condition of the peasantry than the one popularly presented, and it is possible that some readers may wish that it had been less realistically painted; but as the scenes are strictly representative, and I neither made them up nor went in search of them, I offer them in the interests of truth." She felt they showed how much work the Japanese government faced in building a new civilization.

Isabella worked steadily on through June, July and August. In September she was invited to visit her friends Lord and Lady Middleton who had a summer home nearby, and who sent their yacht over to Mull to pick her up. Their cheerful house was filled with young people, including a honeymoon couple, and John Bishop was visiting too.

Isabella was delighted to see him, and told him of her travels in Japan, and her adventures, and in particular her medical experiences along the way. He listened sympathetically. He still believed she would make him a perfect wife, and again he asked her to marry him. She regretfully reminded him that she was not "a marrying woman" though she was sensitive enough to realize how unhappy her refusal made him.

"He has acted nobly and sweetly to me, never saying one word about his own suffering," she confided to Lady Middleton, before escaping to the peaceful calm of Tobermory.

The days slipped by. Isabella realized, with a foreboding of what lay ahead: "I think perhaps that I shall never again have such a serenely happy four months. I shall always in the future as in the past have to contest constitutional depression by earnest work and by trying to lose myself in the interests of others; and full and interesting as my life is, I sometimes dread a battle of years."

In October, it was time to move back to Edinburgh. The two sisters found a house at 19 Coates Crescent, near the center of town. In

October, Isabella's book about her six months in Colorado was published as *A Lady's Life in the Rocky Mountains.*

Its success was overwhelming, far beyond anything Isabella had experienced before or John Murray had expected. The book sold out in a week, a second edition appeared a month later, and a third in January, 1880. The reviews were unstinting in their exuberant praises.

The Spectator enthused: "Spontaneous and unadorned as is the narrative, it is more interesting than most of the novels which it has been our lot to encounter, and in fact, comprises character, situations, and dramatic effect enough to make ninety-nine novels out of a hundred look pallid and flat in comparison. And yet we felt, beyond misgiving, that naught is exaggerated here, nor aught set down in malice. It is a plain record of facts, made on the spot by a genuine and unconscious artist."

The 19th-century novelists like Charles Dickens, George Eliot, Charlotte Bronte and Robert Louis Stevenson were renowned for taking facts and turning them into fiction. Isabella had created a style of nonfiction travel writing where the people she met, the events she experienced and the adventures she enjoyed were described with the same compelling conviction and lively immediacy usually found in novels. Her romance with Rocky Mountain Jim was as touching to read as any fictional love affair. Her account of the man dying in the Colorado Springs boarding house was a scene as memorable and bizarre as any in fiction. She reported conversations in detail, described scenery romantically and wrote humorously about her disappointments and disasters. Her skill was in bringing her travels to life as vividly as novelists did their tales of fiction, using the personal and intimate format of letters to her sister.

The *Saturday Review* observed: "This little volume is so brimful of incident and adventure that, dip into where we may, we can hardly go far wrong. Where chapter after chapter is almost equally exciting, it is difficult to do justice to the variety of the episodes."

The Nation thought the book ought to have had less about the sunsets and more on the people she had met, but conceded: "Her notes on manners are frank and interesting, as far as they go, and they have a reflected interest in the fact that they depict precisely the same character in which Mrs. Trollope found so much to censure."

Reviews appeared in publication after publication. The enthusiasm built month by month. On all sides people asked, "Have you read the Rocky Mountains yet?" and bookstores could not keep enough copies on the shelves.

Isabella was gratified by the praise and attention, and relieved that: "The critics have not scented out impropriety in the letters." So she was outraged when a *Times* reviewer suggested that she had worn men's clothes in Colorado to ride through the mountains. It was considered the height of impropriety for a woman to wear men's clothes, or to ape men's behavior in any way. Isabella interpreted the comment as a personal attack on her, and a serious slur on the ladylike image she tried so hard to preserve when at home and out traveling. She told John Murray he should thrash the editor for insinuating "she donned masculine habiliments for greater convenience."

John Murray calmed her down, and persuaded Isabella to add a footnote and a drawing to the next edition. She wrote: "For the benefit of other lady travelers, I wish to explain that my Hawaiian riding dress is the American Lady's Mountain Dress, a half-fitting jacket, a skirt reaching to the ankles, and full Turkish trousers gathered into frills which fall over the boots—a thoroughly serviceable and feminine costume for mountaineering and other rough travelling, in any part of the world. I add this explanation to the prefatory note together with a rough sketch of the costume, in consequence of an erroneous statement in *The Times* of November 22."

The artist created a charming drawing of Isabella in her costume and hat, standing beside a horse with its front hoof delicately raised, which has become a symbol of Isabella's travels in Colorado in modern editions of the book.

Isabella's concern reflected her fear of being thought of as an outspoken feminist or a radical. In the 19th century, there were dozens of Victorian women gallivanting around the globe in a variety of costumes, often mocked by the press and the butt of jokes and stories.

For many intelligent women stifled by the lack of opportunity, travel provided the only outlet for their energy and ability. Isabella traveled as freely as did Alexandra David-Neel who roamed through Tibet in disguise, or Fanny Bullock Workman who climbed mountains on her bicycle, or Mary Kingsley who explored Africa alone. However, Isabella felt that conforming to society's rules was important, even though her attempts to live that narrow life always made her ill. She wanted to preserve her image as a modest, well-bred lady, traveling merely for her health, and did not want to appear as a radical or improper.

There was an additional footnote to the third edition of her Rockies book. The date of her travels, 1873, had been omitted, and she knew much had changed in the intervening six years: "I learn from friends that log cabins are fast giving place to frame houses, and that the footprints of elk and bighorn may be searched for in vain on the dewy grass of Estes Park."

The success of her book cemented her friendship with her publisher, John Murray III. He was the grandson of the company's founder, John Murray. The publisher and family lived and worked at 50 Albemarle Street, London, where the company had been founded in 1768. Grandfather Murray had published Buffon's *Natural History of Birds* in nine volumes. John Murray II had published Jane Austen's *Persuasion* and *Northanger Abbey*, Byron's *Childe Harold* poems, and started the *Quarterly Review*. John Murray III was interested in travel. He created an extremely popular series of travel guides as well as publishing books by Charles Darwin, Herman Melville, and Washington Irving.

Delighted with Isabella's success, Murray invited her to London and threw a party to celebrate his famous author. She arrived in the elegant drawing room in Albemarle Street and found herself the center of attention. She was introduced to authors, politicians and journalists. She was flattered to be among so many well-known people, sitting at a candle-lit table, glistening with silver and crystal glasses, and praised on all sides.

Other friends invited her to dinners, to tea parties, to evening gatherings. On all sides she was acclaimed as a "literary lion." One admirer presented her with a huge bouquet, and quite overwhelmed by its magnificence, she carried it back to Edinburgh on the train.

That evening she took it with her to a party in her honor. She reported wryly: "It made a great sensation. I really believe that few of the people had seen a bouquet of such size. Murmurs of wonderment ran round the room, and all the learned men were in raptures. Lady Teignmouth has sent across to invite it, Lord Teignmouth having wondered at it last night."

Isabella was full of energy. She had no ailments, no aches, no pains. That spring, busy with revisions on the book on Japan, she stayed in Edinburgh writing while Henrietta went to Tobermory to open up the cottage. Isabella was looking forward to another peaceful summer, just like the one she had so enjoyed last year. She would work on her book, walk with her sister, savor the peaceful pace of life on the island of Mull.

She was already planning a book on the Malay States, which she had visited on her way home from Japan. Henrietta had suggested a romantic title, *The Golden Chersonese,* for her stories of elephant rides and meals with monkeys. This was the old name for the Malay States, which today are known as Malaysia and Singapore. She wanted to write some articles about her spiritual experiences at Mount Sinai, which she felt was important. She was even considering future travels. Should she go back to the fascinating Far East, or travel to the high mountains of Central Asia, a region of the world which had always intrigued her? In her new mood, her life was full of promise and satisfaction.

It was almost the end of May. Working at her desk in Edinburgh, she was surprised to receive a letter from Henrietta. Her sister was ill with a fever and a cold. Would Isabella please come at once? Concerned, Isabella packed a few things, and left to catch the next train to Oban for the ferry to Mull.

At the first train stop, the station master called her name, and handed her a telegram. It was from the doctor on Tobermory: Hennie was seriously ill and Isabella must come as quickly as possible. Isabella read it with foreboding.

The train chugged north past the rippling waters of Loch Lomond and Loch Katrine, over the craggy hills and moors of the Scottish Highlands, where sturdy cows, lanky horses and flocks of sheep grazed peacefully. The journey seemed interminable. Isabella tried to keep calm, but she could not help anxiously calculating over and over again how much longer it would be until she reached the ferry.

At Oban, she hurried to the quay to board the next boat. It was due to leave shortly. Impatiently she waited on deck as the last passengers strolled up the gangway, her mind turning to her sister, longing to be with her.

The ship's siren blasted. The ferry swung away from its mooring, and out into the waters of the bay. Building up speed, it steamed across the water. Isabella stood on deck, the wind tugging at her clothes. She watched the familiar silhouettes of Oban's hotels and houses shrink into the mists as the boat pulled away. Low clouds and fog covered the water. The waves, gray and threatening, slapped against the sides of the boat. Isabella stood holding the railing, looking anxiously for the first glimpse of Mull.

Suddenly, amid the swirling grayness, a stream of sunlight broke through, lighting up the vivid green of the southern slopes of the island. As she watched, a curving rainbow formed in the misty dampness, a graceful arc of soft colors which hung in the air. Then the clouds drifted in, and the rainbow faded, gradually disappearing into the mists.

The boat turned toward the sheltered bay of Tobermory. Isabella peered anxiously through the gathering mist to glimpse the white-painted cottage where her sister lay.

The Bird cottage in Tobermory

Henrietta Amelia Bird

Chapter 10
A Terrible Death

Henrietta develops typhoid. John Bishop nurses her. Death of Henrietta. Isabella devastated. Book on Japan published. Marriage to John Bishop.

When Isabella reached the cottage in Tobermory, the old housekeeper was weeping in the kitchen. Dr. MacLachlan, the local doctor, said: "I can do no more for your sister. She has typhoid fever. I have sent for Dr. Bishop in Edinburgh."

Isabella hurried upstairs to where Henrietta lay in bed, her eyes closed and her face flushed with fever. Isabella called her name, stroked her hair, took her hot hand, but she never responded. Isabella felt a sense of terror grip her heart. She prayed desperately that Henrietta would recover and recognize her.

Outside, a storm had blown in. The rain beat against the windows, rattling the panes. Isabella sat beside her sister. She wiped Henrietta's face with a cool cloth. She tried to calm her when she tossed and turned. The hours crept by, and the evening shadows spread over the house. Still Isabella watched, torn by guilt that she had not come sooner.

That night Isabella sat in the armchair by Henrietta's bed, anxious at Henrietta's agitated movements, the disjointed mumblings, the heavy breathing, not daring to leave her. The minutes ticked by in the darkness.

Images of the summer they had spent so happily together last year kept coming into Isabella's mind. She saw Henrietta arranging a vase of fresh-cut daffodils on the table, walking along the leafy country lanes as they talked together, smiling at a story that Isabella read to her one evening as she sewed, singing hymns in her sweet high voice at Sunday service in the local church, sitting in the garden painting the view of the bay.

Isabella thought of Hennie as her best friend. It was unthinkable they be parted, that she not be there for Isabella always. As independent, outgoing and adventurous as Isabella was, she needed to know she could come back to the safety and security of Henrietta's quiet settled haven. Isabella's career had grown from the audience Henrietta represented. Who was more captivated, more adoring, more absorbed in Isabella's letters about her travels than Henrietta? They were each other's most trusted, intimate confidant, and the perfect complement to each other's character.

As the first light of the gray dawn filtered into the room, Isabella leaned forward to look at her sister again. She lay hardly moving, her eyes closed, her face blank. The next day passed as if in a nightmare, Henrietta lying almost motionless, Isabella by her bedside, hardly eating or sleeping.

Finally John Bishop arrived, bringing the head nurse from the Edinburgh Infirmary to assist him. He quickly confirmed the original diagnosis. It was typhoid fever. Its cause—contaminated water or food—had still not been discovered, so no one knew how it was spread. Tobermory had inadequate water and sewage services, and cleanliness in the community was rare. Little was known about the disease or how to treat it, but it was known as a deadly plague.

Both Isabella and John Bishop knew they too were vulnerable, but they ignored the danger. The old housekeeper left, fearful of being contaminated. The villagers refused to enter the cottage. A few women placed containers of cooked food on the front step, and a knot of people gathered in the garden each morning to hear the latest report on Henrietta's health.

John Bishop explained to Isabella the treatments for typhoid that were often given. Doctors used leeches for blood-letting, enemas, warm water baths and cold compresses to bring down the high temperature. A variety of medicines were available - chloride of sodium, chloride of calcium, carbonate of magnesium, potassium and sodium bicarbonates, as well as opium, ammonia and caffeine grains.

Isabella wrote: "I can only trust to God who may see fit to spare me my last treasure, though I often feel that it is selfish to pray that one so prepared to see God should for my sake be detained among the troubles of this troublesome world."

John Bishop and the nurse cared for Henrietta day and night, and Isabella coped with running the house. The slow days crawled past, and stretched into weeks. When John Murray wrote to Isabella, requesting some additional notes on her book about Japan, she found she was far too distracted to concentrate on her work, and asked John Bishop to write him a note.

"Miss Isabella Bird desires me to tell you that she is here watching her sister, who is dangerously ill with typhoid fever, of which this is the thirty-sixth day. I am to say that she has had many difficulties and hardships in travelling, as you know, but never anything equal to this, apart from the anxiety. This has arisen from the remoteness and isolation of the islands at this season, the smallness of the house, and from the abject panic amongst the natives who fly the cottage as a pest house."

Isabella's appreciation for John Bishop grew steadily during the crisis. He did everything he could to help her, showing his sincere admiration for her and his deep concern for her sister. She was impressed that even though he had broken his leg a few weeks ago, and it was still in a splint, he went out on horseback in all kinds of weather to visit the sick people in the village. She wrote to her friends: "There is such a strength in having so good a man and so skilful a doctor, who knows Henrietta's constitution thoroughly, in the house."

He became the rock on which she leaned each day. He was there at breakfast, reporting that Henrietta had passed a quiet night, or had been restless. He was ready to comfort her when the sight of Henrietta tossing in delirium made her weep. He was there in the long evenings, when they talked of the importance of setting up medical missions in distant countries to ease the suffering of primitive people.

For five weeks Henrietta's life hung in the balance. In June, she slipped into a coma. One night, Isabella looked at her white face, the soft dark hair against the pillow, the thin white hands. She prayed for a miracle, that Henrietta would recover. The house was still. She could hear the clock in the hall striking. She counted the beats slowly, and then sat in the intense silence. Isabella knew; it was over. Her sister was dead. Henrietta Bird had died at the age of 46.

Isabella was shattered. She told a friend: "Oh, the anguish is awful. She was my world, present or absent, seldom absent from my thoughts. Such a lovely angelic being, and now all is gone. I seem hardly to care what becomes of me, and yet I pray God to make me follow her helpful, loving footsteps."

Once again, as she had in the weeks of sickness, she let John Bishop take charge. He was the one who wrote to John Murray informing him of Henrietta's death: "I cannot tell you how nobly and gently the sufferer bore the illness, and how in her very delirium her thoughts were always holy, innocent and unselfish." When the carpenter refused to come into the house to measure the body for the coffin, John Bishop took the necessary measurements. After the coffin was delivered to the door, he and Dr. MacLachlan carried it up the narrow stairs. The two men laid the body in it, Isabella tearfully kissed her sister goodbye and then covered Henrietta's face with the sheet. The coffin lid was closed, and the two men screwed it down.

Isabella wrote despairingly: "She was everything to me, whether present or absent—the inspiration of all my literary work, my best public, my home and fireside, my most intimate and congenial friend." John Bishop, moved by Isabella's courage, observed that she was "woefully distressed, and yet she bears her grief as a gentle Christian woman should."

At the funeral in Dean's Cemetery, Edinburgh, Henrietta was laid beside her mother and father. A relative, Reverend John Lawson, conducted the ceremony. Their friend Ella Blackie felt a wave of pity at the sight of Isabella's "white face, the rigid grief that chilled and devitalized her, and the awful loneliness that wrapped her round." Afterwards, John Bishop confided in Ella Blackie and begged her to plead his cause for he loved Isabella and wanted to marry her.

Isabella went into deep mourning, as she had after her father's death. She collected the memorials written by friends about Henrietta into a book, together with a poem by Professor Blackie and extracts from the funeral sermons. She wrote her letters on black-edged notepaper and envelopes, wore black dresses, and her thoughts constantly turned to her sister.

She cried to a friend: "Oh, what it is to waken daily and know that I shall never see or hear from her again, and that her blessed companionship, the cherished intimate union of a lifetime, can be mine no more! I knew it would be terrible, but never knew half how terrible."

The days passed slowly. Isabella occupied herself writing revisions for the Japan book "but the inspiration has died out of it." She explained: "I feel as if most of myself has gone. How I long to see that loving look and hear the dear voice say once more, 'My own delightful Pet.' She 'is not', and the light, life and inspiration of my life have died with her."

Finally, worn out, she went with her friend Miss Clayton to rest quietly in Switzerland for August and September. There she wrote: "God has comforted and sustained me, or I should utterly have fainted, but the sorrow is very sore and often threatens to overwhelm me. She was so essential in every respect to my happiness, and things without her have lost nearly all their interest."

In October, boxes of her new book, *Unbeaten Tracks in Japan* arrived in Edinburgh. Though at first reluctant to open them, feeling that such selfish interest in her own work was a distraction from her devoted mourning for her sister, she finally looked at the two volumes, and felt a sense of quiet achievement. John Murray enthused: "How can I convey to your ear the tidings of your own praises which are resounding everywhere, and with a unanimity of which I have had no previous experience in my long career as a publisher!" He noted cheerfully that she had "completely bowled over" the competing book on Japan by Sir Edward Reid.

Dozens of reviews of her Japan book appeared. *Saturday Review* thought it: "A record of new and varied experiences told in singularly pure and bright English."

The Athenaeum asserted it was "interesting throughout, and is especially valuable as giving the opinions of one who is neither an enthusiast, nor interested in puffing Japan."

Readers need not bother to go to Japan, said *The Spectator*, because "a perusal of her book is very nearly the same thing, in effect, as a visit to the places which she describes would be."

This time, *The Nation* praised her as "an excellent observer, and her wide and accurate knowledge of botany and natural history, as well as of people, gives her an unusual sweep of view and freshness of style. The evidences of culture are seen on every page of her narrative, and her accuracy has the quality of a sweet perfume."

Isabella admitted: "Though her death deprives me of all pleasure in success, there is a calm satisfaction in this general recognition of the value of laborious research and careful work."

Isabella was particularly gratified by *Nature* magazine's comments on her report on the Ainos, and noted: "I think I have a lurking satisfaction too in having vindicated a woman's right to do what she can do well, and in observing that all the reviews which have reviewed Reid's and my books together have attached more weight to my opinion and researches than to a man."

She confided to a friend: "I have a degree of legitimate pride in having made my own position as a writer and traveller by careful work, without aid from anyone, and without sacrificing the delicacy of a woman."

Isabella could not allow herself to enjoy the celebrations and parties as she had after the success of her Rocky Mountains book. Instead, she determined to follow in her sister's unselfish footsteps, and dedicate herself to helping others in need. She left for Tobermory.

As the ferry steamed into the bay, and she glimpsed the white painted cottage on the hill, she shuddered: "It was such agony that I thought I must leave by the next steamer. But as the days went by and there was help to be given, and dying people to be comforted, the first anguish calmed into a sorrow of exquisite pain and intensity, but without bitterness or repining against Him who has sent it. There is work to be done, and in work there is always interest."

Isabella thought that by imitation, she could find the same satisfaction that her sister had found in being of service.

"She did so much that I feel quite puzzled not only at having to do all alone, but to know how to do it," Isabella confessed sadly. "I must try and make the best of life and to follow her in spirit."

She visited the sick, took food to the poor, sat with the dying. However, she had to confess she found helping the villagers far less rewarding than she had expected, and confided to John Murray: "The Highlanders have some charming qualities, but in cunning, moral timidity, and plausibility they remind me of savages of rather a low type."

That year, the winter in Tobermory was bleak and harsh. A fierce gale blew in, knocking down telegraph poles and stranding the mail boat. Isabella felt completely isolated with no letters, newspapers or any way of communicating with the mainland. She also found that the cottage haunted her because on every side she was reminded of Henrietta.

She went back to Edinburgh. Her life, which had seemed so joyous and promising only a few months ago, had changed drastically. If she traveled, she would have no one to write to and share her adventures. If she lived in Edinburgh or Tobermory, she would always be alone, without the warm affection of Henrietta's company.

As the weeks dragged by, she found her thoughts turning more and more often to John Bishop. She had always said that "the filling up of my life by the affection and companionship of my sister made me regretfully decide against marrying." Now, alone, she remembered his kindness, dedication and sympathy during Henrietta's illness, and his unselfish devotion in the long weeks in Tobermory. Would marriage to John Bishop provide the comfort and stability that she believed she so desperately needed? Without his help, she would never have survived the agony of her sister's illness. Dare she turn to him again and lean on his strength to help her through these terrible days? She hesitated, believing: "It is too soon, and I am too dazed with grief and fatigue to think of any future."

John Bishop had already spoken to Ella Blackie of his desire to marry Isabella. Ella Blackie gently suggested to Isabella that perhaps the two of them might meet again. Isabella replied: "I feel marriage a tremendous step to take without her, and with her I never could have endured a third."

Eventually, she did agree to see John Bishop. When he came round, the graying doctor in his forties, he found the famous travel writer, now nearly fifty, somberly dressed in black. He told her that he understood that she could not love him, might not ever be able to love him, and that the anguish she felt at the loss of her sister might never be soothed. He only asked to let him share her terrible agony, to care for her, and to be able to help her in any way he could after they were married.

Isabella was touched. She remembered the closeness of their days in Tobermory. She would have been happy for them to live together as friends, but they both knew such behavior was unthinkable, and that marriage was the only acceptable path. Isabella had seen what happened to Marian Evans, who wrote novels as George Eliot, and who was completely rejected by society after she went to live with her lover.

Isabella told John Bishop that if he could help her bear her sorrow, she would be deeply grateful. If he had the strength to take on that enormous burden, she would consider marrying him.

John Bishop was overwhelmed with joy. He agreed to everything Isabella wanted. He accepted unquestioningly that if, at some time in the future, she had a desire for "further outlandish travel," he would not in any way stop her from going. He later remarked: "I have only one formidable rival in Isabella's heart, and that is the high tableland of Central Asia."

Isabella told Ella Blackie: "I felt something of rest and protection in his wonderful love, and as if to make him happy would be a not unworthy object in life. It touches me much that he recognized the truth that I shall mourn all my days, and instead of aspiring to fill the place which will be always vacant, he only asks to be allowed to take care of me and to soothe my sorrow."

She added hastily, unwilling to admit that there was a commitment: "There is no engagement and if you hear it said, please contradict it, but to you I will say that if my love for him grows, I will marry him."

Early in 1881, she made up her mind, and told her long-time friend and publisher John Murray: "I have accepted the faithful love which has for so long been mine, and which asks for nothing but that I may be able to say, 'you have made me less miserable.' Ah! but I hope it may be more than this, and that a love may, as time goes on, soothe and comfort, that he may be happy. I earnestly pray that I may be able to return in some degree the most unique, self-sacrificing, utterly devoted love that I have ever seen, and that I may find calm, and he happiness, while my life lasts."

Isabella thought of marriage as the only solution to her hopeless depression. She was nearly 50 years old, and she believed the companionship of John Bishop would give her the strength to continue her own life. It was a most unusual basis for marrying and their agreement to allow her to travel was equally unique.

John Bishop hoped that despite Isabella's intense mourning, he could help her overcome her deep depression, and that they would become a compatible couple. He looked optimistically ahead to years of companionship. Neither of them mentioned sexual concerns or the physical aspects of the marriage, for such topics were not discussed in polite society, and Isabella would certainly not have entertained such ideas.

Isabella's relatives were delighted to hear the news. Many of them had met John Bishop at Henrietta's funeral, and admired his devotion to Isabella. Her cousin, Major Wilberforce Bird, suggested that the marriage take place in the church near the Bird's old family mansion, Barton House, in Warwickshire. Isabella accepted gratefully.

Isabella wrote to her friend Lady Middleton about John Bishop, noting: "A character of truer, simpler worth could not be found." She described him in detail: "He is about, or a little under middle height, very plain, wears spectacles and is very grey, but his faced is redeemed by eyes which Sir Noel Paton says are 'beautiful from their purity' and a high, broad, intellectual brow. He is very intellectual and studious, very receptive and appreciative intellectually, and very able, much cultured, with very artistic tastes, but no artistic facility, passionately fond of nature, very diffident, not calculated to shine socially, or to produce a favorable impression at first, with a simple, truthful, loyal, unselfish nature and unfathomable depths of love and devotion."

Anna Stoddart, Isabella's biographer, met John Bishop on several occasions. She wrote: "His was a nature of a rare simplicity and purity, a man whose thoughts were not so much unworldly as crystal-clear from the source of thought. He was gifted with an absolute selflessness, for ever going out towards suffering with a keen desire to bear it for others."

Isabella's friends were pleased with the announcement of the marriage, and that she had such a good man to rely on, and that his dedication and love had been rewarded. Some of Isabella's friends felt she did not appreciate John Bishop enough, and that he was the loser in the match. There were also those who sniggered at the idea of the fearlessly independent Miss Bird becoming the dutiful wife of a doctor. One story making the rounds was that Isabella had been planning another visit to Japan, but gave up the idea because "it wasn't the kind of place you could take a man to!"

Isabella herself was far from enthusiastic. When she told Lady Middleton that she planned to wear a black dress at the ceremony to show she was still in mourning for her sister, Lady Middleton's Scottish superstition rebelled, and she urged Isabella to wear something more suitable. Isabella refused to consider any alternative, and Lady Middleton realized: "I felt a little sorry for the fiance, for I believed she was marrying him, as it were, under protest. Her real self was buried then in her sister's grave."

To John Bishop, it was unimportant. His unswerving determination had won him the woman he loved to be his wife. He would do everything that she asked and help her in every way he could.

Three days before the wedding, Isabella and John Bishop left Edinburgh to stay with her cousins in Warwickshire where the wedding would take place. John Bishop energetically rode out to the hunt with the red-coated gentry of the village, but Isabella was far from a radiant bride.

"I sit here, half blind with tears, shrinking from all congratulations, and almost from good wishes" she moaned to Ella Blackie. "Your loving wishes will sustain my failing heart."

The wedding took place in the morning of March 8, 1881, in St. Lawrence's Church. Isabella wore a braided black serge dress with a jacket, and a black hat. The photograph of her shows a dramatic woman in black, her face pale and tense, her hair swept back, staring into the camera with unhappiness in her eyes. Major Wilberforce Bird gave her away. His son-in-law Reverend Walter Verney officiated. An aunt and several Bird cousins stood with the bride and her groom at the altar. Though the church bells pealed, there was no party, no wedding guests, no feast, and no celebration.

"It was a marriage altogether in consonance with my feelings— nothing to jar upon my mourning spirit," Isabella declared with relief afterwards.

The couple did not take a honeymoon to Europe but traveled for a couple of months visiting friends and relatives in England. They spent a few days in London visiting John Murray and other friends of Isabella's. It was not until the middle of May that Dr. and Mrs. Bishop returned to Edinburgh to settle into their new home at 12 Walker Street, and begin their married life together.

Chapter 11
The Tragic Marriage

Isabella settles in Edinburgh. Writes book about her travels in Malay States. Bishop falls sick. Travels with him. Death of John Bishop.

Isabella was disappointed to find that married life was not quite what she had expected. She wrote to a friend: "I wish it had seemed more of a step—more novel and exciting—but I was so used to him before, and the great intimacy of the terrible time at Tobermory makes meals and going about together seem merely a continuation of that."

The new Mrs. Bishop had hesitated and agonized and tormented herself so long before agreeing to marry, the reality was an anti-climax. John Bishop was everything he had promised to be. Isabella found him "very gentle, tender and happy; sometimes I feel soothed and rested by his devoted love," but despite his devotion she found "sadness underlies even my best moments."

Isabella threw her energies into organizing the house. She supervised the laying of rugs, hung pictures and arranged her furniture in the rooms. She chose crimson fabric for the curtains to co-ordinate with her patterns, and decorated the living room with bronzes and embroideries from her travels. The Bishops, a middle-class couple, had servants to do the actual work of housekeeping. Isabella hired two housemaids and a serving maid, to join the cook and Bishop's manservant.

To the outside world, their marriage seemed ideal. John Bishop had found everything he had hoped for. He loved and admired Isabella, and though he did not understand her need for outlandish travel, he had accepted it. She had given him the proper social status and the womanly partnership he expected.

The Bishop home in Edinburgh

Isabella had married in hopes of finding companionship and ease for her sorrow, a place to come home to after her travels, and a replacement for the support and complete understanding she had shared with Henrietta.

But her husband, a respected physician, led a busy life seeing his private patients and spending long hours at the Edinburgh Infirmary. While Henrietta had devoted herself entirely to Isabella's needs, John Bishop's focus was on his medical work. He left the house early in the morning and was often away all day, and even in the evenings.

Isabella also led an independent life. She traveled to London to write a profile of a leading clergyman for a religious magazine, and went on a visit to Switzerland with her friends. When she came back, she complained: "I have been at home 14 days and have hardly seen him - never in at lunch and only twice in the evenings. The loneliness is awful, for though I usually manage to get out once a day, I am practically confined to two rooms owing to the badness of my back and feet."

In the first weeks, dozens of visitors called to see the newlyweds. Isabella had to return the calls. She organized afternoon parties for about forty people, friends who enjoyed high-minded conversations and intellectual discussions. The Bishops were in turn invited to dinners, teas and parties. Isabella was soon exhausted by the demands of visiting, the conversations, the unending decisions of housekeeping. She longed for peace and quiet, and time to concentrate on her writing.

John Bishop had renewed the lease on the Tobermory cottage for her. That fall, Isabella escaped gratefully to the island hoping to enjoy the solitude. Instead, everywhere there were painful reminders of her sister.

"I am sitting in the low folding-chair in the sweet sitting-room in the house which she created, and which is consecrated by lovely memories of her lovely life and serene happiness. God only knows what it is to sit here alone, and yet the very anguish, because it is so full of her, is dearer to me than all else. It is a shrine." She hoped to be able to carry on Henrietta's good works but sadly admitted: "All that I can do is so poor and shadowy compared with what she did."

She was at the cottage one morning in October when a telegram arrived from doctors at the Edinburgh Infirmary. Her husband was ill and she was to come at once. Despite a violent storm, Isabella caught the ferry and hurried to John Bishop's bedside. Shocked, she found him very weak and hardly moving. He had been performing an operation on a sailor with a skin disease, erysipelas. By chance, a small cut on John Bishop's face was infected. Within hours, he had collapsed, suffering blood poisoning, and later slight heart failure.

Isabella took him home and nursed him tenderly. He recovered slowly: it was several weeks before he could walk about. By January 1882 he was well enough to go back to work at the Edinburgh Infirmary. Then Isabella developed carbuncles on her spine in the area between her shoulders, close to where the fibrous tumor had been removed years ago.

The months of ill health gave her an acceptable excuse to withdraw from the round of social calls and visits. She welcomed the quiet. She now had time to start her book about her travels in the Malay States, which John Murray urged her to write. To her surprise, a letter came from Kalakaua, the King of the Sandwich Islands, to say he would be in Edinburgh on a Royal Tour. He arrived one afternoon at her home with his attendants, and greeted her. In a simple ceremony, he presented Isabella with the Hawaiian Literary Order of Merit in honor of her book about Hawaii.

To celebrate the occasion, John Murray published a new edition of her Hawaiian book and threw an extravagant party in London for his best-selling author. He invited over a hundred guests. Isabella was the star of the evening. She sat at one end of the room in an enormous chair, her feet, encased in gold-embroidered Oriental slippers, resting on a footstool. She wore a Japanese petticoat delicately embroidered with gold and silver circles. Across her shoulders hung the sash of the ribbon and order from the King of the Sandwich Islands.

Guests were brought up to her to be introduced. Among them were two well-known travelers, Constance Gordon Cummings, an artist and author who spent 12 years exploring and sketching in the Himalayas and India, America and Hawaii, and Marianne North, a naturalist who traveled throughout the world painting flowers and had just built a gallery for her paintings at Kew Gardens. Marianne North thought Isabella looked "a very solid and substantial little person, short but broad, very decided and measured in her way of talking, rather as if she were reciting from one of her books."

The story goes that as the two women stood with Isabella, someone said mockingly: "Three globe trotteresses at once!" The two women, embarrassed, hastily moved away, but Marianne North saw that Isabella was "unruffled and equal to the occasion."

Isabella settled down at home in Edinburgh to finish her book about her adventures in the Malay Peninsula. The region lay between Thailand and Malaysia and had been taken over by the Empire-building British in 1875. Isabella was one of the first Europeans to explore it in 1879 and, unlike her usual free-spirited travels, had been escorted by British officials because of unrest among the population of some half-million Malays, Chinese and Indians, now under the rule of British Residents.

She had arrived in the Peninsula after her energetic travels in Japan and found: "A land where it is 'always afternoon.' Existence stagnates. The nights are very still. The days are a tepid dream. Since I arrived, not a leaf has stirred, not a bird has sung, the tides ebb and flow in listless and soundless ripples." The local Malays were "lying basking in the sun, or leaning over the bridge looking at nothing."

The only way to see the countryside was by boat, and Isabella drifted down muddy waterways with dense green jungle on both sides: "The elephant, the rhinoceros, the royal tiger, the black panther, the boar, the leopard and many other beasts, roam in its tangled, twilight depths. We saw a large alligator sleeping in the sun on the mud, with a mouth, I should think, a third of the length of his body, and we panted past him but he awoke, and his hideous form and corrugated hide plunged into the water so close under the stern as to splash us."

At night, sailing through the humid dark air, Isabella listened to the eerie calls of nightbirds, the hoarse roars and shrill cries of animals hunting and killing, the sudden wild splashings of beasts plunging into the water. Above, blue sheet lightning flashed intermittently, revealing overhanging trees drooping with thick vines, roots and leafy shrubs on the banks, the black swirling water, and the native boatmen strained to see the next bend in the river as the keel of the boat bumped against submerged logs and branches.

At one village along the river, Isabella arrived in the middle of a tremendous celebration because a tiger had been caught in a pit and killed. The animal was over eight feet long. Its beautiful skin was hanging from a tree. The Sultan beat gongs as everyone tried to snatch part of the animal and Isabella observed:

"The Sultan claimed the liver, which, when dried and powdered, is worth twice its weight in gold as a medicine. The blood was taken, and I saw the Chinamen drying it in the sun on small slabs: it is an invaluable tonic! The eyes which were of immense size, were eagerly scrabbled for that the hard parts in the center, which are valuable charms, might be set in gold as rings. The bones were taken to be boiled down to a jelly."

She was eager to ride an elephant, dreaming of howdahs and elaborate cloth of gold trappings.

"But my elephant had neither. In fact there was nothing grand about him but his ugliness. This mode of riding is not comfortable. One sits facing forwards with the feet dangling over the edge of the basket, which soon produces a sharp ache or cramp."

Wedged in her basket, she entered the jungle. Her elephant found a mud-hole and "drew all the water out of it, squirted it with a loud noise over himself and his riders, soaking my clothes." When they came to a river, he did not stop:

"The elephant gently dropped down and was entirely submerged, moving majestically along, with not a bit of his huge bulk visible. We were sitting in the water, but it was nearly as warm as the air, and so we went for some distance up the clear shining river, with the tropic sun blazing down upon us, with little beaches of golden sand, and above the forest the mountains with varying shades of indigo coloring."

She left the tropical languor of the Malay peninsula to sail back through the Suez Canal to England. Now, sitting alone in her room in Edinburgh, with gray skies and falling rain outside, Isabella re-read the letters she had written so happily to her sister and could not help comparing the exuberant freedom of her travels with her present listless dreariness. She worried that her writing would reflect her depression, but when John Murray published *The Golden Chersonese* in April 1883, it proved to be very popular.

There were dozens of reviews, including a long, enthusiastic analysis of her style in *The Spectator:* "Miss Bird is an ideal traveller. She can see, and she can use the words that place what she sees before the reader. She has regard to the essentials of a scene or episode, and she describes them with a simplicity that is as effective as it is artless. Humor is here, of a quality precisely suited to a traveller; never obtrusive, but never deficient when the time comes, oiling the wheels of action just in time to counteract friction. Better still, perhaps, she possesses individuality. Her attitude throughout is as easy as that of a person who is unaware that his photograph is being taken. Not the least noteworthy among Miss Bird's gifts is a heaven-sent faculty for having adventures. Things turn out as if by special inspiration. She trusts to fortune, to what ought to happen, and it does happen. Her whole experience is a singular combination of the natural and the dramatic."

The Nation declared that, like all her previous work, the book had "The same wealth of style, of fascinating narrative and dramatic grouping of effects" and was "the best work in England on the Malay Peninsula." *The Athenaeum* noted: "There can be no better proof of the author's power and skill than the variety she imparts to her pictures of tropical scenery, which, with all its charms, has a certain monotony."

There was one discordant voice. Emily Innes, the wife of a British district magistrate, had lived in the Malay States for a year, and completely disagreed with the rosy view of the place which Isabella described. She wrote a book called *The Golden Chersonese with the Gilding Off,* based on her experiences. She declared that it was a terrible place for ordinary people, what with bullying from British Resident Bloomfield Douglas, the roars of man-eating tigers so close she could almost see their fiery eyeballs, bites from centipedes in her bath, flying beetles tangled in her hair, and carpenter beetles in the soup. She saw nothing beautiful or interesting in the Malay States at all, and Isabella was wrong. She accused Isabella of misrepresenting life in the tropical jungle because she received special treatment and "wherever she went she was introduced to the highest officials in the land."

Isabella never responded to the comments. In June 1883, she and John Bishop went on a trip to Devon, planning to be away for several weeks. Suddenly, John Bishop collapsed. For months he had suffered recurring attacks of weakness but managed to continue working. Now, his strength was exhausted. Several doctors came to see him. The diagnosis was "pernicious anemia," a depletion of the red blood corpuscles resulting from his infection from erysipelas two years earlier. There was little that could be done. The doctors advised the traditional remedy: a change of air.

Over the next months, Isabella took her husband to the south coast of England for the sea air, to London for consultations with doctors, to Edinburgh to see more medical experts, to Tobermory in the summer for the island air, to the French Riviera in the winter for the warm air. When doctors recommended mountain air, she had him carried up steep paths to a village in the Swiss Alps.

By 1884, she saw: "He has become a skeleton with transparent white hands, and his face is nothing but a beard and beautiful eyes. His mind is very clear and bright; he is full of fun, interest and thought for others. We are now fighting death inch by inch. It is an awful time."

In November 1885, they settled on the French Riviera in a hotel in Cannes. Isabella's life now revolved around her husband. Every evening, she slept from nine until midnight while John Bishop's servant sat with him. At midnight, she went to his room to spend the night with her husband while his servant slept. When the man returned at seven in the morning, she went back to bed. During the day, she sat with her husband reading aloud, talking, or writing letters. When he rested, she wrote, went on errands or visited friends. He ate little and grew weaker and weaker, but he was always calm and cheerful. He wrote to a friend that his breakdown in health "has put a stop to everything except reading, tender care and wonderful kindness all around. My dear wife and my excellent attendant are much overworked."

He and Isabella often talked about the need for missionary hospitals in foreign countries. A devout Christian, John Bishop agreed with her that the best way to spread its teachings was through medical work by curing sickness. Isabella told him of the illnesses and skin diseases she had seen in Japan. He offered possible remedies, and Isabella was moved by his unselfish dedication.

As he grew worse, Sir Joseph Lister, his old mentor, traveled from London to give him one of the first blood transfusions using the blood of a young Italian peasant, but it did not help.

Isabella noted: "He is fearfully emaciated, the bones being as nearly as possible through the skin. He has lived on milk exclusively since December 18, with a little brandy in it. He looks very sweet and spiritual, and is quite serene, and though he knows his very critical condition is warmly interested in the things of this life."

The doctors showed Isabella how to administer chloroform to ease his pain. Day by day she watched him growing weaker. As she sat at his bedside, he told her how much he loved her. He promised he would be with her always because "My love is the love of eternity." He talked of the times they had spent together, the joy they had shared, and his last words, whispered to her as his eyes closed, were: "So happy, my own bride."

He died on March 6, 1886, two days before their fifth wedding anniversary. Isabella was insistent that the funeral be held at once; she could not bear to think it would fall on the same day as their marriage. She kept remembering her conviction that she should marry in black, a grim foreboding of what had happened.

John Bishop was buried in a hillside cemetery in France. Only Isabella, his brother and a few friends were present at the graveside. Then Isabella, drained by the long ordeal, collapsed in exhaustion. Yet within a few days, she had pulled herself together. Wearing a black dress, cape and bonnet which she made, she went out to choose a monument for the grave, and to settle her husband's business affairs.

Her next step was to return to England, stopping at places she and her husband had visited. Back in Edinburgh, she closed up the house on Walker Street, sold the furniture, and disposed of her husband's books and papers as he had directed her to do. Then she went to Tobermory, and assessed her situation calmly, noting: "His long and weary illness made him the object of all my thoughts. I have lived for him. But I must not write about my grief and desolation. Henceforth I must live my own life."

A new Isabella was emerging. She refused to give herself up to sorrow, as she had done when her sister died. She had married John Bishop in hopes of finding comfort and support, and instead she had been the one to support and comfort her husband. She always thought she needed the solid anchor of "home and hearth" and yet for months she had moved from place to place and survived. Financially, she had enough money to live comfortably, and to travel wherever she might want to go.

When John Murray enquired about her plans for the future, she explained: "I have at present no plans. But I feel I should be an unworthy heir of many blessed memories if I did not try to make my life useful and interesting. My needs are simple and I am absolutely without any ties, so that I can, if any measure of strength returns, shape my remainder of life as I please." She added: "Such travelling as I am best fitted for involves very much hardship, many risks, the deprivation of all comfort and ease and for the most part complete isolation, and I must have an object worth the deprivations and hazards."

After a year in Tobermory, she made a decision. She would travel in the Far East and establish mission hospitals there in memory of her husband and sister. To prepare herself for the world of medicine, she registered for a three-months nursing course at St. Mary's Hospital in Paddington, London, in the spring of 1887, living in rented rooms nearby.

She spent her days—and some nights—on the casualty wards learning how to set splints, dress wounds, put a man's leg in plaster, and treat hernias and tumors. She watched amputations and operations. She studied the treatment of eye diseases. When her training ended, she went to Tobermory "among sick and dying people, among awful squalid poverty and wretchedness" practicing her new nursing skills.

When John Murray suggested she visit Ireland and write some articles for his new magazine, she quickly agreed, realizing it would be a good way to revitalize her reporting and writing skills. Irish Nationalists demanding independence had clashed violently with the Loyal and Patriotic Union who wanted to keep British rule. For five weeks in winter weather Isabella travelled from village to village, talking to men and women with differing viewpoints.

She confessed to Murray: "My health improved very much in Ireland. I became more vigorous and enterprising daily towards the end of the time. It is rather a sad fact - but rough knocking about, open-air life, in combination with sufficient interest, is the one in which my health and spirits are the best."

The publication of her first-hand accounts vividly depicted the harshness of daily life in Ireland and the oppression which had led to the clashes. Her conclusion was prophetic: "It is not in five weeks, or in five months, that a stranger could found an opinion worth having on the complicated problems which Ireland represents." Her articles were of such importance that they were mentioned in a debate in Parliament. Isabella was revitalized by the experience.

As her confidence returned, she began to plan her next great journey. She would go where she had always dreamed of traveling: the high mountains of Central Asia. To ease her conscience she told her friends her goal was to establish mission hospitals in India in memory of her husband and sister, but this time she no longer mentioned her health as an excuse for her travels.

Isabella booked her passage on a steamer from London to Karachi, India. From there, she hoped to travel north to the Himalayas on the border with Tibet. She wanted to travel through Persia and Turkey, and perhaps take the steamer from Istanbul in Turkey to England. She planned to be away for more than a year.

The preparations for the journey were complicated. She needed official documents from government agencies to build the mission hospitals. She bought some medications and equipment for the medical work she hoped to do. She studied travel books, collected information and maps, and discussed her plans with her old friend John

Murray. He expressed great interest in a new book from his successful author about such an intriguing part of the world.

As 1888 drew to a close, Isabella wrote to a friend: "Here I am finishing needlework, arranging my remaining affairs, answering about fourteen letters a day, and studying India and Persia. When I leave the dear ones here, I shall feel as if the 'bitterness of death' were past. The voyage will be a strange time, a silent interval between the familiar life which lies behind, and the strange unknown life which lies before."

On February 15, 1889, she boarded the steamship *Kerbela* for India. She had learned to travel with as little luggage as possible so she took only four boxes packed with her clothes, sturdy boots, medicines, a canvas stretcher-bed in a brown waterproof bag, a cork mattress, woollen sheets, and her beloved saddle. She also had notepaper, sketchpads, pens and pencils for all she planned to write and draw along the way. With her unquenchable enthusiasm for the unknown, the 57-year-old Isabella was ready to begin again.

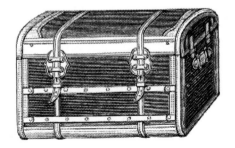

Isabella Bird in her later years

Section III
REWARDS 1889-1904

Chapter 12
Alone in Asia

Leaves for India. Establishes mission hospitals.
Travels to high mountains of Tibet. Climbs and
explores region. Returns to India.

Isabella arrived in India with two goals. She planned to establish hospitals at Protestant medical missions in memory of her sister and her husband, and she wanted to see the Himalayas, the highest mountain range in the world.

Before he died, John Bishop had often talked with Isabella about the importance of medical missions for the heathen as a way of helping the sick and spreading the word of Christianity. He had probably left her enough money to establish them, and to live comfortably on her own. For the rest of her life, Isabella supported medical missionary efforts. Her unpaid work for those organizations provided her with an excuse for her travels abroad, and appeased her conscience for doing what she most enjoyed.

Her travel itinerary was to explore north of India and trek into the Himalaya mountains of the Central Asian plateau. As John Bishop had once joked: "I have only one formidable rival in Isabella's heart, and that is the high tableland of Central Asia." Isabella's dream was about to be fulfilled. She hoped the journey would provide fascinating material for her to write about.

From the port of Karachi she took a train to northern India and on to Kashmir. On the way she stopped at Church Missionary Society medical centers to ask where hospitals were needed and whom she could contact for advice. She was told to get in touch with two brothers, Dr. Ernest and Dr. Arthur Neve, at the CMS mission hospital in Srinigar, the capital of Kashmir.

Isabella arrived in April when Kashmir was abloom with vividly colored flowers and blossoming shrubs. The snowy mountain peaks in the distance reminded her of the Rockies in Colorado. She bought a tent and other camping equipment in preparation for her treks. When she called on Dr. Ernest Neve, she discovered that he had studied with John Bishop in Edinburgh, and greatly admired her late husband. She went with Neve to his next clinic.

Held in the open air under the trees by a swiftly-flowing stream, there were so many patients waiting that several policemen were needed to keep the long line in order. Dr. Neve gave a short sermon about Jesus before starting to treat the patients, and Isabella watched closely as he worked. Later he wrote: "In the course of each day many operations were performed, and I remember her great interest in a man with a large malignant tumor of the neck, which I removed. It was a big operation to undertake in such primitive surroundings. Overhead was the green canopy of the magnificent plane-trees. All around gazed a silent crowd. Mrs. Bishop took a keen interest in all things surgical and offered help as well as looked on."

Afterwards, Dr. Neve rode with Isabella to find a suitable site for a new hospital. She wore a simple costume of a dark divided skirt, long brown cloak and a thick blue veil. No one gave her a second glance as they passed through the narrow, crowded streets, perched on top of her horse, because she looked exactly like a local peasant woman.

Islamabad, some 30 miles from Srinigar, looked the ideal place. There, Isabella bought land for the erection of the John Bishop Memorial Hospital, in memory of her husband. She described the plans in detail in a letter to her friend Miss Clayton: "It will have an out-patient department, a waiting room, consulting room, operation room, and dispensary; two pavilions to hold thirty-two patients; and a rest-house, for patients' friends, who come to nurse and cook for them."

Dr. Arthur Neve agreed to supervise making bricks from local limestone and the construction of the building, and the Church Missionary Society would administer the facility. In the next weeks, Isabella also bought land and arranged for the building of the Henrietta Bird Memorial Hospital in Bias, India, in memory of her sister.

Now Isabella was ready for Central Asia. From Srinigar, her plan was to take a boat down the river to the start of the trekking routes, and climb through the mountains to the ancient city of Leh in Lesser Tibet. Access to the region was across high passes, only clear of snow for a few months in the summer. The rest of the year the routes were blocked and Tibet was completely isolated. Even in summer she was told to expect snowstorms, freezing weather and ice, as well as fierce sun during the day because of the altitude. Dr. Ernest Neve offered to accompany her as far as the first pass, the Zoji La.

Isabella hired a personal servant, Hassan Khan, two other servants, and some mules to carry the luggage. She rode a silver-gray Arab horse called Gyalpo, who "jumped like a deer, climbed like a yak, was strong and steady in perilous fords, tireless, hardy, hungry, frolicked along ledges of precipices and over crevassed glaciers, was absolutely fearless, and his slender legs and the use he made of them were the marvel of all." He was also wild and unpredictable, and tried to bite people, but Isabella relished a challenge.

Isabella's equipment included her tent, almost eight foot square and weighing 75 lbs. She furnished it with a rug, a folding bed with a cork mattress, a folding table and a chair. Her servants shared a smaller tent. She took cooking utensils for herself only. Her servants carried their own since their religion forbade them to use those belonging to a Christian.

The Maharajah of the region sent a military escort to accompany and protect her. Usman Shah turned out to be one of the most colorful characters Isabella had ever met, and full of his own importance. He arrived wearing a white muslin dress with hanging sleeves, added a red-peaked cap with a blue scarf tied over it which hung down over his shoulder, and had a knife and revolver stuck in his belt. Every day he wore fanciful costumes, with turbans decorated with poppies and birds' feathers. He walked in front of Isabella waving his sword and intimidated the villagers along the way.

In June, Isabella and her entourage left Srinigar to climb up from the lush valley of Kashmir into the bleak bare rocks of the Himalayas. It took a week's riding to the foot of the Zoji La pass at 11,300 feet, considered to be the lowest point of the mountains dividing India from Tibet. For hundreds of years caravans of men and animals had trekked along the dangerous trails that clung to the sides of steep precipices and across bare gravel deserts. Isabella noted:

"The Zoji La is a thoroughly severe pass, the worst on the Yarkand caravan route. The track, cut, broken and worn on the side of a wall of rock nearly 2,000 feet is a series of rough narrow zigzags, rarely, if ever, wide enough for laden animals to pass each other, composed of broken ledges often nearly breast high, and shelving surfaces of abraded rock, up which animals have to leap and scramble as best they may."

Trees and trailing leaves drooped over the path while ferns and lilies grew in hidden corners of the rocky walls. Far, far below lay the snow-filled gorges. Struggling up the rocky track, Isabella turned for a last glimpse of Kashmir in the distance with its soft hills, green trees and colorful flowers. Ahead, she saw only crest after crest of mountains, a skyline of sharp peaks and snow-covered slopes stretched on unendingly, craggy ranges soaring higher and higher, with saw-toothed ridges set dazzling white against the sky. As she reached the top of the Zoji La pass, Isabella felt a sense of exhilaration and achievement.

Dr. Neve left to go back to Srinigar. Isabella was on her own, a leader coping with the altitude, the severe weather and servants who spoke little English. From the first day, she established a routine. In the morning at six, her servant Hassan Khan brought her tea and toast. She dressed and packed while the tents were taken down and loaded on the mules. One servant set off early to go eight miles along the trail with the lunch-basket and Isabella's tent and cork mattress. She set out at seven with Usman Shah and a servant, leaving the other servants to load the mules and follow at a slower pace.

When Isabella reached the midway point around ten in the morning, she rested for a couple of hours in her tent: "Such a luxury but for the proximity of things that creep," she commented. Lunch was served—rice, hard-boiled eggs, cold tea and fruit. Isabella waited until the caravan of mules had set out on its way to set up the tents at the evening campsite before starting out along the path.

Usman Shah led the way for Isabella, in costumes that became more spectacular every day. He sported fantastic earrings, shiny bracelets, sparkling rings on all his fingers. His shoes turned up at the toes and he wore black leggings of orange and scarlet stripes and white shorts. His enormously high white muslin turban was now adorned with a cluster of red roses which added almost two feet to his height. However, Isabella felt he did as she told him and was very dependable.

In the late afternoon, when she arrived at the overnight campsite, she checked that the tents were properly erected and that everything was in order. Then she had a cup of tea and wrote up her notes. Her beloved Henrietta was gone, so Isabella wrote long journal-letters to her friend Miss Clayton, to a few other women friends, and to her publisher, John Murray. She also kept a journal, a daily log of distances covered and places where she stayed, with notes of temperatures, altitudes, and geographic features.

Her servants prepared the evening meal of roast meat and boiled rice. Isabella sat with them around the campfire until eight, when she went to her tent. They sat

Usman Shah

talking and smoking their water pipes for an hour and then wrapped themselves in their padded quilts to sleep. The frosty stars glittered like diamonds in the dark night, amid the silence of the mountains. The air was sharp and cold.

Isabella found that every day the paths grew more difficult, winding between precipices, sometimes no more than a narrow ledge above the rushing torrents below. Now two animals could not pass at one time; her servant's horse was pushed over the precipice by a loaded mule, and she watched it fall hundreds of feet into the river and drown.

At a dangerous bend of the road, the baggage mule of another caravan fell to its death. She was sometimes forced to walk when the route was too narrow for horse and rider, and scrambled up narrow paths baked by the intense heat of the sun, where the gravel was burning hot.

Suddenly she saw, set amid the rocks, a painted Buddhist temple. Ahead on the steep slopes were a few houses balanced perilously on the precipices. It was the village of Shergol, her first view of Tibet and the Tibetans. Men and women were around five feet high, which made Isabella—at four foot eleven inches—feel quite at home. She noted:

"The people have high cheekbones, broad flat noses without visible bridges, small, dark, oblique eyes, with heavy lids and impercep-tible eyebrows, wide mouths, full lips, thick, big projecting ears de-formed by great hoops, straight black hair nearly as coarse as horse-hair."

The men wore long coats, woollen leggings and pointed hats. The women had short jackets, full skirts and tight trousers, and twisted their hair into greasy braids, fastened with a long tassel. On their heads they wore a unique head-dress, hung with large turquoises, semi-precious stones and silver ornaments, and jangled with an assortment of hoop earrings, necklaces, bracelets, bangles and other jewelry.

Isabella was interested in their medical care, and asked about their customs and treatments. She learned that the all-purpose remedy was butter. If they had leg pains, they rubbed it on their legs; if their heads hurt, they rubbed it on their heads, and they adapted it for every ailment. The one disease which they recognized and which aroused terror was smallpox. When anyone developed the tell-tale pox marks, they threw the person into the river, or took them to a desolate mountain top to recover or die.

If someone fell sick, they made a half-size model of a sick person, dressed it in the person's clothes, and sat reading prayers, reciting incantations, beating drums and dancing wildly round it. They believed that illness was the work of a demon who could be transferred to the image. Later, the model was led out of the village in a procession and burned. Because most people washed once a year and rarely changed their clothes, they were very dirty, yet, unlike the Japanese she had seen, they were healthy and strong. Isabella watched women carry bundles of sixty pounds or more over the passes.

Family life was unlike anything Isabella had seen before. Only the eldest son in a Tibetan family could marry. When he brought his bride home to his father's house, he became head of the family. His parents often moved out of the house, and the bride accepted all the other brothers as secondary husbands. To Isabella's surprise, the women approved of the situation.

"We have three or four men to help us instead of one," one woman explained. "If I had only one husband, and he died, I should be a widow. If I have two or three, I am never a widow!" The word "widow" was a term of insult and abuse.

Religion was an integral part of their lives. Brightly colored banners inscribed with prayers and colored strips of cotton tied to sticks fluttered in the wind from rooftops. Even in the most derelict homes she saw an altar with a shelf of wooden gods, and a table of offerings to them, or circular prayer wheels with rolls of paper inscribed with the universal prayer, "Om Mane Padne Hun." Outside on rocks there were sometimes dozens of wheels in a row that could be turned by hand, by pulling ropes and larger ones that turned by water power. Tibetans believed you gained merit by repeating prayers so turning a prayer wheel was a way of collecting additional merit.

She left Shergol, and rode on toward Leh. Along the way, she found overwhelming hospitality. "In every village I was invited to the headman's house and taken by him to visit the chief inhabitants; every traveller passed by with the cheerful salutation "Tzu", asked me where I came from and whither I was going, wished me a good journey, and admired Gyalpo."

Riding on, she saw more signs of Buddhist influence. Hundreds of flags inscribed with prayers fluttered in the wind. Colossal figures of Buddha were carved into the rocks along the way, and figures carved in wood, stone or copper adorned the roadway. Painted shrines or "chod-tens" dedicated to holy men stood among the rocks or on the ground. And Buddhist monasteries or "gonpos" were built into the rocks.

Isabella admired their design: "Vast irregular piles of fantastic buildings, almost invariably crowning lofty isolated rocks or mountain spurs, reached by steep, rude rock staircases, with battlemented towers above, with temples, domes, bridges over chasms, spires and scaffolded projections gleaming with gold, looking as at Lamayuru, the outgrowth of the rock itself."

She rode on over bare granite peaks. Though the fierce sun, hot dry wind, and thin air brought noon temperatures up to 120 degrees, and night temperatures often below freezing, Isabella declared: "I did not suffer from the climate, but with most Europeans, the air passages become irritated, the skin cracks, the hair stands out from the head, leather shrivels and splits, food dries up, and tea made with water below the boiling point is flavorless and flat."

She arrived in Leh after a "delightful journey of twenty-five days," full of energy. However, there was a shock. The colorfully dressed Usman Shah was arrested. Recognized by the chief of police, he was apparently wanted for the murder of a local resident some months ago. Usman Shah declared that the murder was to avenge an insult, and that the case had been settled. Despite his protests, the police led him away gesticulating wildly, the roses on his turban waving in the air.

Isabella had no time to ponder the dangers of traveling with a murderer. She was already planning another trek. She met Mr. Redslob, a dedicated Moravian missionary and veteran of twenty-five years in Tibet, who was impressed by the devout Mrs. Bishop. He invited her to join him on a three-week trip to the northern valleys beyond the next range of mountains. Redslob had spent years studying the culture, knew the language, and was translating the Bible into Tibetan, which impressed Isabella. She also watched him at the mission hospital treating hundreds of patients who came to Leh from the surrounding areas.

After a reading from the Gospels, he treated a winding line of people with rheumatism, inflamed eyes and eyelids, malaria, dysentery, and leprosy. He and his staff followed careful antiseptic procedures, which he said the local people adopted because they believed it kept evil spirits from the wounds.

Two days later, they set off to climb the pass which led into the northern region, even higher than anything Isabella had climbed before, which had no effect on her though the others suffered from vertigo. The next morning, she heard strange sounds of grunting and bellowing. Opening the tent flaps, she saw a herd of large, black hairy yaks. Redslob showed her how to saddle and mount her yak, and said they would ride them that day and lead the horses. Isabella found:

"My yak was fairly quiet, and looked a noble steed with my Mexican saddle and gay blanket among—rather than upon—his thick black locks. His back seemed as broad as that of an elephant, and with his slow, sure, resolute step, he was like a mountain in motion."

Riding yaks, she, Redslob, and the Tibetans climbed up the steep slopes of the pass for five hours. Above, the sky was dark with heavy black clouds, and it even snowed. With thick white flakes whirling about in the sharp cold air, she struggled up to the summit at 17,930 feet. At the top, she dismounted from her yak, and the Tibetans reloaded the baggage on to the horses to ride down some 4,000 feet to the village of Digar, where there were cloudless skies and a temperature of 90 degrees.

The next morning they set off to go farther north, crossing the Shayok River. Melting snow had transformed the usually placid stream into a churning torrent, with eight swiftly moving streams stretching for a mile over a gravel surface. Isabella and Redslob stood looking at the waters rushing past, bubbling and foaming over the black rocks beneath the surface, crashing down in foaming rapids, wondering how they would get across.

The Tibetan guides were fearful. They studied the turbulent water to estimate the safest crossing point, prayed aloud fervently, and made offerings to the river gods. Isabella was told to drink from the river to prevent giddiness and to splash her face with water. The dozen horses were roped together, the loads set high on their backs. The servants mounted the first horses, with ropes leading the other animals. Two ropes were tied to Isabella's horse, and they set off.

Waiting to cross at the wildest part of the main river, Isabella looked at the surging foam with apprehension. The horses neighed and pulled at the ropes. Every strap was tightened. The Tibetans shouted and yelled encouragingly amid the roar of the torrent as the first horses led the caravan into the ice-cold waters. Isabella urged her horse forward, the current tugging at his legs. The river was up to the seat of her saddle. Her horse, fighting hard, suddenly slipped, fell, rolled over backwards and disappeared under the water to be swept downstream. In a second, Isabella was pulled under the freezing water.

"A struggle, a moment of suffocation, and I was extricated by strong arms, to be knocked down again by the rush of the water, to be again dragged up and hauled and hoisted up the crumbling bank."

Isabella was rescued by the Tibetans. She suffered a sore rib and some severe bruises. With typical bravado, she commented:

"Mr. Redslob, who had thought that my life could not be saved, and the Tibetans were so distressed by the accident that I made very light of it, and only took one day of rest."

She stayed at the home of a Buddhist monk called Gergan. It was a clean, airy place with mud floors, windows opening on to wooden balconies, and flowers in every room. The food was delicious: apricots grown in the orchards, milk, curds and cheese, sour cream, peas, beans, balls of barley dough, barley porridge and a strange soup. Only Tibetan tea was undrinkable to her, with its thick cream consistency and taste of water, soda, butter, and salt.

Redslob took her to visit a monastery, and while he discussed Christianity with the leader, the monks stood around laughing. Though sympathetic to Redslob's efforts, she admitted: "It was impossible not to become attached to the Tibetan people, we lived so completely among them and met with such unbounded goodwill."

It was time for Redslob to return to his mission in Leh. They would not return across the river, but take an alternate route over an ice-covered glacier, which they set out to cross after a heavy snowfall. The Tibetans cut steps in the ice and sprinkled the path with gravel so that the yaks and horses could maneuver over the difficult route to reach the summit of the pass at 17,500 feet before the descent to Leh.

In August, she returned to Leh, to find the annual market had transformed the quiet village into a bustling town with merchants from far and wide showing their goods and trading.

"Lhassa traders exchange their expensive tea for Nubra dried apricots, Kashmir saffron and rich stuffs from India; and merchants from Yarkand offer hemp, which is smoked as opium, and Russian trifles and dress goods. Mules, asses, horses and yaks kicked, squealed and bellowed; the dissonance of bargaining tongues rose high; there were mendicant monks, Indian fakirs, Moslem dervishes, Mecca pilgrims, itinerant musicians, and Buddhist ballad howlers."

Now she began her journey south so she could reach Kashmir before the winter began. Redslob gave her an introduction to the nomadic tribe of Chang-pas along the way. She traveled with four horses, yaks loaded with hay and barley for her horse, and provisions for two weeks. Her route lay over a series of steep gravel slopes that climbed to 20,000 feet, across bare desert-like plateaus surrounded by bleak jagged peaks. She saw herds of the graceful "kyang"—the wild Tibetan ass—grazing. After crossing Toglang Pass, at 18,150 feet, she began riding across the plains.

Suddenly, a large group of Chang-pas tribesmen on horseback came galloping toward her. As they thundered up to her, the horses reared and the tribesmen came to a halt. "In one moment they were on the ground, which they touched with their foreheads, presented me with a plate of apricots, and the next vaulted into their saddles, and dashing up the valley they were soon out of sight."

They returned, galloping as wildly as before, and brought the chief. He greeted Isabella with great ceremony as a friend of Redslob, and, with horsemen wheeling around the group, escorted her to their camp.

Some fifty black tents were placed in a row by a rushing river. Sheep grazed nearby and yaks roamed the steep slopes. While the horsemen galloped around, tribespeople brought her gifts of apricots, showed her the flock of white goats that they milked, and gave her rugs to sit on.

The chief presented her with a tent for the night, and rugs to put on the floor. As darkness fell, a huge bonfire blazed fiercely in the center of the campground. Exhausted, Isabella fell asleep while the celebrations went on far into the night.

Early next morning, accompanied by a few of the galloping tribesmen, Isabella set off to travel south. For five weeks she rode through Tibetan villages, camped out on windswept plains, and crossed several lofty passes which she rated: "All easy, except for the difficulties from the rarified air."

She rested briefly in Kashmir, and traveled on to Simla, which she reached in October. In the large British colony there, she was greeted as a heroine. For six months she had traversed some of the highest peaks and the most rugged terrain in the world. Everyone was talking about the amazing Mrs. Bishop.

But she was not ready to go home. To the west lay Persia, which she thought would be fascinating to visit. She considered the idea of traveling back across that unexplored region to the Black Sea, where she knew she could find a boat to England. With quiet determination, she began to investigate the possibilities of a new journey.

Chapter 13
Exploring Persia

Invitation from Major Sawyer. Riding off to unknown territory. Difficulties in leadership. Visit to harem. Journey through snowstorms to Teheran.

As the word spread that the indomitable Mrs. Bishop wanted to travel to Persia, the British colonial community hastened to inform her that it would be impossible for a single woman to even dream of such a thing. Isabella listened to stories of caravans being viciously attacked by wild nomadic tribesmen who robbed and killed travelers. She was told of the violent anti-Christian feeling in Persia's Moslem cities, where missionaries had lost their lives. She heard reports that winter travel was impossible because of the unbelievably bitter cold.

Unexpectedly, she received a note from Major Herbert Sawyer asking to speak with her privately. She did not know him but learned he was a respected English officer in the Intelligence Department of the Indian Army. The gossips told her about his wife's sudden death, leaving him a widower at 38 with three young daughters.

Isabella agreed to meet him. He walked in briskly, and she saw a tall, attractive, dark-haired man in uniform. He came straight to the point. He had a secret military assignment to travel across Persia. Would she like to accompany him?

Surprised at the invitation, Isabella asked what he would be doing there. His task was to explore, survey, and map the territory east from Turkey across the mountains of Persia to Teheran to provide information for the British. Isabella realized that it was part of The Great Game, the 19th-century scheming between the major powers of Russia, Britain and France to take over weaker countries. Persia was under attack because, as Sawyer explained, it was in a state of financial collapse from the excessive demands for taxes by the extravagant Shah and greedy regional governors, and had no strong central government.

The reason he wanted Isabella to accompany him was to provide a cover for his activities. The story would be given out that he was traveling as a military escort to the well-known traveler Isabella Bird Bishop, in order to disguise his real work.

Isabella hesitated. She always preferred to travel alone. He assured her that they would both be independent with separate servants, tents, and equipment. She would be free to do whatever she wanted. He was bringing a surveyor, a naturalist, and other experts to help him with his explorations, so she would not need to be involved in any way. The only restriction was that she could not mention what he was doing in anything she wrote.

Isabella commented later: "Nearly everyone thought it the acme of my good fortune as a traveller going with him. But I feel that it involves a certain abridgement of my liberty."

She considered the alternatives, and accepted his invitation. They sailed for Turkey, and in January 1890, they spent several days in Baghdad hiring servants and mules for the journey east. It was an introduction to traveling together, and Isabella was apprehensive.

"The first two days I thought I could not get on with him, but now I think that we shall be able to pull together as far as Teheran. He is a distinguished officer, a great linguist, necessarily a man of science, an artist, and a musician. Very able all round. He is most strikingly handsome and six foot two. His splendid appearance, force of character, wit, brutal frankness, ability and kind-heartedness make a great breeze."

She was concerned that: "He has a crotchetiness which of all mental peculiarities bothers me most, and is restless and fitful besides being sarcastic." Though she found him outspoken and strong-willed, she soon noticed how much he impressed people wherever they went.

The route, almost 600 miles, lay across the high Persian mountains to Khannikin, Kermanshah, Hamilabad, Qum and Teheran. The plan was to stay at local caravan stops along the way, which were about a day's ride apart. As they prepared to leave, Isabella sat astride her mule, a holster on either side with, on Major Sawyer's advice, her revolver in one, together with her tea-making equipment, and in the other, a bottle of milk and some dates. Strapped to the front of her saddle was a thick sheepskin coat, with her blanket and raincoat behind. She had dressed to look as inconspicuous as possible, and wore a long jacket over her American mountain dress, a cork helmet, and covered her face with a gray mask like a veil. She followed the long string of loaded mules as they rode out of Baghdad into the countryside.

The caravan leader had two large bells round his neck on red leather bands ornamented with shells. Every pack on the mules had one large bell and most of the animals wore smaller bells. As the caravan moved along, Isabella smiled at the cheerful sound of constant jingling, the deep note of the larger bells combining with the tinkling sounds of the smaller, sometimes doubling and multiplying to a cacophonous jangle when other caravans passed by. As they trotted into the desert, she enthused:

"The mid-day and afternoon were as glorious as an unclouded sky, a warm sun, and a fresh, keen air could make them. The naked plain, which stretched to the horizon, was broken only by the brown tents of Arabs, strings of brown camels, straggling caravans, and companies of Arab horsemen heavily armed. I felt better at once in the pure, exhilarating desert air, and nervousness about the journey was left behind."

That night, she had her first experience of a Turkish inn. She rode into a muddy square surrounded by derelict stables. Rickety stairs led up to tiny rooms. The doors closed only from the outside and inside were slimy unplastered walls, ceilings blackened with centuries of smoke, and beetles in every corner. A small hole in the wall was used for cooking. Isabella calmly wrapped herself in her blanket, put her camp stool up against the outside wall, and settling behind a heap of holsters, saddles and gear to keep off the wind, busily wrote her journal while her servants unloaded the mules.

"My fingers are nearly numb, and I am generally stiff and aching, but so much better that discomforts are only an amusement," she commented cheerily. "I feel as if I had lived the desert life, and had heard the chimes of the great caravans, and had seen the wild desert riders and the sun sinking below the level line of the desert horizon for two months instead of two days."

Her personal servant, Hadji, was far from ideal. He acted as if he did not understand her, had to be told to do everything several times, was always making mistakes, and never learned to set up her trestle bed correctly. When she reprimanded him, he would exclaim helplessly: "God help us!" Major Sawyer assured her Hadji was faking and called him "a lazy, good-for-nothing, humbugging brute!"

When they set out the next day, the winter rains began, drenching the caravan and turning the floors of the inns into muddy swamps. Out on the plains, Isabella sat on her mule eating lunch, her back to the storm that blew fiercely across the open countryside. That night, the inns were wet and dirty, thick with filth and mud.

It took a week to reach Khannikin. This time, Major Sawyer took her to the house of a local governor. Isabella was given a guestroom under the roof while Major Sawyer stayed in the main rooms. After the men had eaten dinner, Hadji brought some food to Isabella in her room. She was allowed to visit the governor's harem which had about thirty women in it, and the governor begged her to persuade his principal wife, whose baby had just died of cholera, to have an operation to remove an abscess under her arm.

Isabella found the woman wrapped in a black shawl, propped up on pillows in bed. She sat staring ahead and refused to move, though she was burning hot with fever. Isabella had been told she was an educated woman, and owned land, and did not understand why she would not respond. However, over the next few days, after she had spoken to the doctor, she realized there was conspiracy within the harem.

"I have become aware that unscrupulous jealousy of the principal wife exists, and as is usual in the East, everybody distrusts everybody else, and prefers to trust strangers. The doctor says an operation is necessary to save the lady's life, but when I urge him to perform it, he replies that if she were to die he would be accused of murder. I have seldom seen a harem without its tragedies of jealousy and hate, and every fresh experience makes me believe that the system is as humiliating to men as it is to women."

She was glad when it was time to leave. As the caravan rode across the border into Persia, four soldiers in uniform joined them as an escort. That night, they reached the first Persian caravansary, a great stone castle-like building near a village, entered through a huge archway to a courtyard open to the sky. The surrounding stone walls had arches leading into narrow recesses, like small rooms. Beyond lay a huge mule stable, with a high domed roof and dozens of similar recesses with "at least four hundred mules jangling their great bells, and crowds of muleteers, and travellers, all wet and splashed with mud, some unloading, others making fires and feeding their mules, all shouting when they had anything to say. The floor was deep with the manure of ages and piled with bales and boxes. The odor was overpowering and the noise stunning."

Revolted, she bribed a family to give her their room over the gateway away from the mules.

As they rode through the Kurdistan region, she visited the village of Saripul dating back to the fifth century A.D. to see the Ali-Ilahis, a tribe that had kept Jewish names and still worshipped Moses, Benjamin, Elias and David among others. Often called Davidites because of their veneration for King David, they guarded his tomb set in the rift of a rock and called Dukkani-Daoud, or David's shop, because they believed he still lived and worked as a smith. People traveled from all parts of the region on pilgrimages offering animal sacrifices to him, and legend said that the Ali-Ilahis were one of the lost tribes of Israel.

The route now climbed higher, crossing the rocky pass to the plains. With relief Isabella found there was crisp snow instead of soggy mud to ride on. That night the caravan camped at a large Kurdish house. An excellent dinner of soup and meat was served, cooked on the open fire. Isabella's bed, hidden by reed screens, was set up by the raised stone platform where the warm fire blazed, and from where she could look out through the open doorway to a view of snow and sparkling stars in the sky.

Riding in the mountains, Isabella was in her element. The frozen streams, the snow-bound world of rocks and mountains, and the icy streams under a brilliant blue sky and warm sun were exactly what she loved. But the path led down to the plains covered with deep snow, where the caravan followed the mule track, cut like a trench through the whiteness, just wide enough for one mule.

One morning, as the loaded animals plodded along the narrow path between the walls of snow, Isabella saw another caravan with loaded mules coming towards them, their bells jingling. She realized the muleteers were waiting to see who would give way first. No-one wanted to drive their mules off the track to struggle in the deep, powdery snow, knowing they might have to be unloaded before they could scramble back on to the track. Major Sawyer was far ahead, out of sight beyond the next snow-covered hill. As the caravan came closer, she decided to give way, and tried to pull her mule off the track, but he refused to budge.

"Down the track came sixty animals, loaded with their great packing-cases. They could not and would not give way and the two caravans came into collision. There were mules struggling and falling, loads overturned, muleteers yelling and roaring, Hadji groaning 'God help us!' "

Isabella's mule began plunging and kicking the others, and she was hit on the ankle by a packing-case, and another heavy case banged against her. She called to Hadji to help her, but he sat helplessly moaning amid the confusion while his animal rolled into a snowdrift. The mules came relentlessly on, their bells jangling, until finally the last one went by.

Isabella assessed the damage. "My snow glasses are gone, a number of bruises, a badly-torn riding skirt, and a bad cut, which bled profusely and then the blood froze. The muleteers had asked us to keep together in case of difficulties with caravans. Difficulties indeed! A mild term! I was nearly smashed."

That night, her room at the inn was icy. "A fire fails to raise the temperature of my room to the freezing-point, yet it is quite possible to be comfortable," she commented cheerfully, as she scribbled her notes until her ink froze.

The winter cold had arrived earlier than expected. On all sides, the plains glittered in the sunlight. Ice covered the steep passes, making it almost impossible for the mules to keep on their feet. The next day, as they descended the slopes, she could see below the large building of the caravansary and the surrounding houses only five miles away, but it took three hours to reach it. Isabella was stiff and in pain from the intense cold. At the inn, she was lifted from the mule to her bed, covered with blankets, and a pot of hot embers from the fire put beside her. Her hands and feet were rubbed, while she sipped hot tea, but it was two hours before she could go to the kitchen for food. The local residents thought the English mad to go traveling in the winter, and the muleteers joined in the criticisms, cursing their leaders for dragging everyone through such suffering.

Isabella and Major Sawyer rode on to Kirmanshah, about 350 miles from Teheran, through drifts and over a vast plateau of rippling snow. Here they stayed at the house of the British Agent. His son Abdul Rahim greeted them, and Isabella followed him through the frozen courtyard to the palatial mansion. He led her to an elegant room, thick with carpets, sofas, a blazing fire, and a table covered with apples, oranges and sweetmeats. On the wall, incongruously reminding Isabella of the England she had left behind, was a photograph of Queen Victoria.

Abdul Rahim and his family were Arabs who had become British subjects and now came under British protection. In the week Isabella rested there while Major Sawyer explored the region outside the town, she found herself treated as a guest of honor. At dinner, served with fine silver and china, she sat at the head of the table.

When she walked through the bazaars wearing a veil and a mask, as Persian women were expected to do, men shouted and insulted her because she was a woman. Because Christians were considered filthy, she was warned not to touch the food or the merchandise. Abdul took her to see the carpet-weaving for which Kirmanshah was famous, and she watched men weaving the elaborately knotted rugs on simple wooden frames. He took her for a winter picnic in his country house with its rose garden, and on a horseback ride with a view of mountain ranges.

"I rode a splendid Arab horse, with a neck clothed with thunder, a horse to make one feel young again, with his elastic stride and pride of bearing. We crossed the river by a deep ford up to the girths, and had an exhilarating six miles' ride by moonlight in the keen frost, the powdery snow crackling under the horses' feet."

That evening, Isabella dined alone with Abdul and, with Hadji interpreting, answered his questions about British politics and everyday life, describing his own Islamic beliefs as: "What God does is good. He knows, we submit. Whoso loves and befriends the poor is acceptable to God."

She was gratified by Abdul's gentlemanly behavior: "He has seen but very few English ladies, and it shows great quickness of apprehension that he should never fail in the respectfulness and quiet courteous attentions." His religious beliefs though, she found hard to accept and confided to a friend that she thought Islam "the most blighting, withering, degrading influence of any of the false creeds."

When the caravan left, a snowstorm had blanketed the area, and the narrow mule track again lay between high banks of snow, but the scenery was magnificent.

"It was the most artistic day of the whole journey, much cloud flying about, mountains in indigo gloom, or in grey, with storm clouds round their heads, or pure white, with shadows touched in with cobalt, while peaks and ridges, sun-kissed, gleamed here and there above the indigo and gray."

The next day a blizzard struck as she was riding ahead of the caravan. "It became dark and wild and presently the surface of the snow began to move and to drift furiously for about a foot above the ground. The wind rose to a gale. My cape blew inside out and struck me such a heavy blow on the eye that for some time I could not see and had to trust the mule. The wind rose higher, and the drift was higher than my head, stinging and hissing as it raced by. Fine sharp hard-frozen snow crystals beat on my eyes. Gusts of storm came down, sweeping the powdery snow from the hillsides into the valley; the mountains were blotted out, the path was gone, I could not even see the mule's neck, and he was floundering in deep snow up to the girths; the hiss of the drift had increased to a roar."

Her mule refused to budge. For an hour she spurred and forced him, hardly knowing where the trail was. Then, frightened to be alone, she turned into the shelter of a ruined mud hovel, to wait until the others caught up with her. It seemed like hours before she saw Major Sawyer's horse in the snow. Leaving the shelter of the hovel, she followed him, riding in the face of the fierce storm. Just as suddenly as it had begun, the blizzard subsided and the wind dropped. The sky cleared, the two peaks of the Shamram mountains rose amid the clouds, and the sun came out.

At the village Isabella was lifted off her horse in intense pain. A teaspoonful of whiskey in warm milk revived her, and two women chafed her nearly frozen hands. She heard that five men in another caravan ahead of them had died in the snow, but her philosophic comment was: "Tired and benumbed as I am, I much prefer a march with excitements and difficulties to the monotony of splashing through mud in warm rain."

The next morning, Isabella dressed for the weather with "six woollen layers of my mask, my three pairs of gloves, my sheepskin coat, fur cloak, and mackintosh piled on over a swaddling mass of woollen clothing." Soon after they set off, a bitter wind swept across the frozen surface, whipping up flurries of snow into their faces, numbing their feet and hands. Despite her clothes, she ached with the cold, her hands unable to hold the mule's reins.

Major Sawyer, walking in the snow, his mask frozen solid, was valiantly trying to measure the altitude. He asked his assistant to fasten a strap on the equipment. "I cannot, Sahib" the man replied sadly, his arms and hands paralyzed by the bitter wind. They struggled on to the crest of the pass at 7,000 feet. The tears in Isabella's eyes were freezing on her face, her mask had frozen to her lips, and she knew "I would gladly have lain down to die in the snow." But as they began the downward climb, the wind dropped. They struggled into the village. She heard that three more people had died in the snow that day.

That evening, the muleteers begged Isabella and Sawyer not to go on. The deaths of the other travelers had brought much too close the dangers which they faced. Major Sawyer argued that it was better to reach Teheran than to stay and freeze here, but they pleaded with him to stop. In the end they came to an agreement: they would set out, but if the icy wind began again, they would return to the inn.

Before she left, Isabella put on every piece of clothing she possessed. "The difficulty of mounting and dismounting for a person thus swaddled may be imagined!" As she struggled along the track, she saw the scattered bales of chopped straw lying in the white snow where the three men had died the day before. It was again a long, difficult march. When they arrived at the inn, several of the men could hardly move and one was suffering from snow-blindness.

"Even Major Sawyer's herculean strength is not what it was," Isabella commented. "I have chills but in spite of them and the fatigues am so much better than when I left Baghdad. I ought not to complain of the hardships, though they are enough to break down the strongest men. I really like the journey."

Undeterred, Isabella spent the next day acting as nurse to the men. She made mustard plasters and poultices, and gave out doses of Dover's powders, chlorodyne, salicylate of soda, emetics, and beef tea all day. Major Sawyer carried them from her room across the three feet of snow in the courtyard to the men lying in their beds.

She and Major Sawyer discussed the situation. The sick men needed attention, but staying in the cold inn with little food or protection would not help. They decided their best hope was to travel to Qum, only 25 miles away, to find a Persian doctor.

In the morning chill, it took hours to load the mules, balance the boxes, and get the caravan started. The men were exhausted, and often Isabella and Major Sawyer were the only ones with enough energy to tie the straps and adjust the loads. When they finally reach Qum, the Persian doctor was denied permission to visit the caravan, because they had come through a region in which there was supposed to be cholera. Their only hope was to reach Teheran, about 120 miles away.

The caravan set out the next day. After crossing a pass at 9,000 feet, the trek went downhill. Ahead Isabella saw a dreary brown landscape of mud hills, mud plains, mud slopes, rocks and stones stretching ahead. The snow had been left behind. Two more long days of riding brought them to within 60 miles of Teheran. They crossed the Great Salt Desert of Persia, an empty region with no houses, no trees and no living creatures, and were within a day's ride of Teheran.

Early in the morning, Isabella and Major Sawyer sent the sick men off. They helped the men pack the boxes and load the mules. At ten o'clock, they set off riding together, hoping to reach the city by afternoon. At first, it was dry and sunny, with views of the distant snow-covered peaks of the Elburz mountains, and the ground was crisp and firm. But gray clouds covered the sky, and the rains began. The roadway turned into a quagmire of glutinous earth. The two of them scrambled through ditches and over dikes as the road become water-logged.

Isabella was faint from want of food, and clutched her saddle to stop herself falling off. She was so exhausted that in the afternoon she was forced to stop at an inn to rest for half an hour. They rode on, splashing through muddy puddles and over rushing streams, as it grew dark.

Night had fallen when, at last, Isabella saw the walls of Teheran. With relief, she rode behind Major Sawyer through the gate and into the city. The British Legation building was still two miles away. Isabella almost gave up: "One lives through a good deal, but I all but succumbed to the pain and the faintness." Following Major Sawyer down muddy alleys and narrow streets, she forced herself to respond to his constant question: "Are you surviving?"

Suddenly they turned a corner. There was the large imposing gateway of the British Legation. A fine stone staircase led up to the central door.

"Every window was lighted, light streamed from the open door, splashed carriages were dashing up and setting down people in evening dress, there were crowds of servants about, and it flashed on my dazed senses that it must be after eight and that there was a dinner party!"

Indeed there was, but Isabella was quite unable to attend. She was caked with mud from head to foot, dripping wet, nearly blind from fatigue, wearing clothes that had survived weeks of the roughest traveling. She was vaguely aware of a voice announcing, "Dinner is served." But she was beyond dinner.

She allowed herself to be taken to a room upstairs, and, pulling off her muddy cloak, lay down on the thick rug in front of the fire, and slept until four o'clock the next morning.

Isabella Bird in Kurdistan on her horse, Boy

Chapter 14
Dangerous Missions

Travels with Sawyer in rough country. Discovery of new lake. Unexpected attacks from tribes. Sawyer recalled.

After her incredible journey, Isabella had lost 32 pounds and her hair was streaked with gray. She received dozens of letters and telegrams of congratulations, but she had no time to savor her achievement. Within weeks, she was already planning to join Major Sawyer on his next expedition to explore the Bakhtiari country, a bleak, mountainous region in central Persia inhabited by dozens of warring nomadic tribes. He told her to meet him in a month's time in Isfahan, 300 miles south of Teheran.

The indefatigable Isabella spent her days sightseeing in Teheran, disguised as a Persian woman. British officials took her to visit the Shah's Palace. She strolled through the gardens, beautifully landscaped with orange trees, roses climbing on trellises and flowerbeds filled with narcissus, irises, and tulips. In the spacious Audience Hall were tables of beaten gold and glass cases with a dazzling display of gold, silver and precious stones, accumulated by royalty over 2,500 years. She was awed by shields studded with diamonds and rubies, scabbards and sword hilts encrusted with sparkling gems. One especially striking treasure was a golden globe, on a golden stand set with rubies, where the Equator was outlined in rubies, Persia in diamonds, the ocean was a sea of emeralds, and a heap of large gold coins lay around the base. At the far end of the hall stood the magnificent Peacock Throne from India, made entirely of gold enamel, its fan-shaped back encrusted with rubies and diamonds.

As she stood gazing at its decoration, two men approached her. She recognized the Shah of Persia, Nasr-ed-Din, and his Prime Minister. The Shah, his watchchain sparkling with diamonds, wore an Astrakhan lambskin hat, dark pants, and a loose coat of dull silk brocade. He was "a somewhat rough-looking man, well on in middle life, rather dark in complexion, and wearing a thick, dark moustache, and spectacles with thick horn rims."

He was eager to meet Isabella, the famous British traveler, so the Prime Minister introduced her. He added that, with the Shah's permission, she planned to visit the Bakhtiari country.

"The King pushed up his big horn spectacles and focused his eyes upon me with a stare which would have been disconcerting to a younger person, asked if I were going to travel alone, and if fitting arrangements had been made."

Isabella explained her plans. The Shah listened but said nothing, then turned and walked away. The Prime Minister said: "I hope you will write kindly, and not crush the aspirations of my struggling country, as others have done." Isabella nodded diplomatically. Her private opinion she expressed to friends.

"This is a ruined, played-out country, perishing for want of people, of water, of fuel, and above all for want of security, crushed by the most grinding exactions to which there is no limit but the total ruin of those on whom they press, without a middle class and without hope."

She was eager to leave the city for her journey to Isfahan. Isabella hired a Persian cook, and a new personal servant, Mirza Yusuf, who had been a teacher in an American school and spoke good English, though he had never traveled in rough country. With her baggage loaded on to her mules and a soldier as her escort, she rode out of Teheran in the warm spring air to go south. She wrote cheerfully to a friend: "The roughness and freedom of camp suits me. Is it not wonderful that at my age and with my cranky spine I have become a greater horsewoman than ever! I rode the 300 miles to Isfahan mainly at a gallop."

She reached the city on a Moslem holiday. As she entered the streets filled with men in bright clothes and women shrouded in black, they shouted at her: "A Feringhi woman! A Nazarene woman!" and called her names. Men sneered and laughed, young boys yelled at her rudely, and several people spat at her as she rode by with her group. The abuse continued for half an hour, with Mirza Yusuf watching anxiously, knowing that if he protested, the crowd would attack them both. When they finally reached the gate to the suburb of Julfa, with its large Armenian Christian community, the shouting stopped, and Isabella rode peacefully io the Church Mission House.

She spent three weeks with the director, Dr. Bruce and his family. Though Isabella was impressed by the hospital, the two schools, the orphanage, and the library, she was critical of the women who came out to the mission to serve but were quite unprepared for what they would find. Frequently they collapsed and had to be sent home, overwhelmed by the climate, the rough conditions, and the difficulties of the language. Isabella recommended that mission boards should choose women who were strong enough to cope with the difficulties, and urged every mission to establish rules for health and hygiene, including daily horse-riding and fresh air. While she admired the missions, their style of life was too confining for her.

When Major Sawyer breezed into town with his commanding appearance and lively manners, she was ready to set off. He outlined the proposed itinerary. They would follow the Karun River from the Ardal plateau in the south to Burujird, which lay some 700 miles to the north. Sawyer was to survey and map the area, and establish cordial relations with the chiefs of the nomadic tribes, mostly related to the Bakhtiari, whose total population was estimated at about 232,000.

Studying the map, Isabella noticed mountain ranges with passes up to 11,000 feet high, as well as valleys and rivers at high altitudes. There were no roads - only tracks worn over the centuries by the annual migration of nomads and their flocks. Several areas were marked "Unknown" and "Empty."

Isabella packed two large mule-trunks with her money wrapped in bundles, and took cans of meat, milk, and dried soup, some candles, and her camping equipment. As presents for the tribes, she had thimbles, china buttons which they sewed on children's caps, needles, thread, boxes with mirror tops, scissors, scarves, bead bracelets, necklaces, leather purses and tobacco pouches. She was very pleased when Dr. Bruce gave her a new Burroughes and Wellcome medicine chest with fifty bottles of pills, a hypodermic syringe and surgical instruments, to which she added quinine, bandages, lint, cotton and some remedies from a local doctor.

Her new horse, whom she called Screw, was "well-bred, big-headed, big-eared, small-bodied, fine-coated, slightly flat-footed, and has carried loads for many a day." She set out, exhilarated at the thought of the journey ahead.

Major Sawyer brought along a tripod camera as part of his equipment. Isabella was fascinated by this new invention and he showed her how to take photographs and develop them, which she soon learned to do on her own.

For the first few days, she and Major Sawyer traveled east through villages and desolate countryside. Though warned of robbers and brigands, Isabella was relieved to find it was quite safe to set up camp near the villages, close to water, and trees, crops and flowers. As they rode farther on into the bleak waterless plains, there were only miles of barren gravel. In the distance loomed snow-capped mountains.

One night, camped outside a village, the news that a foreign "hakim" or doctor had arrived leaked out. Soon a crowd of people surrounded her tent, calling to her.

"In vain I explained to them that I was not a doctor, scarcely even a nurse. The fame of Burroughes and Wellcome's medicine chest has spread far and wide." She finally lifted the chest out of her trunk, and for hours doled out medicines and advised people on their eye ailments until late at night. She fell into bed exhausted.

When she woke next morning, Isabella noticed that one of her two trunks was not in the tent. She got up, and went outside. The empty trunk lay on the ground, its padlock broken. All her money had been taken. She realized that the people who watched her lift out the medicine chest could have seen the money, and come back to steal it. Even more disturbing, she was horrified to realize she had slept through two thieves coming into her tent and carrying out the trunk.

She decided: "I have got out my revolver which I hoped never to need and am letting it be known that it is under my pillow, for the report would rouse the whole camp."

Major Sawyer was furious at the theft, and asserted that the Bakhtiaris were all thieves and robbers and that it was a bad omen for the journey. The local chief, the Ilkhani, sent officials to search everyone's baggage, but nothing was found. A week later, another village chief ceremoniously returned the money to Isabella, much to her relief. It had been collected from the people in the village where it had been stolen. But the thefts of food and equipment continued. As she and Major Sawyer sat talking one evening, a valuable instrument for measuring altitude was stolen from his tent.

A new problem arose. Major Sawyer's surveyor developed an eye infection and could no longer help him with the work of noting down geographic details. Although Sawyer had promised Isabella she would be independent of him, she was conscripted to help with the observations of latitude and longitude. Every day, she stood in the midday heat for an hour and a half, taking down the chronograph record of the sun crossing the meridian. At night, using the stars as guide, she stood with Major Sawyer noting observations of longitude. His attitude to her was the same as to his servants; sarcasm and anger when she made a mistake or requested that he repeat a figure to make sure it was correct.

Isabella confessed: "It is terribly hard work. My hand gets shaky and icy cold, and I get some very sharp words. A single mistake of sight and the base from which the survey starts would be vitiated, and all the elaborate astronomical calculations would be upset."

Next, the botanist Sawyer had brought along turned out to be inefficient. Major Sawyer assigned Isabella to collect and press nature specimens, write the Persian names, details of where the specimen was found, medicinal use and other information on special labels from the Indian Government.

"Don't think that I complain!" Isabella scribbled hastily to a friend. "It is far more interesting to have responsible work, but I have even now almost no time."

One afternoon as she rode toward the camp, she found Major Sawyer on the ground, badly hurt after his horse had kicked him. He thought his leg was broken. She examined him and found the muscles had been badly injured. He rode into the camp, trying to ignore the pain.

The accumulating problems of the journey were having an effect on Sawyer—the loss of his men, the rough quarters, the thefts, the dangers and his injury. His temper and angry outbursts increased, and his attitude became ever more insolent and sarcastic. When he asked for supplies from the village chief that evening, Isabella was horrified to hear him bellowing: "Tell him if he doesn't bring wood, I'll go with my men and tear down every roof and door post in the place, and tell him to go to the devil!" Isabella knew that his orders from the British government were "to conciliate the powerful chiefs," and Isabella was certain this was not the right way to go about it.

Next, Major Sawyer's interpreter quit. Sawyer immediately commandeered Isabella's servant, Mirza Yusuf, to interpret at his meetings with the tribal chiefs. Isabella quietly instructed Mirza Yusuf to translate the more outrageous of Major Sawyer's brutal statements into polite Persian phrases, hoping to ease the tensions.

"Imagine the toil I have here where he ought to be most friendly and polite to the great feudal chiefs, whose guest he is, and is most desperately rude and insolent in manner," she wrote in exasperation. "It is a frightful political mistake."

That evening as her tent was being erected, one of the Bakhtiari told her: "We are very much displeased with the Sahib. He behaves very badly to us. He treats us like dogs. It is not his country, it is ours and he is our guest. We cannot bear it. You know no Persian but your manners and looks are polite; the horsemen like to serve you. If it were not for you, we'd leave the Sahib."

Isabella tried to apologize, explaining that Major Sawyer did not express himself well, but she was frightened by the anger in the man's face. What could she do? If she told Sawyer, he would be furious at her and even angrier to realize that the Bakhtiari found her easier to deal with than him. If she did not speak to him to curb his temper, they could both be killed. She decided to speak to him that evening, reminding herself that she had to assert herself or be completely dominated by him.

She stood outside with him as he set up the equipment for observations under the stars, and said quietly that she had heard his behavior offended the Bakhtiari chiefs, which was dangerous. Furious, he turned on her and burst into an angry tirade against her. She was impossible to travel with. She didn't understand these natives, treating them with medicine while they robbed her blind. And the most infuriating aspect of her personality was her voice—he had hated it from the moment they first met.

Isabella had been prepared for an outburst. She knew him well enough by now. Determined not to be intimidated, she pointed out calmly that it was he who had asked her to come with him, and that she had always preferred to travel on her own. If he found her annoying, he should remember that she was here at his invitation. There was nothing to be done about it now. However, if he continued to insult the Bakhtiari chiefs, they might both be killed.

Major Sawyer glared at her. Then he realized the truth of what she said. Reluctantly, he agreed to try to curb his temper and treat the Bakhtiari chiefs with more respect.

Isabella had won a victory. She knew perfectly well Major Sawyer could not manage without her. She was essential as his cover for the mission, and also for his surveying and botanical research. She realized that she was the only person who could speak to him like this. From then on, she was relieved to see he controlled his temper with the chiefs. However, he was always furious with her. He still criticized her sarcastically and shouted at her when she worked with him.

Despite the difficulties, she rode from dawn to dusk across the deserted plains, accompanied by the long caravan of mules, horses and sheep, enjoying herself thoroughly.

"This is a purely wandering and random life. I never led such. We never know in the morning where we shall be at night. But if a place looks nice and there is water, we decide on encamping there. My food consists of roast mutton, rice, tea and milk, without luxuries or variety. Life is very simple and free from purposeless bothers."

At a large Bakhtiari camp at Ardal, the Chief invited them to a party. Two spacious canopy tents were erected in the shade, with rich carpets laid on the floor, and chairs for the European guests. A cloth of "blanket bread" was stretched over a table, on which was heaped a mixture of rice and meat. A line of some fifty servants brought out lamb cutlets, curried chicken, celery with sour sauce, clotted cream, and sour milk, with plates, knives, forks and iced water.

Isabella was taken to the harem to meet the women, and found: "They wore gay 'chadars' of muslin, short gold-embroidered jackets, gauze chemises, and bright-colored balloon trousers, black silk gold-embroidered skull-caps, set back on their heads, and long chains of gold coins from the back to the ear, with long necklaces of the same."

Their long dark hair hung down in thick waves to their shoulders, and each woman had painted black eyebrows, a tattooed star on her forehead, three on her chin, and dozens on the backs of her hands. They assured Isabella she would look better if she dyed her hair and painted her face. They asked about marriage customs of England, divorce, the position of women, horsemanship, amusements. Isabella offered to take their photograph but they said: "It is not the custom of our country; no good women have their pictures taken, we should have many things said against us if we were made into pictures."

Isabella returned to the party. She took a photograph of the Chief with his three brothers standing behind his chair, their three young sons in front of them. One child, who was deaf and mute, held his right hand open on his chest in a plea for divine help. The Chief presented her with a cow so she could have milk on the journey. As she left, several horseman wheeled and galloped around her, shooting their pistols and whooping with yells of excitement, a traditional farewell.

Isabella Bird's photograph of the chief and his family

She was pleased to find that Mirza Yusuf was proving to be everything she had hoped for in a personal servant. She found him "good, truthful, and intelligent, sketches with some talent, is always cheerful, never grumbles, is quite indifferent to personal comfort, gets on well with the people, is obliging to everyone, is always ready to interpret, and though well educated, has the good sense not to regard any work as menial."

At the next camp, once again lines of people were waiting outside her tent for medical supplies. The men and women pushed forward, shouting and clamoring, complaining of eye infections, headaches, and rheumatism. Isabella saw 278 patients in two days, doling out eye lotion, advice and medicine: one woman brought half an eggshell to carry the precious liquid back to her tent. As she gave them medicine, Mirza Yusuf carefully wrote directions in Persian for each one, but Isabella knew that many people swallowed the eye-lotions and put stomach medicine in their eyes. She saw people wearing charms and amulets, and people often chewed and swallowed verses from the Koran, believing that to be a cure. She was beginning to wonder if what she was doing had any benefit at all.

"They have no idea of the difference between curable and incurable maladies. Many people, stone blind, have come long distances for eye-lotion, and tonight, a man, nearly blind, came in leading a man totally blind for eight years asking me to restore his sight. Octogenarians believe that I can give them back their hearing, and men with crippled or paralysed limbs think that if I would give them some Feringhi ointment of which they have heard, they would be restored."

She wondered why she was accepted as a doctor even though the Moslems treated women with such contempt. Among the Bakhtiari, she was told, there were several women doctors because men were considered too unsettled. The women knew how to extract bullets, heal wounds with a paste made from an oaktree nut, and cure fevers with a liquid made from willow bark. If a father had any medical knowledge he passed it on to his daughter, and women who were doctors taught their daughters.

It was June. The fierce summer heat began. The sun blazed down on the gravel plains, almost desert-like in their bleakness. Major Sawyer roused them at 2:45 every morning with the call of "Boot and Saddle!" so they could ride in the cool of the day before the sun came up. The green grass disappeared in the scorching heat. Isabella, plagued by black flies and sand-flies, was overwhelmed: "I often long for an Edinburgh east wind, for drifting clouds and rain, and even for a chilly London fog!"

By July they had reached a region that had never been explored before. The map noted, "Empty snow clad mountains," but Isabella reported: "The scenery is most magnificent and abounds in torrents and springs. But no mountain exceeds 14,000 feet. No Europeans have ever passed through the region."

One day she climbed with Major Sawyer to the top of a high jagged ridge. Looking down, far below, she saw a beautiful sapphire-blue lake walled in by high cliffs, unmarked on the map. Major Sawyer named it Lake Irene, after his eldest daughter.

The tribes in these territories were reputed to be more dangerous than others. One afternoon, at they rested at the midday camp, Isabella was reading aloud from *Ben Hur* to Major Sawyer and his assistant. The mules had been unloaded and the muleteers were resting. A servant stood half-listening at the open door of the tent, amazed that a woman could read. Suddenly, he pointed excitedly. About ten tribesmen rode into the camp and began talking to the muleteers. Their voices became loud, and an angry discussion broke out. As Isabella went on reading calmly, Major Sawyer strolled over to speak to them.

"There was a scramble, and an attack on him with clubs. He seemed to shake his assailants off, lunged towards his mule, took his revolver from the holster, fired it in the air, and with an unconcerned, smiling face, advanced towards the savages saying something like how excellent firearms were, then fired two bullets close over their heads. They fell back, and molested us no further."

The tribesmen had wanted the muleteers to join them in robbing the camp but Major Sawyer's cool manner had deflected the attack. He gave orders for everyone to keep their revolvers at the ready, ride in a close group during the day, and arranged a system of guards for the camp at night.

The route led up narrow goat tracks, skirting mountain spurs, cutting round precipitous ledges and over sharp crests. Riding down these dangerous paths was even more hair-raising than scrambling up them. The mules slipped and fell frequently and Isabella on her horse felt dizzy looking down at the zig-zag turns of the path, knowing that one slip would mean disaster.

As she took one turn, she saw ahead a precipice and Sawyer's voice shouting to her to dismount. She did, and managed to get down the precipice by letting herself down over the ledges with her hands, and leading her horse at the same time. After the gruelling day's ride, Major Sawyer ordered a day of rest in camp. For Isabella, there was no respite.

"The tents were scarcely pitched before crowds assembled for medicine. I could get no rest, for if I shut the tent the heat was unbearable, and if I opened it there was the crowd, row behind row, the hindmost pushing the foremost in."

She administered medicine for several hours, and then went to bed. At dawn she woke to hear voices shouting "Hakim! Hakim!" Throughout the day she saw patients.

"I was able to open two abscesses, dressed five neglected bullet wounds, sewed up a gash, prepared eye-lotions and medicines for seventy-three people. The mercury had never fallen below 100 degrees. I had been standing or kneeling for hours, and had a racking headache so I reluctantly shut up my medicine chest to go and visit the Chief's wives. But the whole crowd surrounded and followed me, swelling as it moved along, calling out 'Hakim! Hakim!' People even clutched my clothing and hands were raised to heaven to implore blessings on me if I would attend to them."

The demands for medicine, the debilitating heat and the thefts were exhausting Isabella. She felt nauseous, and had terrible headaches as well as suffering from pain in her arm, which she could only move in one direction, and a swollen knee which she had injured falling on a rock. Major Sawyer, however, had little sympathy with her complaints. He had decided from the first that her ailments were entirely imaginary, and that each additional complaint only added to the story.

During the day there were frequent sounds of gunshots. Isabella's scrawled letters often interject such comments as "Firing again, and this time the crack of one of our own rifles," and "Another shot! I wonder what it means." There were rumors of attacks from tribesmen and plots to rob the camp. Somehow, she did not feel frightened. She slept soundly in her tent at night, despite occasional shots, and she enjoyed the riding during the day, though she kept her revolver ready.

As the caravan stood ready to depart one morning, a group of men rode up and tried to steal a sheep. Isabella sat on her horse watching the fight that developed, and noticed several armed men around, making threatening gestures as they muttered "Feringhi!" at her.

"I took my revolver out of the holster, and very slowly examined the chambers, though I knew well that they were all loaded. This had an excellent effect. They fell back, and began dispersing."

The next destination, Burjird, lay about three weeks' travel away. Every day, incidents and attacks occurred. Tribesmen shot at the caravan as it wound its way among the mountains or threatened to attack the camp and take all they had. In response, a huge fire was lit at night and guards posted to keep watch with orders from Major Sawyer: "Fire to kill!" He now stayed up half the night checking the guards, and Isabella thought he looked completely exhausted.

One afternoon as they rode up a steep pass, shots rang out from the surrounding mountains. Major Sawyer shouted for the caravan to scatter and ride slowly forward. Isabella could see the volley of firing ahead, but rode on calmly, her pistol in her belt. As she reached the crest of the pass, she saw a rough group of men carrying old guns, sticks and knives. Major Sawyer told them he was a friend of the local chief. At first they did not believe him and accused him of coming to destroy their homes. In the end, they let the caravan pass.

The hot, sultry days continued. The miles slipped away. Finally, Isabella rode into the village of Burujird, 700 miles north of Isfahan. There, Major Sawyer found telegrams canceling his plans for further exploration. He was ordered to go at once to India's Afghan border, where fighting had broken out.

Isabella was shocked. She had hoped to travel with him back to Teheran. She knew it was much too dangerous to return on her own through the country they had just crossed. She studied the map carefully. Her best solution was to travel north through Persia to Armenia, and reach the port of Trebizond on the Black Sea where she could take a steamer to England. It was a journey of almost a thousand miles. Major Sawyer arranged for the local governor to provide a military escort as protection. Isabella hired a muleteer, four mules and two horses, and repacked her limited supplies.

On her last evening, resting in Major Sawyer's room at the military fort, they talked about their journey.

"We had a very frank pleasant clearing up conversation," Isabella noted with relief. "My last words to him were, 'I am very glad to be so sorry to part,' and his to me, 'I'm thoroughly sorry to part; you forgive all my badness. God bless you.' So we parted friends, thank God. It had several times appeared as if it must be very different."

Isabella realized that she would miss the security of his presence, because no woman had ever traveled alone through this desolate unexplored region, but she set off determinedly. As she rode out of Burujird the next morning, she looked back. Major Sawyer stood on the roof of the fort, waving his hat to her. She waved her hand until his tall figure disappeared in the dust swirling behind her.

Isabella (on right) with friends at Persian camp

Isabella Bird, 1891

Chapter 15
The Triumphant Return

Alone to Black Sea and steamer home. Acclaim for Kurds article and Persia book. Meets Prime Minister. Addresses MPs in British Parliament. Honored by Royal Scottish Geographical Society. Appointed first woman Fellow of Royal Geographical Society.

Isabella's route lay through the Kurdistan region where some two million Kurds lived in nomadic tribes and settlements. It would be a dangerous journey, with only one Persian soldier on horseback to guard her. "It is an unusual, if not unheard-of thing for a European lady, even if she knows Persian, to travel through this country without a European escort," she noted.

Her personal reason for wanting to go home by way of northern Persia, Syria, Turkey and Armenia to the port of Trebizond on the Black Sea was because she had heard there were Christian missions in Hamadan, Urmi, Kochanes, Van, Bitlis and Erzerum and she hoped to visit them.

Her new horse was called Boy and he became an adored pet. "He follows me like a dog, comes when I call him, stops when I stop, and usually puts his head either on my shoulder or under my arm. Every day he becomes more of a companion. He walks very fast, gallops easily, never stumbles, can go anywhere, is never tired, and is always hungry."

She dressed Boy in the woollen shirts and felt coats that Persian horses wore. He liked to eat grapes, cucumbers, bread and milk, which he licked from a soup plate. While she ate her dinner, with Boy tied to her tent, he "waits with wonderful patience for odds and ends, only occasionally rubbing his soft nose against my face to remind me he is there." Boy became the most beloved horse of all her travels.

She set out for Hamadan, 86 miles away, which took a week's riding in burning summer heat. Isabella felt so ill when she arrived that she rested for three weeks at the American Protestant Mission.

While she recovered, she went out to see the city which was "ruinous, filthy, decayed" with poor people in rags on the streets. In the Jewish quarter, she visited a monument erected to the memory of Esther and Mordecai, who, according to the Biblical story, saved the Persian Jews from destruction by King Ahaseurus. There were two tombs inside on a blue tiled floor, and on top was an ancient carved wooden ark covered with pieces of paper with Hebrew writing that were prayers left by visitors. In the street, she saw that the local Jews who looked after the monument were "kicked, beaten and spat upon, and their children are pelted going to and from the school which the Americans have established for them."

The Protestant missionaries were horrified to hear Isabella's travel plans. They warned her of the terrible dangers ahead, and the cruelty of the tribes she would encounter. Her only protection lay in an official letter from the Turkish Ambassador in Teheran which asserted: "Among the honored of English ladies is Mrs. Bishop. On this tour of travel she has a letter of recommendation from the Exalted Government of England, issued by the English Embassy in Teheran, and earnest request is made that in her passage through the Imperial Territory she be well protected."

Undeterred, Isabella set off in the summer heat. Now she was forced to cope with all the disagreeable aspects of camp life that Sawyer had dealt with before. Fearing theft, she ordered her servants to keep guard day and night over her tent and her equipment. But one night her cooking utensils and food were taken. Another morning she woke to find her journal letters, notes, gold fountain pen, and sketches stolen, which devastated her since they were irreplaceable.

Her servants declared they had no idea how the thefts could have happened. Shocked, Isabella realized they had disobeyed her orders to stay on guard. They refused to recognize her authority because she was a woman and they did not believe she traveled under government protection. Remembering Major Sawyer's approach, she called the leader to her tent and harangued him:

"You have broken your agreement, and you will have to take the consequences. Your conduct is disgraceful and abominable, so cowardly that you don't deserve to be called a man. Do you mean to keep your agreement or not?" The man threw himself at her feet whining, but she shouted at him: "Khamosh! Bero!" which was Persian for "Be silent! Begone!" and shut the tent. She realized she sounded just like Sawyer, but it had the desired effect. The men were terribly frightened, and they came back to beg her not to send them to the governor.

"By acting a part absolutely hateful to me, the mutiny was quelled and things are now going on all right," she conceded. "It is so vexing that the policy of trust which has served me so well on all former journeys has to be abandoned, and that one of suspicion has to be substituted for it."

She realized she had to be on her guard at all times. Every night she chained her trunk to her bed, and roped her chair and table together. She set new rules for her men to check the campsite several times during the night, and ignored their grumbles with firm authority.

It was August. The temperatures soared to over 100 degrees, and swarms of black flies and sandflies plagued her. On all sides she saw low mud hills of bare brown earth, scorched thistles, and a land parched by the fierce sun. It was a relief in September to arrive at an oasis in the Syrian town of Urmi, about four hundred miles north of Burujird.

"Irrigation canals shaded by fruit trees and irrigation ditches bordered by reeds carry water in abundance all through the plains. Big buffaloes draw heavy carts laden with the teeming produce. Wheat, maize, beans, melons, gourds, potatoes, carrots, turnips, beets, chilis, celery, cotton, oil-seeds of various sorts, opium and tobacco all flourish. The orchards are full of trees. Beautiful are the pomegranates, the apricots, the apples, the peach and plum, and glorious are the vineyards."

For over 50 years, American, English, and French Protestant missions had been working in Urmi. She was particularly interested in the Sisters of Bethany, part of the Archbishop of Canterbury's Mission to the Assyrian Christians, and also visited the American mission college and seminary, English schools, and an orphanage.

Isabella crossed the border into Turkey, and rode on to Kochanes. Now she began to hear of violent raids by Kurds armed with rifles who swept down on the villages and drove off the sheep, and killed anyone who tried to stop them. The cruelty and savagery of these sudden attacks were devastating to the villagers, most of whom were Christians, and the loss of their livelihood was driving them to poverty and starvation. It was rumored that a Kurd leader, Hesso Khan, had seen his father die in a Persian prison and swore to avenge his death by robbing and killing Persians. When he had been driven north, he attacked Turkish villagers.

Isabella said she wanted to meet him, thinking that perhaps she could show him the error of his ways. She was taken up the mountain to his hiding place, and led into a room thick with tobacco smoke, the only light coming from a hole in the roof. Half a dozen men lounged against the walls next to their rifles, with revolvers and jeweled daggers stuck into their belts.

"Hesso himself leaned against a roll of bedding. A superb stage brigand he looked, the handsomest man I have seen in Persia, with a large face, dark prominent eyes, a straight nose, and a false smile." He wore a jeweled turban, a short jacket, wide trousers of cream-colored wool, an embroidered silk shirt, and an coat of rich brocade.

Isabella innocently hoped that her quiet persuasion might touch the streak of good she believed lay in every man and wanted to ask him to stop taking the villagers' sheep. But Hesso turned on her and accused England of making Turkey weak so that her frontier and Armenia are in a state of anarchy. As she looked at his harsh angry face, and the ever-present rifles of his men, she realized he would have no hesitation in shooting and killing her at a moment's notice.

"Of course my errand failed," she confessed frankly. "I could not speak about the sheep and Hesso said that he could not speak on any political subject before the Persians who were present."

She rode on to Kochanes, and stayed in the rambling stone castle of the Syrian Patriarch of the region, a Protestant churchman and political leader. The castle was full of people, all attending on the

Patriarch. Throngs of men waited for hours in the corridors to speak to the Patriarch, while in other rooms men cleaned swords and guns, or engaged in wrestling matches, or played chess, or practiced horsemanship. The Patriarch's sister efficiently ran the household, organizing the food, welcoming guests, and dealing with the occasional conflicts that occurred.

Here, Isabella met a churchman who knew about the Kurd attacks from personal experience. An Armenian Protestant Bishop, he had escaped a death threat from the Kurds after he protested publicly against their attacks in his diocese and petitioned the government. The attacks had begun seventeen years ago, and were destroying the villages. There were thefts during the day and sheep-stealing at night so that the people, without flocks and any way to make a living, had no money to pay their taxes and their fields were in ruin.

Isabella was horrified, and hoped she could find some way to help them. But it was time to ride on. After hearing all the stories of attacks from the Kurds, even Isabella was concerned at the thought of the dangers she faced ahead, and briefly considered returning to Urmi. But she realized:

"It is obvious that my journey to Erzerum will depend on my own nerve, judgment, and power of arranging, and that at best there will be serious risks, hardships and difficulties, which will increase as winter sets in. After nearly coming to the cowardly decision to return, I despised myself for the weakness. The die is cast."

She did wait several days for her official guard, a sturdy Turkish officer in full army uniform, to arrive and escort her to the next village. On the way, they met three Armenian villagers wearing only shirts who wept that Kurds had robbed them an hour before and taken their mules, equipment, clothes and money. She and her guard rode on warily. At dusk, they were riding down to the village in the valley when they were attacked.

"Four mounted men, each armed with two guns, rode violently among the mules which were in front of me and attempted to drive them off. In the fight the muleteer was knocked down. The guard jumped off his horse, threw the bridle to me and shouldered his rifle. When they saw the Government uniform, these Kurds drew back, let the mules go, and passed on. The whole affair took but a few seconds."

After the attack, the bells were taken off the mules, and the soldier walked in front, his rifle at the ready. In bright moonlight, Isabella followed him until they reached Van and went to the house of the British Vice-Consul. There, she learned that no one ever took the route she had followed from Urmi to Van because it was too dangerous. "I was glad no one knew enough to dissuade me from it," she commented dryly.

Isabella stayed in Van for several days completing the formalities of official papers so she could travel on. Reloading the mules, she set off for Bitlis, which was some 400 miles from the Black Sea. The route was too dangerous for her to camp out so she stayed overnight in Turkish "odahs."

These rough inns, spaced about a day's ride apart, were caves dug into the hillsides, and designed with a raised mud platform in the center where travelers gathered, to rest, cook their meals, talk and sleep. On the floor and by the mangers along the walls the horses, mules, oxen, asses, and buffaloes crowded, with occasional sheep and goats. Isabella, after her many experiences in primitive surroundings, was unperturbed.

"Ceaseless munching goes on, and a neigh or a squeal from some unexpected corner startles one. The heat and closeness are so insupportable that the morning temperature is 80 degrees." She liked to set up her tent in the doorway where it was cooler, with her horse as company, noting: "Boy is usually close to me, eating scraps from my dinner, and gently biting the back of my neck when he thinks that I am forgetting his presence." By October, she reached Bitlis, set on steep slopes by the rushing waters of the Eastern Tigris, which she described as: "The most romantically situated city that I have seen in Western Asia. Picturesque stone bridges soared over the river, some of them dating back to Alexander the Great's time. The people were remarkably striking, with sharp features, white teeth, deep-set eyes, long eyelashes and dark hair, and the women sported silver rings in their noses.

At the end of October, the first snows dusted the mountains. The night temperatures fell below freezing. Isabella set out on the last stretch of her long journey to Erzerum, facing winter storms by day, with snow, sleet and blizzards howling around her caravan, and nights crowded into cave-like shelters with mules, horses and sheep, and the noises and babble of animals and people. She admitted: "The very long marches on this journey have been too much for me."

With relief she arrived in Erzerum and rested at the American Mission House for a few days. Then, amid icy weather and wild storms, she rode off for the last ride, the 200 miles to the Black Sea. The storms were so fierce that once in a wild snowstorm, Isabella clung to her saddle to avoid being blown away. It took eleven days of riding to reach the port of Trebizond.

There were few arrangements to make. Isabella unloaded her boxes, paid her servants, and gave her beloved horse Boy away. She caught the steamer to Constantinople, boarded the Orient Express train to Paris, and crossed the Channel to England to arrive on Christmas Day, 1890.

———

John Murray III, publisher, 1881

Early the next morning, Isabella visited John Murray's house on Albemarle Street in London to have breakfast with him and his wife. She had been away for a year, and had a great deal to tell her enthusiastic publisher about her adventures. He urged her to write a book on Persia.

Isabella spent New Year's Day in the cottage in Tobermory, and a few days in Edinburgh with Professor and Mrs. Blackie, who listened eagerly to her stories. She then traveled south to Bournemouth to her old friend Miss Clayton to whom she had been sending her letters. Isabella was shocked to find Miss Clayton hardly able to move: she had fallen down a steep flight of stairs and suffered a severe concussion.

Isabella noted sadly: "She is so frail, and aged and so deaf. She will never be the same again."

But she was relieved to discover that most of her letters from Persia had arrived. She had details of her travels up to the time she set off from Burujird. Her other letters had been stolen on the journey together with her journal and sketches, so her only source for the last part of the journey was her pocket-diary with brief notes of the places along the way.

Isabella, who had no real home of her own, settled down in Miss Clayton's house to write her book about Persia. She told a friend: "I am frightfully busy. I make no visits, don't read, and only go out for exercise. I write from 10 to 1, from 5.30 to 7, and from 10 to midnight. From 8 p.m. to 9.30 I write letters and do odds and ends. For an hour in the afternoon I take a brisk solitary walk."

She did find time to write two long articles on a subject close to her heart - the sufferings of the Armenian Christians in Turkey. These were published in *The Contemporary Review* and described what she had seen.

"Squeezed between the rapacity and violence of the Kurds and the oppression of the Turkish officials, who undoubtedly connive at outrages so long as the victims are Christians, the condition of these Syrians is one of the most pitiable on earth. They are simple, grossly ignorant, harmless, helpless shepherds and cultivators, clinging passionately to the fragments of a faith."

The articles aroused tremendous interest. Many refugees had fled to England with their terrible stories of persecution. Isabella's reports were the only first-hand accounts to provide essential information for those who had to decide British Government policy. John Murray invited her to a dinner party to meet the British Prime Minister, William Gladstone, who wanted to know all about her travels among the Kurds. He listened to her comments intently.

She then received an invitation from Members of Parliament who asked her to address them on the issue. She did not want to make a speech but agreed to answer their questions. On June 18, 1891, Isabella addressed the Members and their wives in a crowded committee room of the Houses of Parliament. A small, dignified figure in a black dress, her graying hair combed back, she stood calmly with her hands folded in front of her, and spoke quietly but authoritatively for almost two hours, responding to their many questions about what she had seen.

Isabella was now invited to speak before professional organizations, a mark of the increasing respect her work and her opinions commanded. In August, 1891, she addressed the British Association, a national scientific society, on *The Upper Karun Region and the Bakhtiari Lurs*, and a report on her speech noted:

"There were several papers dealing with original exploration, and of these Mrs. Bishop's account of the Bakhtiari was by far the most important. Mrs. Bishop spoke for the greater part of an hour merely from notes, but without the slightest hesitation. Her subject-matter and its manner of treatment were in her hands a model of excellence."

Isabella was also busy addressing church meetings to raise money for medical missions. Her speeches to these groups were very different from her travel articles and books. At one meeting at Exeter Hall, London, she declared:

"When traveling in Asia, it struck me very much how little we heard, how little we know, as to how sin is enthroned and deified and worshipped. There is sin and shame everywhere. Mohammedanism is corrupt to the very core. The morals of Mohammedan countries, perhaps in Persia in particular, are corrupt and the imaginations very wicked. How corrupt Buddhists are! It is an astonishment to find that there is scarcely a single thing that makes for righteousness in the life of the unchristianized nations. They degrade women with an infinite degradation. There is also an infinite degradation of men. The whole continent of Asia is corrupt. It is a scene of barbarities, tortures, brutal punishments, oppression, official corruption."

This was Isabella the preacher, as her father had been. She gave her missionary audiences sermons, telling them the details that would rouse them to support distant missions. Indeed, this speech was so successful that thousands of copies were printed and distributed in England and America.

In her books, she takes a much more rational and objective view of different religions. She describes Buddhist observances, Tibetan beliefs, Moslem practices, the customs of marriage and families in different cultures, unusual observances and celebrations with an open-minded respect for other faiths. Like many writers, Isabella shaped her material to suit her audience.

Almost a year later, Isabella had finished her book on Persia and sent it to her publishers. John Murray was editing the manuscript. He sent chapters back to Isabella for revisions and corrections. She rented rooms in London, and was busy answering his questions, which necessitated visits to the War Office and the Royal Geographical Society library for information. She also met several times with Major Sawyer, now back in England, to clarify details of the journey.

A new problem arose. Isabella had agreed in Teheran not to mention Major Sawyer by name in anything she wrote. She referred to him as M, or The Sahib, or The Agha, whenever his appearance was essential to her story. Now she was told that the entire manuscript had to be approved by the India War Office before publication.

The War Office then expressed great concern about the maps in the book because of England's political maneuvering. Isabella wanted to include the places she and Major Sawyer had discovered in the areas marked "unknown." But the Commander in Chief of the Intelligence Department of the India War Office refused to allow it; he feared Russia might get hold of the map and see the still-secret information. The new names had to be left out.

"I have very much of the feeling of having a millstone round my neck," Isabella complained. She was busy traveling around the country on speaking engagements as she revised the book, and sent changes and additions in a stream of letters and postcards to John Murray from a variety of addresses. She assured him:

"I have adopted all your corrections but one. A great many of yours make me much ashamed of my want of perspicacity. I am vexed to see how many of my sentences have gone off the track. Your corrections have been an education in grammar and style, which will not be thrown away. The original letters were invariably written when I was greatly fatigued and my rewriting has been done under great pressure."

By October the entire hand-written manuscript reached the printer. She added the preface, glossary and details of her itinerary. Isabella's diary note of "Thank God!" recorded her relief. In December 1891, *Journeys in Persia and Kurdistan* was published in two hefty volumes, each about 400 pages long with maps, sketches and photographs, including one of Isabella sitting astride her favorite horse, Boy.

The book was immensely successful. Within a few months, it had received more than 90 reviews. Sir Robert Murdoch Smith, an expert on Persia, wrote in the *Scottish Geographical Magazine* that: "Much has been expected from her facile and graphic pen, and we may at once say that those expectations are not disappointed. The picture drawn of the sufferings of man and beast from the intense cold of the icy blasts that sweep over these uplands, however exaggerated they may seem, are true and exact as photographs."

The Athenaeum selected the book as the first to be reviewed in its Literature section of January 16, 1892. Several columns of close print replete with quotations from the text concluded that: "The reader will find much to instruct, interest and amuse."

Blackwoods Magazine's lengthy review found "her style wonderfully free from every affectation." But the reviewer observed that the "gentle but persistent plea for medical missionaries, which runs like a thread through her book, sets one wondering whether this was the 'definite object' of her journey."

Though he was right, Isabella never admitted it publicly. She realized that if she expressed her pro-mission views in her books more explicitly, "I much fear that with the generality of readers it would have provoked a sneer at the outset."

Unexpectedly, the Royal Geographical Society in London invited her to address them, the first woman ever to speak to their group. It was a great honor. However, Isabella hesitated because she knew the Society refused to admit women as members. She declined the invitation, and instead agreed to speak to the Royal Scottish Geographical Society which had admitted women since its creation in 1884.

It was a memorable evening. She addressed a special meeting of the London branch of the Scottish Society on her travels in Persia. The Scottish Society honored her by appointing her as the first woman Fellow. Isabella was delighted at "the innovation they have made in recognizing a woman's work."

The Royal Geographical Society was embarrassed. The President promptly proposed - and the Council agreed - that Isabella be appointed the first woman Fellow of the Society, and that women should be admitted. At a Special General meeting on November 28, 1892, held in a wood-paneled hall of the University of London, 15 women sat with the 26 men waiting to be initiated as new members.

There was strong opposition. Admiral Sir Leopold M'Clintock was apoplectic at the sight. He stood up, his mustaches bristling, and declared that the Constitution did not permit women to join. But the Council had made the decision, and a motion to welcome the women members passed by a large majority. The names of the new members were read out: Isabella L. Bishop became the first woman Fellow of the Royal Geographical Society.

The Admiral and his supporters were outraged. Indignant letters appeared in *The Times*, and discussions erupted in the smoking rooms. Admiral Inglefield said he hoped never to see a woman on the Council!

George Curzon, who had recently written his own and less successful book on Persia, declared: "We contest the general capability of women to contribute to scientific geographical knowledge. Their sex and training render them equally unfitted for exploration, and the genus of professional female globe-trotters with which America has lately familiarized us is one of the horrors of the latter end of the nineteenth century."

A poem in the humor magazine *Punch* commented:
"A lady an explorer? A traveller in skirts?
The notion's just a trifle too seraphic;
Let them stay and mind the babies,
or hem our ragged shirts;
But they mustn't, can't and shan't be geographic."

The Admirals organized a special meeting in April, 1893. A new vote was taken, and women were denied membership by 147 to 105. The 22 ladies who had already been admitted were allowed to remain. Isabella, astonished at the decision, commented:

"The proposed action is a dastardly injustice to women. I don't care to take any steps in the matter as I never took any regarding admission. Fellowship as it stands at present is not a distinction, and not a recognition of work, and really is not worth taking any trouble about."

Isabella was in her sixties, and still full of energy and enthusiasm, though she told Lady Middleton: "I have become a very elderly— indeed I may say an old—woman, and stout!" She was busy taking classes in photography, speaking at missionary meetings and attending social affairs. She was presented to Queen Victoria at Buckingham Palace. *Leisure Hour* magazine published her articles about her travels in Tibet, which the Religious Tract Society brought out as a book, *Among the Tibetans*, in 1894. She was saddened in April, when her old friend John Murray III died; she had worked with him for almost forty years. Though his son, John Murray IV, took over the company, Isabella felt his loss deeply.

She wrote to Lady Middleton: "We have lived into a new era, and whether we like it or not (and I don't like it, and think the old was better) if we are to be of any use, we must cease sighing over the past and throw ourselves as heartily as may be into those currents of the new life and age which are surging around us."

For the first time, she felt the need for a permanent home. In 1892 she bought a house in Edinburgh with her friend, Miss Cullen, but she was rarely there. Miss Cullen noted: "It was rather a farce, she did not live in the house for more than eighteen weeks, but her two rooms were kept for her."

Isabella's frenetic pace of speaking, traveling, and writing brought on an attack of pneumonia. When she recovered, she consulted with her doctors. They diagnosed rheumatic gout, a lung infection, and "fatty and calcareous degeneration of the heart." Their advice: give up some of her activities, rest and take the waters at a spa.

Isabella knew the only cure for her was to travel. She understood that her mind overcame the demands of her body. When she traveled, her interest and natural resilience carried her over every obstacle, and forced her to ignore her ill health. It was time to prepare for a new journey.

Her decision was to return to the Far East, visit Japan and China and perhaps more. She would be away for a year. This time, she took a tripod camera and developing materials for photographs as well as journals, paper and notebooks for her writing.

When she went to book her passage aboard the steamer, the captain, honored to have her aboard, gave her the best cabin. She packed her belongings in boxes, said goodbye to her friends, closed up her house, and set sail from Liverpool in January 1894. A sturdy widow of 62, with gray hair and a lined face, Isabella looked very much like the elderly Queen Victoria. But nothing would stop her as she set out again on her eternal quest for adventure.

Isabella Bird's photograph of her sampan, Han River, Korea

Chapter 16
Korea and the Far East

Travels to Korea. Takes photographs. Explores Han River and Korean countryside. Japanese invasion. Death of Korean Queen. To China and Russia.

For the next three years, Isabella explored Korea, China and Japan, without any clearly defined plan. Though she had hoped to spend much time climbing high mountains and exploring unknown regions, the situation in Korea led her to become a war correspondent and political interpreter, and to consult with the Korean royal family.

Other British explorers roamed the Far East convinced that European civilization must reform the Oriental barbarians. Isabella believed: "It is essential for us to see quite clearly that our Western ideas find themselves confronted, not with barbarism or with debased theories of morals, but with an elaborate and antique civilization which yet is not in decay, and which, though imperfect, has many claims to our respect and admiration."

Her first impression of Korea's capital, Seoul, was "monotonous in every way." But her aim was to avoid cities and travel off the beaten track. She set out to explore the north and south branches of the Han River with a crew of two boatmen, accompanied by a young missionary, who brought his servant to translate for them, and Wong as her personal servant. Wong was "a big cheery fellow, with inexhaustible good-nature and contentment, never a cloud of annoyance on his face, always making the best of everything, ready to help everyone, and with a passable knowledge of English."

The boat they lived and traveled on was only 28 feet long and less than five feet wide. Isabella's photograph shows a long low vessel covered with an uneven roof of woven matting.

It was spring, and the trees had fresh green leaves and new blossoms of bright red, pink and white. Colorful butterflies and dragonflies fluttered and darted over the river. Mallard ducks, geese and teal paddled among the reeds. White egrets, long-legged cranes and ibis with soft pink feathers stood in the ricefields while kestrels and falcons flew above.In the crystal-clear stream Isabella noticed brilliant green and brown snakes.

The boat stopped frequently so she could stroll through the villages by the river, where farmers lived in derelict mud huts in depressing poverty. One more prosperous village had an elegant mansion belonging to a rich local governor. A group of giggling women took Isabella on a tour, but she was not impressed:

"Fine parquet floors, mostly spoiled by being covered in whole or in part with Brussels tapestry carpets of loud and vulgar patterns in hideous aniline dyes. Great mirrors in tawdry gilt frames and French clocks asserted their expensive vulgarity in every room. This general foreign tawdriness is spreading rapidly among the young swells who have money to spend, vulgarizing Korean simplicity."

Korean women led secluded lives. They stayed in their parents' house until the age of seventeen, when they married and moved to their father-in-law's house. The only time they went out, with their husband's permission, was after dark; some women had never seen the streets in daylight. After marriage, a woman was called "the wife of so and so" or, if she had children, "the mother of so and so." Her husband addressed her as "Ya-bu" which meant "Look here!" and she rarely spoke. Isabella noted: "Korean women accept inferiority as their natural lot."

The six weeks aboard the boat passed quickly. As well as her tripod camera, Isabella had brought an array of scientific instruments to record daily temperature, altitude and barometric readings. On this trip, she collected plants and flowers which she pressed and dried. She kept a careful daily log of distances traveled and the names of places visited. She checked her measurements to make them accurate as possible, remembering all she had learned on her travels with Major Sawyer. She was now so professional that the long account she wrote to the Royal Geographical Society from Korea about her journey up the Han River was published in its entirety in the Society's journal.

When the Han river became too wild and rocky to go any farther, Isabella hired mules and ponies to ride through the Diamond Mountains to Won-san on the coast. She found Korean ponies very different from her beloved Persian horse, Boy. Thin, scrappy animals, they fought and kicked constantly, attacking each other and their riders. Astride, Isabella had to be constantly alert to outbreaks of sudden fights.

The local inns were dismal. Not only were they dirty, noisy, and flea-infested but a system of pipes under the floors constantly brought hot air from a furnace-shed to all the rooms. Isabella's thermometer once registered a temperature of 105 degrees in her room! At the inns, the ponies were chained to troughs in the stables where they could not raise their heads and bite each other, but their hyena-like braying and noisy kicking echoed throughout the night.

The route into the Diamond Mountains necessitated climbing steep paths through the mountains. European boots were useless so Isabella climbed in Korean string shoes, energetically "jumping from boulder to boulder, much winding round rocky projections, clinging to their irregularities with scarcely a foothold, and much leaping over deep crevices and walking tight-rope fashion over rails," adding: "I never slipped once."

The scenery was superb: "Across the grand gorge through which the Chang-an Sa torrent thunders, and above primeval tiger-haunted forests with their infinity of green rises the central ridge of the Keum-kang San, jagged all along its summit. Their yellow granite pinnacles, weathered into silver gray, rose up cold, stern and steely blue from the glorious forests, then purpled into red as the sun sank."

Centuries before, Buddhists had built retreats in the mountains, and now, isolated from the mainstream of Korean life, they sheltered hundreds of Buddhist monks and nuns. Isabella walked across a bridge to the Pyo-un Sa monastery, decorated with extensive wood carvings in blue, red, white, green and gold.

Melodious bells chimed in the wind harmonizing with the bells calling the monks to prayer. They were strict vegetarians so Isabella was served rice, pine nuts, honey, tea, and honey water. Though one monk gave up his room so she could stay for the night, she thought they lacked the true religious spirit because they were "well dressed and jolly, and have a well-to-do air which clashes with any pretensions to ascetism." One young priest in prayer repeated every word ten times for every bead on his rosary and explained: "They have no meaning, but if you say them many times you will get to heaven better."

Leaving the mountains, the route led down to coastal plains. Here the hot, dirty inns were often hung with salted and drying fish, fishing boats bobbed on the smooth greeny-blue sea, and she observed primitive methods of making salt from sea water.

She soon reached Won-san, a busy port town of 15,000 people, where Isabella rested at the American Presbyterian Mission. The port had recently opened to foreign trade. She noticed a newly established Japanese Consulate, Japanese mail steamship company, Japanese bank, and many European goods for sale in the stores. For years Korea had cut off all contact with the outside world to deter continual invasions, and refused to allow foreigners into the country. After the Chinese began to infiltrate from Peking and began trading throughout Korea, the Japanese and the Europeans tried to enter the country. By provoking a naval incident in 1875, the Japanese negotiated access to Korean ports. There were frequent clashes because the Koreans hated all foreigners, particularly the Japanese and Chinese.

Inside Korea there was also unrest. Growing protests by farmers and peasants challenged the ancient traditions of land ownership. The King and Queen and their nobles owned most of Korea's land, which they leased out, and lived on the income. In the 1860s, a religious group called the Tonghaks demanded land reform, and held protest rallies throughout the country, which attracted wide support.

When Isabella sailed back to Seoul, she was surprised to see a fleet of six Japanese warships moored in the harbor, and Japanese transports unloading troops, horses and supplies. In Seoul she saw Japanese soldiers marching in the streets, houses in the Japanese area turned into barracks and filled with soldiers, and a huge camp had been set up. She persuaded a young Russian soldier to show her around, and discovered: "There were 1200 men under canvas in well-ventilated bell tents, with matted floors and drainage trenches, and dinner was being served in lacquer boxes. Stables had been run up, and the cavalry and mountains guns were in the center. Every man looked as if he knew his duty and meant to do it."

Japanese officials said they had come to protect the Japanese in Seoul from the Tonghak rebels. Isabella knew there was no real danger, and that they had brought in troops and provisions so that they could take over Korea. Just then a worried British Vice-Consul hurried over to her hotel. An invasion was imminent, and the Legation could not be responsible for her safety. She must leave at once.

Though reluctant to go, she did not want to embarrass the British government. Without any baggage, she hastily took the next boat to the nearby port of Chefoo in China, and went north to Mukden to stay at the China Inland Mission, where it was presumed to be safe.

No sooner had she arrived when news reached Mukden that the Chinese had attacked the Japanese fleet and lost a troopship with 1,200 men aboard. The Chinese, outraged, declared war, and the Sino-Japanese war began on August 1, 1894.

In Mukden, long lines of Chinese troops straggled through the town on their way to join the soldiers in the south. They carried silk banners, umbrellas and fans, but hardly any of them had weapons. Isabella looked at their outdated uniforms and weapons, and commented: "It was nothing but murder to send thousands of men so armed to meet the Japanese with their deadly Murata rifles, and the men knew it."

Isabella took photographs of the soldiers. She was busy photographing the city, and visited the inner walled section, the first European woman to do so, taking pictures of quiet streets where foreigners never ventured. She had a tripod camera, weighing about 16 pounds, as well as a lighter hand camera. She also had plates and chemicals for developing her photographs as she traveled.

"Photographing has been an intense pleasure. If I felt free to follow my inclinations, I should give my whole time to it. I began too late ever to be a photographer, and have too little time to learn the technicalities of the art; but I am able to produce negatives which are faithful, though not artistic, records of what I see."

Isabella's photographs of mountain peaks, rivers and canyons as well as of street scenes, temples and people were included in her books on Korea and China. Her book of photographs of China was published in 1902.

As the war continued, Chinese hostility against foreigners increased in Mukden. Once out photographing a huge stone archway in the city, Isabella was mobbed by a hostile crowd, who believed her camera was a black devil with an evil eye so that "whatever living thing it looked on died within a year, and any building or wall would crumble away." A friend from the Mission, Reverend Gilbert Walshe, who had watched her photographing in China, commented: "Even in the face of the largest and noisiest crowds, she proceeded as if she were inspecting some of the Chinese exhibits in the British Museum. Her absolute unconsciousness of fear was a remarkable characteristic."

Soon afterwards, news came that soldiers had wrecked the Christian chapel at a mission outside Mukden, and beaten a Scottish missionary to death. Isabella's friends at the Mission were horrified and urged her to go to the safety of Peking. She left in August, and settled in quickly.

The famous Mrs. Bishop was invited by the Oriental Society of Peking to address them on her travels. She spoke on the evening of October 5, 1894, in the Hall of Dragons of the British Legation. Her audience was the entire diplomatic corps, officers of the Chinese Customs Department, and professors from the Imperial College. Afterwards, they elected her an Honorary Member of the Society. Isabella wrote breezily to the Royal Geographical Society:

"The scare here is fearful, and I think without reason. I met with nothing perilous or disagreeable, and for a fortnight I have gone about freely here on foot and in a mule-cart. There is nothing to daunt or repel an experienced traveler. I never found people kinder or more sympathetic."

A month later, rumors were rife that Russian soldiers were massing on the border of Korea preparing for an invasion. Isabella decided to investigate. She took a German boat north to Wladivostok, the Russian port near the Korean border. To her surprise, she found a bustling city with a railway station, wide streets, shops, houses and impressive public buildings. Traveling on, she discovered that some 20,000 Korean refugees had crossed the border and set up farms and villages in Russia where they lived under much better conditions than they had ever found in Korea.

Isabella rode along the frontier, looking for the thousands of Russian soldiers ready to invade, according to a report in an English newspaper. The only military post she could find was a rundown mud hut with fifteen men and one corporal. She showed them the newspaper report.

"The roars of laughter which greeted the English statement were not complimentary to newspaper accuracy. I photographed the 'Russian army' and the barracks, and the corporal slouching against the forlorn quarters in an attitude of extreme dejection."

She shared their dinner of black bread, barley soup, tea and a little vodka, and spent the night in the hut. When she returned to Seoul, she wrote an account of what she had found for the *St. James Gazette* in London. The editor thanked her for the first-hand information and urged her to send more.

The Korean King

Isabella went back to Seoul. She was a well-known figure, and through British friends received an invitation to meet with the Queen for a private audience. Arriving at the Palace, an interpreter took her to a small room where the King, the Crown Prince and the Queen stood on a dais. The Queen wore a robe of blue brocade with a crimson bodice, and a black silk cap edged with fur over her shining black hair. The King, a plain, short man, was dressed in white. He had a thin mustache and a tuft of hair on his chin and nervously twitched his hands. The young Crown Prince, also dressed in white, looked fat and flabby and sat holding his mother's hand without saying a word.

Isabella answered the Queen's questions about her travels and found her "quick-witted as well as courteous" but she felt the King was "weak in character and is at the mercy of designing men, persuaded by the last person who gets his ear." She was invited back to photograph the palace, and had other meetings with the King and Queen, who asked her many questions about the British system of government. Isabella felt the dynasty was worn out and that the royal family would be deposed.

When the Japanese forced the defeated Chinese to sign the Treaty of Shimonoseki, the Sino-Japanese war ended in April 1895, and an uneasy calm settled over Seoul. There were many public announcements of change but little actually happened. Isabella had left the city to organize her travels in China when she heard that the Queen had been assassinated by the Japanese. She hurried back to Seoul.

The details horrified her. One October night Japanese soldiers swarmed into the Palace demanding to see the Queen, and found her in her rooms. "The Minister of the Royal Household stood with outstretched arms in front of Her Majesty, trying to protect her. They slashed off both his hands and inflicted other wounds, and he bled to death. The Queen, flying from the assassins, was overtaken and stabbed, falling down as if dead. A Japanese jumped on her breast and stabbed her through and through with his sword. The Japanese laid her on a plank, wrapped a silk quilt round her, and she was carried to a grove of pines and burned."

The imprisoned King escaped from the palace to find asylum at the Russian Legation, hoping the Russians would help him keep Korea independent. The weeks slipped by, and as the slow pace of diplomatic negotiations stretched into months, Isabella decided she could wait no longer for her travels in China.

"My chief wish on arriving at a foreign settlement or treaty port in the East is to get out of it as soon as possible," she once declared. She longed to explore the distant mountains on the border of China and Tibet. She left for Peking to make her arrangements.

Her plan was challenging. She would travel up the Yangtze River from Shanghai to Wan-Hsien. The Yangstze, 3,450 miles in length, climbed some 15,000 feet on its route west. Once she reached Wan-Hsien, she planned to trek overland through the mountainous region of north west China to its border with Tibet. It was a journey of more than 5,000 miles, and she was the first woman to attempt it.

Chapter 17
Adventures in China

Boat up Yangtze River. Overland exploration to mountains on China-Tibet border. Revels in challenges of journey. Returns to Shanghai.

From Shanghai Isabella took a steamer to Ichang where she rented a house-boat to go up the Yangtze River. The boat came with its owner, his wife, their three children, sixteen boatmen and a skipper. She also traveled with two missionaries, Mr. Stevenson and Mr. Hicks, and her new interpreter, Be-Dien.

"It was an old boat, the paper on the windows was torn away. The window-frame of the cabin in which I slept, ate, and carried on my various occupations, had fallen out; the cracks in the partitions were half an inch wide."

Isabella was never bothered by primitive conditions, or the nightly smell of opium which the boatmen smoked. Instead, she marveled at the magnificence of the gorges; "Cliffs of extraordinary honeycombed rock, carved by the action of water and weather into shrines with pillared fronts, grottoes with quaint embellishments, huge rock needles. Higher yet, surmounting rock ramparts 2,000 feet high, are irregular battlemented walls of rock, and everywhere above and around are lofty summits sprinkled with pines on which the snow lay."

She was busy taking and developing her photographs. Every night she pinned newspapers and blankets over the chinks in her cabin to keep out the light while she developed her negatives and toned her prints, using river water in the process, and hung her printing frames over the side to dry.

Isabella Bird in Swatow, China

"I found that the most successful method of washing out the 'hypo' (chemical) was to lean over the gunwale and hold the negative in the wash of the Great River, rapid even at the mooring place, and give it some final washes in filtered water. The difficulties enhanced the zest of these processes and made me think, with a feeling of complacent superiority, of the amateurs who need dark rooms, sinks, water, tables and other luxuries. When all these rough arrangements were success-ful, each print was a joy and a triumph, nor was there disgrace in failure."

After the boat left the soaring cliffs of the gorges, Isabella heard the thundering water of the rapids ahead. The boats on the river climbed up the rapids, which was extremely dangerous. As her boat slowly approached the roaring water, she saw signs of disaster everywhere. She noticed partially submerged wrecks above and below the rapids.

Gaunt human skeletons sprawled on rocks. On all sides sharp-edged rocks, spurs and gray rough-edged humps broke through the rushing water. On the turbulent waters, red-painted lifeboats bounced, ready to dart into the turmoil at any moment.

The passengers disembarked before the rapids, and Isabella stood on shore watching as ropes were attached to her houseboat. The ropes looped from the boat to the seventy trackers standing on the steep cliffs who would pull it up the rapids, and the ropes attached to a strap tied round their chests. Narrow, steep flights of steps had been cut in the rocks, which were often slippery and wet. At high water, when the steps were completely submerged, the trackers had to scramble over boulders on the river banks, or cling with fingers and toes to the steep precipices hundreds of feet above the river.

Isabella watched as the men struggled for hours heaving the boat up the rapids. The noise was almost deafening because adding to the crash and roar of the rushing water were the yells of the trackers, the shouts of the men watching, and the thudding beat of drums to encourage the men and the banging of gongs to frighten away evil spirits.

Isabella declared: "I have found that many of the perils which are arrayed before the eyes of travellers about to begin a journey are greatly exaggerated, and often vanish altogether. Not so the perils of the Yangtze. They fully warrant the worst descriptions which have been given of them."

Once the rapids had passed, the river narrowed between soaring perpendicular cliffs and became a rushing rippling stream. They reached the province of Sze-Chuan. Ahead, Isabella saw a smooth, still lake. The city of Wan-hsien loomed above her, its temples and pagodas clustered picturesquely on the high cliffs. The boat pulled up to the dock. Taking her belongings, Isabella walked up the 150 steep stairs from the river to the town, and went to the China Inland Mission.

Her clean, spacious guest room had windows on two sides. One overlooked a peaceful courtyard, and the other looked out over the city rooftops, to the Yangtze river gleaming silver far below. Isabella had successfully traveled some 1,300 miles. Now she planned her great trek overland.

"The longer one travels, the fewer preparations one makes," Isabella asserted. She had now adopted Chinese dress and wore a long loose-fitting Chinese robe with a large oversize jacket. Into its many pockets she tucked a portable oil lamp, diary, tea, her revolver and other travel essentials. For this journey, she hired a light bamboo chair for herself, carried on fourteen-foot-long bamboo poles by three servants while she sat inside with her feet on a footboard suspended on ropes. She bought a new Chinese robe and straw shoes, some extra curry powder for her evening meal, and large heavy sheets soaked with linseed oil to protect her from fleas in the inns.

Her servant-interpreter, Be-Dien, though educated and intelligent, had become "persistently disagreeable, useless, lazy, unwilling, and objectionable all round." It was too late to replace him. Isabella set off from the mission at Wan-shien with Be-Dien, her two official guards, four coolies, and three chair-bearers.

It was a beautifully clear, sunny day. Her chairbearers hurried along an old paved road beside cultivated farmlands, over stone bridges, down hills and past fields of beans, barley, and rice. But that night, the Chinese inn was deplorable. Her long narrow room had chinks in the wall partitions where eyes peered in at her, two beds infested with vermin, and a damp mud floor.

Isabella methodically set up her camp bed, pinned cotton curtains over the holes in the partitions, spread an oiled sheet on the floor for her belongings and two small oiled sheets over her bed. She hung her clothes on her camera tripod, lit a candle, ate her curry, and wrote up her notes and letter sitting under her mosquito net. It was not an auspicious beginning, and she confessed: "I am not ashamed to say that a cowardly inclination to abbreviate my journey tempted me the whole evening."

As she traveled through the villages, the residents were merely curious about her, since she was often the first European woman they had ever seen. They stared and pointed, laughed at her strange round eyes and her enormous feet, very different from the tiny bound feet of Chinese women. As Isabella traveled farther inland, their curiosity became hostile.

One evening, as her bearers were carrying Isabella's chair to the village inn, a crowd of men ran after her hitting it with sticks and screaming "Foreign devil!" and "Child-eater!" Isabella could see the innkeeper at the inn just ahead trying to close the gate. Her runners pushed the chair through. She hurried to her room, and hastily pulled the strong wooden bar across the door, hoping she was safe.

Outside, she heard the sounds of yelling and shouting grow louder. The crowd had broken through the gate and poured into the courtyard. The men began hammering at her door with planks of wood, screaming as they banged. The pounding grew fiercer by the minute. Isabella kept calm:

"I sat down in front of the door with my revolver, intending to fire at the men's legs if they got in, tried the bars now and then, looked through the chinks, felt the position serious. Darkness, no possibility of escaping, nothing of humanity to appeal to, no help, and a mob as pitiless as fiends."

Just as the top of the door started to cave in, the shouting and banging stopped, and a sudden silence fell. Looking out through a crack, Isabella saw the crowd had disappeared. A troop of soldiers sent by the local mandarin had dispersed the riot, "which he might have sent two hours before," she commented wryly.

Though shaken, Isabella was determined to travel on. At the next village, she sent a runner ahead of her, waving her official letter in the air. He cleared a way through the crowds and she followed safely behind him. After that, there were no attacks or threats on her life.

Isabella was following part of the wide Imperial Road from Peking to Cheng-tu, built a thousand years before. Weeping cedar trees, planted at intervals by the roadside, soared hundreds of feet into the air. Their drooping branches provided a thick canopy over the road, the huge trunks measuring sixteen feet around. Fields of opium poppies stretched to the horizon.

"These were days of delightful travelling without any drawbacks. The weather was beautiful, the air was sharp, and the people well-behaved. There was no fatigue or annoyance, the accommodation was fair, and there was literally nothing to complain of."

At Mien-chow, she stayed at a Mission House with Reverend J. Heywood Horsburgh and his wife, who, like Isabella, had adopted Chinese dress. Mrs. Horsburgh offered to take Isabella on a tour. They set off in two chairs, and Isabella admired the spacious farmhouses shaded by cedars and cypresses, the fertile fields and bamboo groves. Watermills and canals provided the water for the crops, and Isabella watched as the peasants pedaled high-wheeled pumps to distribute it.

When they two women turned back to go home, they passed a large crowd of men. Catching sight of Isabella's open chair, hundreds of men rushed toward her throwing stones, calling names and shouting. One stone hit Isabella on the head and knocked her unconscious. As she slumped forward the crowd hesitated, thinking they had killed her. Her bearers hurriedly carried her to the next village where she recovered.

"I had a violent pain in my head, and the symptoms of concussion of the brain, and felt a mortifying inclination to cry," Isabella admitted. She spent a sleepless night in great pain. The next day she still felt ill and had a headache.

She had to admit that, despite her sympathies, the Chinese hated foreigners. She was weary of being jeered at by crowds who pointed at her large feet, her eyes, her hair, her camera, her pens and pencils, and her ability to write in a society where women were not educated. Isabella heard that other European women had broken down, gone insane or died from attacks by Chinese mobs. But as she lay recovering, she looked out of the window, and thought of how much farther she could travel.

"The clear, sparkling Min river sweeps past with a windy rush, and the mountain views are magnificent. Why should I not go on, I asked myself, and see Tibetans, yaks, and aboriginal tribes, rope bridges, and colossal mountains?"

The Horsburghs, unable to persuade her to stay, suggested she take a young missionary, Mr. Knipe, to help her. While she recovered, he hired the mules and drivers to continue the journey west to Tibet, and brought his own servant to join the group.

They set off to climb into the highest regions of the world. As the long caravan snaked up into the foothills, Isabella exulted in the breathtaking views of snow-covered peaks, the rushing streams foaming into waterfalls, the dazzling clarity of the air and the soft mosses and flowers underfoot. "There was the pleasurable excitement which attends a plunge into the unknown," she declared cheerfully.

Isabella was the unquestioned leader. She carried official papers to show she was a traveler of rank. She chose the route and made the decisions. She wrote letters and her daily journal, kept the log of distances traveled, measured and noted geographic statistics, took and developed her photographs, the basic research material for her books and articles. Her great concern was to make sure the information was as accurate as possible.

Her goal was to reach Somo, a village beyond the farthest point of previous explorations on the mountainous border of China and Tibet. She had no accurate map of the region, no knowledge of the route, and no official escorts to guide her. But with her long experience of travel in unlikely places, she knew that mules and muleteers could lead her to the next village.

On all sides lay spectacular views of the snow-covered mountains, with rocky villages perched among the rocks. Isabella was pleased to reach the Man-tze region of China, where Tibetan influence predominated.

"To be away from crowds, rowdyism, unmannerly curiosity, to be among mountains whose myriad snow-peaks glitter above the blue gloom of pine-filled depths, to breathe the rare air of 8,000 feet, to be free and embarked on a journey, and last, but not least, the complete disappearance of the rheumatism, made up an aggregate of good things."

Friendly smiles from the people she passed greeted her. Isabella stayed in their stone houses perched precariously on the steep mountainsides, and, as a guest, slept on the roof with views of the distant mountains at sunset and sunrise. She ate sandwiches of macaroni paste with chopped garlic. And no one stared at her.

She observed the Man-tze carefully, and asked about their social customs, traditions and beliefs. She was particularly interested in the rosy-cheeked healthy-looking women walking through the streets in contrast to the Chinese women Isabella had seen with their pitifully bound feet. The Man-tze women had complete equality with men, spending time together happily.

"They share their interests and amusements everywhere. Men and women are always seen together. A woman can be anything, from a muleteer to a Tu-tze (leader). Social intercourse between the sexes is absolutely unfettered. Boys and girls, youths and maidens, mix freely," she observed. Two laughing young girls were appointed as her official escort to the next village. They wore pleated skirts, short loose jackets and high leather boots decorated on the front and sides with scarlet and green cloth. She wanted to photograph them but every time she went under the black cloth to focus the camera, they ran away giggling shyly.

Isabella journeyed farther west and the scenery became ever more magnificent. The canyons reminded her of the Rocky Mountains in their craggy glory with the river rushing through.

"Piled above the forest-clothed cliffs and precipices which wall in the river, and blocking up every lateral opening, were countless peaks or splintered ranges, cleaving the blue sky with an absolute purity of whiteness. High up, in extraordinary situations of dubious access, are Man-tze villages, much like fortifications, the flutter of prayer-flags giving life to the scene. The river adapts itself to its changed surroundings. Its coloring is a vividly transparent green. Over it drooped stems of trees covered with ferns, orchids and trailers, long sprays of red and white climbing roses, and ferns. The river descends in falls and cataracts, under bending trees and trails of clematis and roses, pausing now and then in deep green pools, but its thunder-music, echoing from gorge and precipice, pauses never."

Isabella's travel books are filled with vivid, dramatic,and accurate descriptions of nature. Some of her descriptions may sound exaggerated, but the richness of her language recreated for her readers the details of the scenery she most admired. Mr. Knipe, the missionary, later wrote an account of his experiences which makes their journey sound like a church outing. Isabella's descriptions, on the other hand, can still recreate images of the excitement she wanted to share. Her literary skill was that of the travel journalist, bringing vividly to life the immediate experiences, sights, sounds, and incidents, and in particular the natural beauty she loved.

At the next village, local officials refused to allow her permission to travel farther. They told her she was beyond Chinese jurisdiction, she had no papers, and there was danger ahead. This time Isabella was prepared.

"I produced an official Chinese map, and showed them that the village lay far within the limits of the Viceroy of Sze Chuan. I produced my passport, and they could see that it gave me rank; and I said if obstruction persisted, I should write a formal statement to the British Consul in Chungking."

They rushed off to see their superiors and came back, crestfallen, to say she could travel on. She commented with satisfaction: "They were quite quenched."

That day, as she climbed to the top of one of the highest passes, she was in her element. The snow-covered mountains of China's frontier with Tibet stretched around her for miles. Peak after peak, the jagged ranges like pointed dragon's teeth loomed against the vivid blue sky. Among them stood Mount Everest and Kanchenjunga, their summits rising close to 30,000 feet. The sun blazed down on the snowy mountaintops, on the jagged bare rocks of gray and on the dark forest-covered slopes of evergreen. The whiteness dazzled her eyes in the bright sunshine. Far below, she could see the river like a green silk cord streaked with silver winding its way among the rocky gorges.

Then she looked back. In a long line straggling up the zigzag trail behind her were her eleven men jumping, laughing and singing, some with leaves stuffed into their nostrils to prevent nosebleeds from the thin air, the two Chinese soldiers in their ragged uniforms, the mules with the muleteer in his picturesque Tibetan costume. She relished for a moment a sense of triumph at what she had accomplished. She had successfully defied authority, overcome obstacles and succeeded in leading her men to this superb view. She confessed: "I felt the joy of a born traveller."

Isabella's assertiveness had developed from her years of travel. At first she had politely obeyed foreign officials, believing she was a guest in their country and should follow the rules. Major Sawyer had shown her that bullying had its place in the face of corruption and opposition. Isabella now spoke out and would not be intimidated. She had become an authoritative leader, competently facing every difficulty along the way.

Her stamina and energy were amazing. One afternoon, after a long day's trekking over mountainous territory, she reached the village where she planned to stay for the night. A squabble over arrangements broke out between her servants and the local officials. Her men begged her to let them go to the next village, Matang. Isabella knew that it would take at least eight hours to cross the next pass, over 11,000 feet high, and it would mean traveling at night. She tried to settle the argument, but tempers were high and passions roused. In the end she was unable to calm her men down and set off on what she contemptuously called "this most foolhardy venture."

As darkness fell, they reached the steepest part of the climb. The temperature had fallen, the air was bitterly cold, and a fierce snowstorm hit them, whirling icy flakes in their faces. They struggled on against biting cold winds.

"I was dragged rather than helped by two men who themselves frequently fell. The guide constantly disappeared in the darkness. Several times I sank in drifts up to my throat, my soaked clothes froze on me, the snow deepened, whirled, drifted, stung like pin points. The men were groaning and falling in all directions."

When they reached Matang, Isabella was "exhausted, shivering, starving, drenched to the skin." After two days, she had completely recovered and was ready to set out again. She climbed on through the spectacular mountains until, from a high peak, she looked down and saw the village of Somo, her goal from the beginning.

Her men followed her down the mountain slope to the narrow streets of the village, relieved the journey was over and expecting a welcome. But a Chinese official had the local leader deny them shelter and food. All doors were barred and savage dogs snarled viciously.

Isabella could not accept this. She sent Mr. Knipe to climb the wall of the Man-tze leader's home. He dropped into the courtyard, and persuaded him to provide rooms and food in a nearby house. Isabella settled into her rooftop room, and considered the next step. She longed to travel on, and to see the wild unexplored regions of the mountains ahead. She confessed: "I cherished a project of getting down to Ta-tien-Lu by a route involving a journey of twenty-one days."

After making inquiries, she was told that tribal war had broken out and bridges had been destroyed. Mr. Knipe confirmed this after a day's scouting expedition. Several of her servants were ill with fever. Her food supplies were almost exhausted. Even Isabella realized she might not have the energy for more strenuous mountain climbing. Regretfully, she concluded that she could go no farther. It was time to return, though she admitted: "Every reader who is also a traveller will understand the indescribable reluctance with which I abandoned the project."

She took a different route back overland to reach the Yangtze river, where she hired a houseboat to sail down to Ichang.

It was May. The trees were in blossom, the fields green with spring crops, and the warm summer air was refreshing with the brisk breeze from the water. The journey down the Yangtze was a swift careening descent over rapids, the water at its high summer level.

When she arrived in Shanghai, her arrival caused a flurry of excitement in the British community. Isabella had been traveling for five months. She was the first woman to successfully explore a region of China rarely visited before by Europeans. She was the center of attention.

A reporter from the *North China Daily News* came to interview her in June. He described Isabella as "a retiring soft-voiced woman, whose silver hair is a passport to respect." As he sat listening to her accounts of crossing high passes in a snowstorm, her tales of attacks by Chinese mobs, her treks through the spectacular mountains, and her descriptions of breath-taking scenery, he changed his mind.

"When she begins to talk, selecting her words with the nicest discrimination, she at once exercises a sort of spell over the listener, making him feel the power of her intellect and the acuteness of her observing powers. Then we recognize that Mrs. Bishop is a wonderful woman, possessing an unsuspected force with which to overcome the most forbidding obstacles."

That summer Isabella rested in Japan for several weeks taking the sulphur baths in Yumoto to ease the pain in her back. In the fall she went to Seoul, Korea, to find a letter waiting for her at the British Legation from her publisher, John Murray IV. He urged her to write a book on Korea, now much in the news because of the political upheavals and the assassination of the Queen.

Isabella settled into the British Legation to write the book, hoping to make it the most significant book on Korea for some years to come, since all the others were now out of date. She worked busily for several months. She had completed most of her notes and outlines by the winter. She realized she had been away for almost three years. It was time, Isabella decided, to go back to England.

Isabella Bird in Manchu dress

Chapter 18
The Final Years

Writes books on Korea and on China, with photos. Plans return to Japan and China. Rides through Morocco's Atlas Mountains. Death and burial in Edinburgh.

It would have been easy for Isabella to settle permanently in the Far East. She was honored as an author and traveler, had made an extensive circle of friends, and found Oriental life fascinating. No welcoming hearth waited for her in England.

"I feel very loth to leave," she told John Murray. "I am far more at home in Tokyo and Seoul than in any place in Britain except Tobermory, and I very much prefer life in the East to life at home."

But Isabella could never decide to settle anywhere. She was always finding places she loved—the valleys of Hawaii, the Rocky Mountains of Colorado, the high mountains of Tibet—and then moving on. That winter she packed her boxes, boarded a steamer, and arrived in London in March, 1897.

Isabella rented rooms in London to finish her book on Korea. She also wrote articles for two London journals, spoke to church groups on missions and wrote for missionary publications. Then one morning she received an official invitation from the Royal Geographical Society. Would the honorable Mrs. Bishop address the Society on her travels in Western China?

The Society had a handful of women members from the brief time they were allowed to join. Isabella agreed to speak, recognizing it as a major recognition of her status as an explorer. On the evening of May 10, 1897, she described her five months of adventures in the mountains of northwest China, illustrated with 45 lantern slides and two hundred photographs she had taken. It was the first time in the Society's history that a woman had addressed the membership. Later, Isabella's speech was published in the RGS Journal together with several of her photographs. She also spoke to the British Association at several meetings on her travels in the Far East.

In January 1898 *Korea And Her Neighbors* by Isabella Bird Bishop was published. John Murray chose to bring out the work in two large volumes illustrated with detailed maps of the region, and Isabella's photographs. There was tremendous public interest in Korea because the newspapers had written extensively about the revolution there. The first 2,000 copies sold out in two days. In the first year, the book was reprinted five times, and there was also an American edition. The reviews, all favorable, no longer called Isabella a travel writer but referred to her as a political authority on Korea.

Pleased with the recognition, Isabella commented: "I thought it would bring down a good deal of hostile criticism. The success was quite unlooked for, and I am very glad to have the hard and conscientious work of a year so fully recognized."

Next, John Murray suggested a book on her Yangtze travels. She agreed and rented a house in London's Holland Park for two years, prepared to settle down for a while. The book demanded a great deal of work, with careful checking of the various spellings of Chinese names, details of distances covered and evening after evening developing her photographs for the illustrations.

A year later in November 1899, *The Yangtze Valley And Beyond* was published. The 550-page book was equally as fascinating as her book about Korea, but public interest in the Far East had faded. The newspapers were full of stories about South Africa where British troops were dying in the Boer War. Though she received excellent reviews, few copies were sold. Isabella admitted: "I put hard work into it and I should like to have imposed some of my opinions on a larger circle of readers than it is likely I shall have."

Gratified by the serious attention and praise her two books had received, she felt piqued that the Royal Geographical Society never honored her achievements, but gave awards and citations to men who achieved far less than she had. She confided to John Murray: "I think that I have contributed so much to the sum of general knowledge of different countries that had I been a man, I should undoubtedly have received some recognition from the RGS."

That winter she went to the cottage in Tobermory to rest. She saw that the village had changed. "Tobermory is four years worse. Drink is ravaging it. The place does not improve. The people are so intellectually lazy and so spiritually dead, and so contented merely to vegetate. I see no hope that things will ever be any better."

Regretfully, she decided to give up her lease on the cottage after twenty years. "It is hard—God alone knows how hard—and it closes a chapter in my life, with all the lovely and pathetic memories, first of her, and then of my husband," she wrote to Ella Blackie in April 1900.

Isabella moved to London. She started a course of French conversation, joined a photography class, and even took some cooking lessons. She was also busy putting together a book of her photographs from China, which was published by Cassells, with 60 black and white photos and brief descriptive paragraphs.

As her seventieth year loomed ahead, thoughts of old age and the inevitability of death filled her mind, and she remembered old friends and those she loved who had died.

"How pathetic life becomes when its landmarks are graves alone. I felt profoundly depressed during this winter. It is very odd to look at all things in the light of old age, and I am trying resolutely to face it."

One day as she visited with Anna Stoddart, Isabella remarked: "When I die, it may be that my memory will perish with me, but it also may be that others will care to know something about me." Anna Stoddart, who had just written a successful biography of the late Professor Blackie, said she would be glad to write Isabella's biography.

However, Isabella's unquenchable urge to travel was not yet ready to die. Longing to escape the cold, damp London winter, she decided to go somewhere warm. She chose North Africa, and left by steamer for Morocco on the Mediterranean Sea. She arrived in Tangier on New Year's Day, 1901, a plump, aging widow of 69. She was hardly able to walk, and immediately fell sick. The major news of the day was the death and funeral of Queen Victoria in England. Isabella was so ill she did not hear about it until weeks later.

She lay in bed, helpless. But her spirit was still strong, and she decided: "I realized I must either make up my mind once and for all to 'give in' or resort to what proved a panacea before, and quit civilization for the wild."

Within days she was up, acquired a magnificent black horse, hired a servant, mules and camping equipment and set off to explore Morocco's Atlas Mountains. The challenge of riding and the rough, outdoor life revived her immediately. She exclaimed in a letter to Anna Stoddart:

"You would fail to recognize your infirm friend astride a superb horse in full blue trousers and a short full skirt, with great brass spurs belonging to the generalissimo of the Moorish army, and riding down places where a rolling stone or a slip would mean destruction. I never expected to do such travelling again. It is evidently air and riding that do me good."

Her companion this time was an Englishman from the Consulate, Mr. Summers, whom Isabella described as a "strong, resourceful man, never worried and with absolute control of temper." He spoke the language and took charge of all the arrangements, including the retinue of soldiers accompanying them. Their route led through rugged mountains over a thousand feet high among wild Berber tribes.

Isabella found: "I can now ride 30 miles a day and enjoy the twin fascinations of camp life and barbarism. We were entertained everywhere at the great castles of the Berber sheikhs as guests of the Sultan."

When she returned to Marrakesh, the first European woman to travel through the Atlas Mountains and visit the tribes, she was invited to meet with the Sultan.

"I wish it could have been photographed," she lamented. "The young Sultan on his throne on a high dais, in pure white; the minister of war also in white standing at the right below the steps of the throne; Kaid Maclean in his beautiful Zouave uniform standing on the left and interpreting for me; I standing in front below the steps of the throne, bare-headed and in black silk, the only European woman who has ever seen an Emperor of Morocco!"

At the end of the interview, she wished him long life and happiness. "He said that he hoped when his hair was as white as mine, he might have as much energy as I have! So I am not quite shelved yet!"

There was one more ride, a trek of five hundred miles north from Marrakesh. It was her last grand adventure, her final experience of riding fearlessly among uncivilized tribes, coping with unexpected dangers and enjoying the challenge of the unknown. But she never wrote about Morocco. She gave John Murray five reasons for not doing so:

"1. That I took no notes of anything but my journey in the Atlas Mountains.
2. That there is little variety in the country, and few salient points.
3. That Miss Frazer is writing a book on Morocco for the next publishing season.
4. That I am really not well enough for sustained effort in writing. My head is tired. Had it been for a year hence, I might possibly have managed it.
5. That Morocco did not interest me much or take a strong hold on me."

She added: "I am hoping if I live till the autumn of next year to return to China and then I shall probably be inspired!"

She did put together an article on the political situation in Morocco for the *Monthly Review*, and confided to a friend: "The country is rotten to the core, eaten up by abominable vices, everything petrified and tending to decay."

A few months after she returned, she suffered intense pains in her chest. She was so weak she could hardly sit up at a table. Reluctant to see a London doctor, she went to Edinburgh to consult with her doctors there. They diagnosed a fibrous tumor growing in the region of her lungs and heart and told her that her old symptoms of heart disease were reappearing. She was seriously ill.

Isabella hated the idea of becoming an invalid. She was already packing her boxes for her next trip to China. She had speaking engagements to fulfil. She had photographs to develop. She went back to London, attended a five-day photography conference in Cambridge, spoke at missionary meetings in Oxford, lectured to the boys of Winchester School about her travels, and watched the coronation procession of King Edward from the windows of John Murray's office in Albemarle Street.

The pains returned. This time she was bedridden for several weeks at a relative's house in Huntingdon. In April 1903, she drew up her will and signed it. Very weak and ill, she moved into an Edinburgh nursing home.

"I have been walking through the valley of death's shadow and the doctors consider me still dangerously ill and without hope of recovery or prolonged life," she wrote to a friend. "Some singular affection of the veins and heart not previously known. One feature is blue rings and broken veins all over my heart and chest. Breath often nearly ceases, and there is no strength."

Yet once again within a few months she had recovered. She moved into rented rooms in Edinburgh. Her mind was as alert and active as ever. Friends came in every day to talk and read to her, brought her food and books, and marveled at her interest in the world. When one woman admired Isabella's patience, she replied: "I am not patient; I would much rather be going about."

Her arms were so weak she could barely write. In one of her last letters to John Murray, her firm, scrawling writing had become shaky and uneven. She apologized for it and explained it was the first time she had been able to use a pen in eight months: "My severe heart disease obliges me to lie completely flat in bed, and as I am deplorably weak, writing is almost impossible. This is most vexatious as this enforced rest after over 30 years of varied hard work without a holiday has put my brain into excellent working order and has completely renovated my memory!"

She still talked of her journey to China and longed to take the Trans-Siberian train to Mukden and travel on to Peking. Her boxes were packed and waiting in London. As the weeks passed, she realized she might never make the trip.

"You cannot imagine my disappointment about China. It captivated and enthralled me and I did hope to see it once again. My heart was greatly set on this. It is harder to give up than all else."

The months of summer slipped by. One October morning, she asked her friends to sing the hymn *Abide With Me*. She leaned back on the pillows, listening. Outside, the winds rattled the windows. The bleak gray stones of the castle loomed above Edinburgh. Heavy clouds scudded across the sky.

As the hymn ended, Isabella suddenly said in a loud clear voice: "Oh, what a shouting there will be!" It was a family phrase she and Henrietta used when they talked of meeting again after a long separation. The church bells struck noon. Isabella closed her eyes. Quietly, she died. She was 72. She who had risked danger so fearlessly in life met death peacefully in bed.

The funeral took place on Monday, October 10, 1904. Isabella was buried in Dean Cemetery in Edinburgh, beside her father, her mother, and her sister, and John Bishop, whose body was brought back from Cannes. The gravestone read:

> *"Edward Bird*
> *Dora Lawson*
> *Henrietta Amelia*
> *John Bishop, their son-in-law,*
> *Isabella Lucy, F.R.G.S., F.R.S.G.S.,*
> *Hon. Member of the Oriental Society of Peking,*
> *their eldest daughter, wife of the above John Bishop,*
> *who after arduous journeyings in many lands*
> *died in Edinburgh, on 7th October 1904, aged 72.*
> *A servant of Christ who went about doing good.*
> *As she had opportunity, she did good unto all men."*

Dozens of publications announced Isabella's death. *The Times* of London published a long obituary of "the well-known traveller and author," citing her work for medical missions as well as her travels.

In America, the *New York Times* declared: "Noted Woman Traveler Dead: Mrs. I. L.Bishop Made Long Journeys in Various Wild Lands," and said she was regarded as "one of the most daring women travelers who ever lived."

The *Denver Post* called her a "Well Known Woman Author," and quoted from her Rocky Mountains book: "Never, nowhere, have I seen anything equal to the view into Estes Park" and "Womanly dignity and manly respect for women are the salt of society in this wild West."

The *Denver Republican* announced: "Pioneer Woman Traveler in Colorado is Dead; Author of 'A Lady's Life In The Rocky Mountains' Passes Away in Scotland." The article described her visit to Colorado in 1973, her climb of Longs Peak with Platt Rogers, Judge S. S. Downer and Rocky Mountain Jim, and concluded: "It is doubtful if any woman ever travelled as extensively as Isabella L. Bird Bishop. Most of her travels were amid pioneer scenes or in the wild beyond. She was a woman of poetic temperament and unusual courage."

The Royal Geographical Society, which had not deigned to honor Isabella in her lifetime, gave her the highest praise in the Journal obituary in 1904:

"The distinguished traveller, Mrs. Isabella Bishop, died at Edinburgh on October 7. For the extent and value of the information she brought home from her wanderings, she may be ranked with the most accomplished travellers of her time, while among the many distinguished lady travellers who have come before the public during the past half-century, her title to the foremost place can hardly be challenged."

Isabella's estate, valued at some thirty-three thousand English pounds, was divided among her cousins, friends, doctors, servants and church mission groups. She gave John Murray the copyright to all her books, and the Royal Geographical Society her photographic plates.

She also left funds to erect a clock tower in Tobermory on the island of Mull, in memory of her sister Henrietta. It stands there today, on the curving bay overlooking the ocean, below the white-painted cottage on the cliffs, chiming the hours as the seagulls cry and the waves break on the shore.

Isabella Bird, 69, two years before her death

SOURCES

Books by Isabella Bird

The Englishwoman in America. London: John Murray, 1856. Wisconsin: University of Wisconsin Press, Madison, 1966.

The Aspects of Religion in the United States. London: Sampson & Low, 1859. New York: Arno Press, 1972.

Notes on Old Edinburgh chapter in *Odds and Ends.* Edinburgh: Edmonston & Douglas, 1869.

The Hawaiian Archipelago. London: John Murray, 1875. New York: G. P. Putnam, 1894. Vermont: Charles E. Tuttle Company, Rutland, 1974.

A Lady's Life in the Rocky Mountains. London: John Murray, 1879. New York: E. P. Dutton, 1882. Oklahoma: University of Oklahoma Press, Norman, 1960. London: Virago Press, 1982.

Unbeaten Tracks in Japan. London, John Murray, 1880. New York: G. P. Putnam, 1900. London/Boston: Virago Press/Beacon Press, 1987.

The Golden Chersonese and The Way Thither. London: John Murray, 1883. London: Century Publishing, 1983.

Journeys in Persia and Kurdistan. London: John Murray, 1891. London: Virago Press, 1988.

Among the Tibetans. London: Religious Tract Society, 1894.
New York: Fleming H. Revell, 1894.

Korea and Her Neighbors. London; John Murray, 1898. Vermont: Charles E. Tuttle Company, Rutland, 1986.

The Yangtze Valley and Beyond. London: John Murray, 1899: London/Boston: Virago Press/Beacon Press, 1987.

Views in the Far East. Photographs by Isabella L. Bishop. Tokyo: S. Kayima, 1902.

I.B. Photographs Persia 1890. Unpublished photograph album interleaved with descriptive body text; Special Collections, University Research Library, UCLA, California.

Biographies of Isabella Bird

Stoddart, Anna M. *The Life of Isabella Bird (Mrs. Bishop)* London: John Murray, 1906.
Barr, Pat. *A Curious Life For A Lady.* London: Macmillan/John Murray, 1970.

References to Isabella Bird

Arps, Louisa W. *Letters from Isabella Bird.*
Boulder: *Colorado Quarterly*, Vol. IV, Summer 1955.
Arps, Louisa W. *Tracking Isabella Bird.* Denver: *Roundup Magazine*, December 1956.
Allen, Alexandra. *Travelling Ladies.* London: Jupiter Books, 1980.
Badger, Amy H. Quarterly Review, Vol. 257, pages 278-299.
The Centenary of Isabella Bird Bishop. 1931.
Climate Magazine, Vol. 1, No. 4, pages 117-122.
The Art of Travelling: An Interview with Mrs. J. F. Bishop. July 1900.
Dunning, Harold M. *Facts About Longs Peak.* Boulder: Johnson Publg, 1970.
Dunning, Harold M. *The Life of Rocky Mountain Jim.* Boulder: Johnson Publg, 1967.
Hamalian, Leo, Editor. *Ladies on the Loose.* New York: Dodd, Mead, 1981.
Haveley, Cicely P. *This Grand Beyond: The travels of Isabella Lucy Bird.*
London: Century, 1984.
Jardine, Evelyne E. M. *Women of Devotion and Courage: No. 4, Isabella Bird.*
London: Cassell & Co., 1957.
Knipe, W. Church Missionary Intelligencer. *En route to Tibet with Mrs. Bishop.* 1898.
Middleton, Dorothy. *Geographical Magazine*, Vol. XXXIV, No. 9, pages 502-506.
The Lady Pioneers: Isabella Bird Bishop 1831-1904 January 1962.
Middleton, Dorothy. *The Cornhill*, No. 994, pages 274-300.
A Lady's Life in the Rocky Mountains. 1952-3
Middleton, Dorothy. *Victorian Lady Travellers.*
London: Routledge & Kegan Paul, and New York: E. P. Dutton, 1965:
Miller, Luree. *On Top Of the World.* London: Paddington Press, 1976.
Mills, Enos A. *Early Estes Park.* Colorado: Big Mountain Press.
Rittenhouse, M. *Seven Women Explorers.* New York: Lippincott, 1964.
Rogers, Platt. Address at April Meeting. Denver: *The Trail*, Vol. 9, #12, May, 1917.
Sprague, Marshall. *American Heritage*, Vol. 18, pages 8-13.
Love in the Park. February 1967.
Stewart, Agnes Grainger. *Blackwoods Magazine*, Vol. 176, pages 698-704.
Some Recollections of Isabella Bishop. 1904.
Tabor, Margaret E. *Pioneer Women.* London: Sheldon Press, 1925.
Ubbelohde, Carl, Benson, Maxine, Smith, Duane A. *A Colorado History.* Boulder:
Pruett Publishing, 1972: and *A Colorado Reader*, editors, Boulder: Pruett Publishing, 1982.
Wide World Magazine. Snapshots in the Far East.
Interview with Isabella Bird Bishop. July 1899.

Original Letters of Isabella Bird

Letters from Edinburgh, Australia, Hawaii, Colorado, Japan, Hong Kong, Singapore, and Persia in several collections.

INDEX